Additional praise for *Embracing Fry Bread*

"We can all enjoy the wit and humor of my long-time friend and Native rights colleague Roger Welsch. He presents an important message, as we strive to live together as one great people joined together on the same land by a common heritage."—Walter R. Echo-Hawk, author of *In the Courts of the Conqueror: The Ten Worst Indian Law Cases Ever Decided*

"A self-described wannabe, Roger Welsch has over many years absorbed a deep knowledge and appreciation of the Indian tribes of the Northern Plains. His writing, sincere and often humorous, reveals a personality that many Indian people and even one tribal council have come to trust, love, and adopt into their circles."—Charles Trimble, Oglala Lakota journalist and author

"Once again my Heyoke friend, Roger Welsch, has captured the true essence of being a 'wannabe,' not afraid to take risks, staying close to the fire but not too close. Like our people, he understands what it means to live in two worlds. He does so with humor, gusto, and fearless dignity."—Judi M. gaiashkibos (Ponca), executive director of the Nebraska Commission on Indian Affairs

"*Embracing Fry Bread* is quintessential Welsch. Roger hooks the readers with a title about a tantalizing culinary delight, then reels 'em in to the deeper heart of the book. This is a watchful, thoughtful man's memoirs of how he has been drawn into three Indigenous families and communities through no particular volition of his own. This is the story for anyone who wakes up one morning and realizes he or she has somehow become something beyond what nature and nurture had originally provided . . . and is the better human for it. Welsch writes a compelling personal account that can resonate with us all. As Welsch would say, it is not so much about being a WANNAbe as a GOTTAbe."—Mark Awakuni-Swetland, author of *Dance Lodges of the Omaha People*

EMBRACING FRY BREAD

Confessions of a Wannabe

Roger Welsch

University of Nebraska Press
Lincoln and London

Publication of this volume was assisted by a grant from the
Friends of the University of Nebraska Press.

Library of Congress Cataloging-in-Publication Data

Welsch, Roger L.
Embracing fry bread: confessions of a wannabe / Roger Welsch.
p. cm.
ISBN 978-0-8032-2532-9 (pbk.: alk. paper) 1. Indians of North America—
Folklore. 2. Indians of North America—Public opinion. 3. Indians in
popular culture. 4. Indian philosophy—North America. 5. Public opinion—
North America. I. Title.
E98.F6W46 2012
970.004'97—dc23   2012021497

Designed and set in Adobe Caslon by Ashley Muehlbauer.

For Alfred "Buddy" Gilpin Jr., Francis Morris, and Charles Trimble, three men of dignity, accomplishment, and strength who have blessed my life by calling me friend and brother.

Contents

Acknowledgments

Parts of this book and its main points were presented to a plenary meeting of the American Folklore Society in Boise, Idaho, October 22, 2009. That presentation was also published in the *Journal of American Folklore* (vol. 124, no. 491, Winter 2011). I am grateful to the society, its officers, and the journal's editors for giving me that forum to discuss the issue of cultural ownership and doing so with the gracious understanding that the paper would be expanded and to some degree duplicated in this book. I am also grateful to Tim Lloyd and Barre Toelken, friends and stalwarts of American folklore and the society, for their insistence that I do both the plenary session and the publication. Without their encouragement I would never have been so audacious.

It would be impossible for me to list the names of all the people who have been a part of my long travel though the journey of becoming a Wannabe, or perhaps more correctly, confessing that somewhere along the line I did become a Wannabe. The list contains not only the living but also those who have gone, as the Omahas have it, "over that fourth hill." There are many white people—some Wannabes, some not. Some, like Carlos Castaneda and the *Born to Run* author, I haven't even met. Most are Indians of many tribes. All have been helpful. I could perhaps double the list by including those who have helped me by making my path a difficult one; sometimes in their example of the worst of ways they helped me see more clearly those who take the best of ways. I have listed these names in no particular order and have omitted, I know and regret, many. But as I read over the list myself I take enormous pride in being able to say honestly, these have been my friends. As I have grown older I have resolved to clean out my life, discarding people whom I cannot respect or honor and those who clearly do not respect or honor me. Many of the people in this list are among those who are left, the very people whom I respect and honor and those who respect and honor me. I feel the list is impressive and the people on it are beloved. (Of course there are other, larger lists of people who are positive elements in my life but not an element in this particular part of it. They are equally distinguished and beloved in my life.) If we are, as my father told me on several occasions, judged by our friends, then it looks to me like I've done just fine in my lifetime. And my enemies are pretty impressive, too, if I may say so.

Edgar Red Cloud; Earl Dyer; Alfred "Buddy" Jr. and Naomi Gilpin; Frank, Clyde, and Lillian Sheridan and their children and families; Oliver Saunsoci, Sr. and Jr.; Benny Butler; Calvin Ironshell; Ronnie GoodEagle; Jess, Colleen, and Michael Flores; Bill and Alberta Canby; Joseph Marshall; Elmer Blackbird; Frank LaMere; John Turner; Nicky Solomon; Shirley Cayou; Francine and Francillia Philips; Carrol and Karma Stabler; Charles and Elizabeth Stabler; Russell Parker; Ago Sheridan; Dorrin Morris; Felix and Rufus White; Clydia and Reeves Nawooks; Francis Morris; Charles Trimble; Louie LaRose; Nancy Gillis; Judi gaiashkibos; Dawn Adams; Jimmy Horn; Bill and Clem Howell; Alice Alexander; John Mangan; Mark Awakuni-Swetland; Mick Maun; Kristen Friesen; Pat Wendt; Walter Echo-Hawk; St. Elmo Wilde; Ron Rice; Rob Bozell; Deborah Echo-Hawk; Ronnie O'Brien; Gale Pemberton; Peggy Lang; Margot Liberty; Dorothy Howard; Jim Gibson; John Carter; Art May; Mert Moore; Paul Olson; Alan Dundes; Phyllis Stone; Francis LaFlesche; Reuben Delgado; Barre Toelken; Jean Lukesh; Liz Deer; Pat Leading Fox; Marshall Gover; Vance Spotted Horse Chief.

Most important of all, my beloved wife, Linda, who sure didn't bargain on this when we were married thirty years ago but who has become a full partner in the adventure.

Embracing Fry Bread

1. *First, a Story*

oyote lived at the edge of the village in a deep lodge with his blind grandmother. One day he told her he was going to go out and look around a bit so she warned him, "Whatever you do, Grandson, go anywhere you want but do *not* go over the hill on the other side of the river where that big bull buffalo has his herd. He is one mean fellow and you certainly don't want to cross trails with him."

Well, you know Coyote, and you know what a warning like that means to Coyote. From the moment he left the lodge all he could think of was going over that hill and going to take a look at that big bull buffalo. So that's what he did. Just over the top of the hill he stopped and lay down in the shade of a plum bush to watch the big bull and his herd. And oh, what a beauty that great bull buffalo was. Coyote thought of his own humble life, living in the cramped, damp, dark lodge under the ground with his grandmother, eating whatever scraps others left or whatever carrion he could find on the plains and in the hills. He lived in fear of everything and everyone. He was always running away from something . . . hunters, bears, buffalo, mountain lions, and storms. But Big Bull Buffalo down there, grand and proud, was afraid of nothing. He ate constantly without hunger, for grass was everywhere and he could go wherever he wanted. When storms came, Coyote cowered in his lodge with his grandmother or shivered, wet and cold, in the open, but Big Bull Buffalo stood strong and warm in his thick hide, facing into the storm, marching on almost defiantly.

Oh, to live a life like that! thought Coyote.

His fear dulled by wonder, Coyote crept closer and closer to the big bull until he was close enough to smell the buffalo's breath and close enough that the bull turned his huge head to look at Coyote and pierce him with his deep-set eyes. His thunderous voice came from his mouth, held close to the ground, lowered to be near Coyote, now flat on the ground. And he said, "What do you want? Why have you come so close to me? Don't you know the danger you are inviting by daring to approach me like this?"

Coyote was startled because he hadn't noticed, in his awe, how close he had come to Tenugagahi, Big Bull Buffalo, and now he wasn't quite sure how to recover. So, uncharacteristically, he just blurted out the truth:

"Sir, Tenugagahi, I am sorry I insulted you by coming so close without a warning or greeting but I was just admiring you and your herd and wishing I had had the good fortune to have such a fortunate birthright. You see, I live in a small lodge at the edge of the village over the hill here with my blind grandmother. We eat carrion and garbage. I am afraid of everything. We are alone. We suffer terribly from the weather. I look at you and I can see what could be. You are surrounded by your herd. You eat grass, and what else is the prairie but grass? You never go hungry. You fear nothing. You laugh at storms and blizzards."

"What you say is true," Tenugagahi said.

"Is there any way I might become like you?" asked Coyote. "I would give anything to be like you and not what I am."

"Well, yes, there is a way. But you're not going to like it," Big Bull Buffalo said. "It is not easy."

"Master Tenugagahi, I am prepared for anything if you would be so kind as to turn me into a great, bold beast like you," cried Coyote piteously.

"You must do as I say, then," said Big Bull Buffalo. "Stand right here and don't move. No matter what I do, you must stay here as still as you can be."

With new hope, Coyote agreed and steeled himself for what might come. Big Bull Buffalo stepped away twenty or thirty steps and put his head low to the ground. Then he started running straight at Coyote. Coyote was afraid but he did everything he could to stand firm as the giant bull charged straight at him, but at the last moment his courage melted and he jumped back as the buffalo rushed by.

"I told you that you must stand still," snorted Big Bull Buffalo. "You cannot become a bull buffalo like me if you jump back like that."

"Oh, my friend, I was so startled when I saw you running right at me that even though I tried to stand firm, I had to jump back at the last instant because I was sure I would die if I stayed standing in front of you. Please, great Buffalo, give me another chance. I promise you that this time I will not move a muscle."

Big Bull Buffalo went back many more steps this time. He put his head down. He raised his tail into the air as buffalo bulls do before they charge, and again he rushed directly at Coyote. Coyote shook and whimpered as the saw the bull coming at him and he held his ground longer than before, but finally he had to jump away at the last moment, this time feeling the rush of air go by as Big Bull Buffalo passed.

Again Tenugagahi shook his head in disgust and told Coyote that he was doomed to be forever the wretched creature he was if he couldn't do something as small as standing still as instructed for this little ritual. And again Coyote begged and apologized and asked for one more chance. The big bull felt sorry for Coyote and so said yes, he would indeed give him one more chance. This time he went way off up the hill to a clump of plum brush. He snorted, lifted his tail, and pawed the ground and then again ran straight toward Coyote. Coyote closed his eyes and clenched his teeth but when he felt the ground shake beneath his feet from the buffalo's charge, he threw himself back and out of the way, just in time to feel the animal's horns brush the hair of his side.

"That's it," snarled Big Bull Buffalo. "No more. You have worn out my patience." And he started to wander off back to his herd. Now Coyote was really ashamed. He whined and cried and begged the buffalo for yet a fourth chance. [In the stories of Western culture, I should perhaps note here, things always happen in threes. But within Native culture and narrative, everything occurs in fours!] Coyote promised and swore that he would stand still this time. He threw himself at the hooves of Tenugagahi and rolled in the dirt, belly up, to show how totally ready he was to put himself at the buffalo's mercy. And so Big Bull Buffalo said he would give Coyote one more chance. "But this is your *last* chance," he said, and Coyote could see that he meant it.

Big Bull Buffalo stepped to the top of the hill. With his horns he tore up a small cedar tree standing there. He pawed at the dirt and threw it into the air. He bellowed and roared, lowered his head, and raised his tail. And he ran straight at Coyote. The ground shook. Coyote closed his eyes and prayed. He sang his death song, "Kiyeeyee Aiiiiyeeyee!" But this time he stood his ground. The buffalo's head slammed into him and threw him down the hill in a heap, apparently broken and shattered. But then he got up and shook himself off and there he was . . . a buffalo bull. Big Bull Buffalo had told the truth: he had the power to make Coyote a buffalo.

Coyote couldn't believe his good fortune! He wandered down toward the herd, happy at last not to suffer his birth fate of being a lowly coyote. He lowered his head and began to graze on the rich, soft grass of the prairies. Uh-oh . . . it was not what he expected. The grass tasted terrible. And it was dry and gritty. It rasped in his mouth. Well, okay, but still he was no longer lonely, and he stepped again toward the herd and all his new companions. But he was instantly confronted by a dozen of the other young bulls, who challenged him. They butted him and kicked him. They knocked him down and tramped on him with their sharp hooves. Startled, Coyote-Now-Buffalo jumped up and was about to ask why everyone was suddenly so unfriendly, but before he could speak, a dozen Indians ran over the hill with spears and arrows and began killing buffalo around him, even wounding Coyote-Now-Buffalo in his side, so he ran with the others until, utterly exhausted, they stopped at the edge of a river and tried to renew their energies. Again, before they could find any rest and peace, they were struck by a flash blizzard and began their customary walk into the face of the storm.

With the ice and snow in his eyes and ears, cold and lost, Coyote-Now-Buffalo began to doubt the wisdom of his decision. He began to think of his grandmother's fish-head and dead rabbit soup, of their warm dark lodge, of the fact that no one threatened him because no one cared about him, about how he and other coyotes occasionally gathered on especially nice nights when the moon was full to sing their old songs.

So he made his way again to Tenugagahi, Big Bull Buffalo. When he got close, Tenugagahi turned his massive head and fixed his angry eye on Coyote-Now-Buffalo. "What do you want now?" he asked curtly.

"Well, sir," Coyote-Now-Buffalo said uneasily, stuttering a little and lowering himself to show he certainly was not intending to challenge Big Bull Buffalo's primacy in the herd. "I was, uh, well, wondering if maybe perhaps there would be some way . . . well, some way you could turn me back into a coyote."

"There is a way," sighed Big Bull Buffalo, "but you're not going to like it."

You can guess the rest of the story. The buffalo charged Coyote-Now-Buffalo four times. The first three times Coyote-Now-Buffalo jumped back in fear, first feeling the air of the buffalo's passing, then the shaking of the earth under his hooves, and then his horns grazing along the hair of Coyote-Now-Buffalo's side. The fourth time, however, Coyote-Now-Buffalo closed his eyes and prayed; he sang his death song, "Kiyeeyee Aiiiiyeeyee!" The buffalo's head slammed into him and knocked him down the hill, and when he again stood up, sure enough, he had been again transformed and was . . . again . . . Coyote.

He made his way back over the hill to his blind grandmother's lodge, where he smelled her good fish head and dead rabbit soup cooking. As he came into the lodge she asked him, "Grandson Coyote, where have you been?"

"Nowhere," he said as usual.

"What have you been doing?" she asked.

"Nothing," he said, as was his custom.

2. *Introduction*

Is there a child who hasn't at least once pretended to be an Indian, sneaking around spying on the unsuspecting white settlers, maybe camping in a nearby woods or backyard or under the dusty porch? It's not even an American phenomenon; people from Europe and England have told me of their own childhood that they argued over who would get to be the Indian in the mix. At least one case of playing Indian in my life was a long hike out to the local Boy Scout campground that I took with my boyhood pal Billy Danek. We had no tent, just a light tarpaulin and a couple of ragged sleeping bags. We built a small fire in a cramped clearing we made with a machete. To this day I am amazed we didn't seriously wound ourselves or each other and wind up in a hospital emergency ward on that occasion. We started a smoky fire and roasted—or more precisely, burned—some hotdogs (at least the outside was black and crispy) impaled on sticks. Before we had a chance to eat, two campground supervisors showed up, figured out that we weren't old enough to be Scouts and clearly weren't skilled enough to be camping on our own, and sent us back home in disgrace, shuffling down the gravel road eating half-raw wienies and dragging our sleeping bags behind us.

The models for our fantasies were Hollywood and literary Indians, either fancifully evil or romantically heroic—Tonto, Cochise, Geronimo,

Sitting Bull, Uncas, Hiawatha, Yellow Hand ... For some reason it never occurred to me that the dark-skinned little girl who sat in the desk next to me through grade school was an Indian, even though our teachers made a point of her heritage now and then, usually during Thanksgiving, that one time of the year when it's downright noble to be Indian. As I think about that time, I realize I knew she was Indian, even by her looks. But in my mind, in the reality of a Saratoga school classroom she wasn't—well, you know—an *Indian*. No beads, no feathers, no goofy stilted language. She was just a little girl and a friend of mine.

A couple of years ago I ran into this same girl at a social gathering and she introduced herself. I recognized her at once. Again I could see she is Indian, but more than that she was my old friend and classmate and still not the Pocahontas or Sacagawea of legend. Just an Indian. She remembered that I had been something of a hero to her because once when she wet her pants in class, I had cried right along with her, embarrassed for her embarrassment and the other kids' taunting. I'd have probably done the same for any pretty girl in class, but give me some credit ... this little girl *was* an Indian, even though at the time that distinction had nothing to do with our friendship or the embarrassment.

The situation has always been like that between mainstream white America and Indians. There is a certain admiration for the Noble Savage in the distance but a forgetfulness or even contempt for Natives in proximity. In the early nineteenth century James Fennimore Cooper magnified both the nobility and the savagery of American Indians, bringing to the European as well as the American public the image of the Noble Savage, at one with nature, steeped in arcane knowledge of the ways of animals, plants, and geography, bearing ancient and unknown wisdom, while at the same time brutal, villainous, and only in some rare cases to be trusted. So while some Americans read Cooper's works with an almost fanatical enthusiasm, others methodically murdered Indians, stole their wood, food, land, and women, and put enormous effort into destroying them and their way of life, the very landscape and resources that sustained them. Eventually some Americans would lament the destruction of North American Indian cultures, while others cheered it on. Remarkably, those same two conflicting attitudes can easily be found today in any governmental body or on the editorial page of most newspapers.

Hold up! Wait a minute! What is this "destruction of the Indian culture"? Not so fast. That extinction exists only in the wishful thinking of some, the sad but premature mourning of others. Nebraskans laugh at the naiveté of easterners who think there are still cowboys and Indians on the Great Plains—while missing the obvious point that there *are* still cowboys and Indians on the plains! And not just in historical pageants, organized festivals, and museums but in very real, active, contemporary Native life. Non-Indian children still pretend to be Indians, now perhaps taking their models from *Dances with Wolves*, *A Man Called Horse*, or *Little Big Man* (maybe even from Mel Brooks's *Blazing Saddles*), and there are still adults who envy and emulate Indians (although more often than not using historical models) or despise them and wish them gone, annoyed perhaps at their unwillingness to bend to the mainstream paradigm, now seeing them not so much as a romantic model but instead as a troublesome impediment to "progress," much as the buffalo of the past had been.

I have not been immune to these feelings or processes. All of them. My classmate at Saratoga Grade School was not particularly an Indian to me, not that that would have made much difference because she certainly wasn't Pocahontas or Cochise. She was just a girl to me, probably infested with the same cooties infesting all grade school girls. Like many boys who become men, in my youth I continued to have a fascination with Hollywood Indian lore and had no idea that Victor Mature and Sal Mineo might not be Indians and might not have exactly those wonderful natural powers they demonstrated on the movie screen. Over the years I have remained to some degree or another a mainstream, middle-class, educated white man. While I haven't embraced all the ugly influences of white culture around me, I have at least consciously acknowledged them, speaking to what they are and what they do. I am not a radical activist for Indian issues, although I do tend to embrace Indian interests and to speak up about them freely. In part I avoid vocal polemics because I am not an Indian, and I do not—cannot—speak for American Indians; American Indians speak quite well enough for themselves, thank you very much, so I usually sit back and listen.

I do occasionally speak up more when white people make themselves look particularly stupid, more to save my own race further humiliation than to explain or protect a culture and people who scarcely need yet another white guy speaking up for them. A couple of months ago, for example, I heard from a former student of mine from many years ago, a particularly bright fellow who went on to graduate from Harvard with a degree in philosophy (I believe) and has continued on in his life to become a professor in a small midwestern college. I was disappointed that he has cultivated a snooty professorial posture, not nearly as fresh and bright as he was when he was simply an exceptional undergraduate. While I was telling him about some of where my life had gone during the past thirty years, I mentioned that my wife, Linda, and I have returned our farm and home to the Pawnee Nation and have in return been adopted by the tribe as Pawnee. He snorted that that was not such a notable distinction because after all he had his own Native associations: *his* great-great-grandfather had married (I saw it coming already and began a long, slow, low groan) a Cherokee—I mumbled the word in unison with him—"princess." My skepticism really riled him and he would not listen further, so I got in only a few words to the effect that as a folklorist I can say with all confidence that the canard of the great-great-grandfather's Cherokee princess bride has to be one of the most common pieces of empty racist nonsense in America, and yet it constitutes a curious kind of Wannabeism because it is a method of establishing a personal Indian connection near enough to lend to the family tree some of the mystic wisdom that comes with Cherokee blood while at the same time keeping that connection distant enough that it isn't a stain on the family escutcheon.

Which is to say, arrogance and ignorance toward and about American Indians past and present are not mistakes restricted to any one class or educational level. Again, not long ago a very well-known popular historian in our state, a professor with a doctorate and long career in higher education, expanded his speaking menu (while adding nothing to his qualifications or credentials to do so) to include lectures on how to help Indians become "successful," by which he meant more like him, he being the ideal in his mind. He recommended as his first offering that we abolish Indian reservations, thus leaving Indians no choice but to "acculturate"—that is, acquire a culture, which would, of course, be the culture of mainstream, white America. Like his.

I suggested to him that Indians might not choose to become like mainstream, white Americans. He was utterly befuddled. Why would anyone not want to be exactly like him?! I explained that Indians frequently love the reservation as a last refuge against the tsunami of white culture. Returning to the reservation is sometimes referred to as "going back to the blanket," not as a cowardly retreat but as a return to the comfort of home. Many Indians see the reservation as a life raft where they can still, perhaps, practice their language, foodways, rituals, and religion within their community and without outside interference or even observation. Moreover, many people around the world—not just Indians—look at American or Western culture and find nothing there at all attractive to them. Moreover, a tribe's reservation lands may contain sacred sites, either from deep history or from more recent history, but held to be sacred nonetheless. Eliminating a reservation, perhaps submerging it under yet another Army Corps of Engineers dam, would be a callous raid and destruction of sites and rites considered sacrosanct.

It's not as if life on a typical Indian reservation is idyllic. Indians have every reason to be angered by the poverty of their own people on their own lands, and many are not entirely enchanted with their ancient cultural expressions and the continuation or restoration of historical artifacts from their past. They may indeed be looking for something else, something more or different than the ways of their elders. They may even want to join in the profligate ways of American society, or for all our own mainstream love of it, it may be the last thing they want for themselves. Despite the worn, dim-witted cliché that the world hates us for our freedom, the truth is that a good part of the world hates us for our arrogance, ignorance, profligacy, hypocrisy, and cold dismissal of other wisdoms.

In fact, just as most Americans are scarcely aware of their own culture's worldviews or how the rest of the world sees them, American Indians too may not see anything at all about their own ways that is anything but natural, normal, logical, or God-given. They accept their ways of life on the reservation as *the* way of life, if not necessarily the best or even a good way of life. Again and again Indian friends of mine have dismissed any notion that their ways, knowledge, culture, or traditions are in any way different or of particular value. That's the way real culture works: it is so much a part of their normal life they can't imagine how it could seem as anything other than that to others. They are wrong. All of us are.

I suggested to my provincial and narrow-minded historian friend that instead of trying to "integrate Native Americans into the ways of Mainstream America so they can enjoy all the benefits of it that the rest of us do," maybe he should work at eliminating the German "reservations" in Pennsylvania and Texas, or the Irish "reservations" in Massachusetts, or the Italian "reservations" in New York City. He didn't seem to think that would work, but after a couple of occasions when he presented his ideas about civilizing Indians to be just like us to audiences in which there were Indians, he dropped that particular lecture from his offerings.

Such cultural myopia is less likely within Native circles than within the American mainstream, however, because a mainstream, white American may go through life never encountering an Indian except one operating a roadside curio stand for tourists or lying drunk and filthy in the street of a town near a reservation, thus witnessing and accepting the most visible but also most distorted view of "the Indian" as the model for a lifelong understanding of what an Indian is. People get stuck in lost but not forgotten worlds of ethnic, regional, neighborhood, religious, and even historical points of view. The shared perceptions appear as if out of nowhere, expressed by people you were sure would know better, so out of place and time that it's for all the world like spotting a dinosaur eating out of your backyard birdfeeder. Cultural presumptions about others and perhaps even more importantly about our own culture are so ingrained that they are thought of as biological or at least logical inevitables. We speak to others with firm eye contact; to do otherwise shows dishonesty, or sneakiness. It's normal. It's natural. And that's only if for some reason we stop to think about what we do with our eyes in social contact, something very few people ever do. A firm handshake is . . . well . . . a clear demonstration of . . . what? . . . sincerity. Everyone knows that. No, not everyone. In many cultures that piercing eye contact and hand-crushing grip are received as aggression. And why not? Firm handshakes and unwavering eye contact are the standard operating gestures of honest, decent, good people. You know, like used-car salesmen. Politicians. Television evangelists.

It's almost as if we live in our own world, unmoved by even the most dramatic changes and shifts of the cultural winds around us. Buzz-cut throwbacks from 1960 presume they are the mainstream and continue mocking or dismissing long-hairs as fey eccentrics, even while cheering on equally well-tressed country singers or NFL linemen with manes springing from under their helmets. Evangelical zealots continue to presume they are part of a cutting-edge majority even though the world has long ago left them behind with wiser and more profound spiritual knowledge and commitment. Bigots snarl that recent immigrants' "American" usage is not up to their demanding standards, even though English is the Thai's, Somali's, or Guatemalan's second or even third language while the genu-wine 150 percent American is only marginally literate in his first.

I'm probably more than a little snarly about this because I was a hippie in the 1960s and heard my share of the standard insults of the time: "Hey, are you a boy or a girl?" "Hippie, why don't you take a bath, get a job, and buy a haircut?" Never mind that I was gainfully employed, while the cultural throwback throwing the insult was not. Or that I enjoyed success in nearly every part of my life, in part because of my insistence on the freedom that I expressed in my choice of hairstyles. But this person who without doubt prided himself on his patriotism, piety, and handsome good looks while actually having none of those virtues, while loudly proclaiming America as the land of the free and the home of the brave, was actually a hopeless coward and feared nothing more than the freedom I represented simply by wearing my hair long.

I could have been cursed with the same set of prejudices. In America it is easy to be culturally isolated. However, through a series of unique (I like to think) coincidences, circumstances, strokes of incredible good luck, and twists of fate and the grace of others I found a magical entry into another culture dramatically different from my own and avoided the narrow perspective of the old friend who disappointed me with his cruel and ignorant fear of . . . long hair. Perhaps my good fortune was a gift from Coyote the Trickster, to my mind to this very day the best metaphor I have found for the quirky sense of humor and divine wisdom of the sacred fool, the power that swirls around us, and, although I hate to admit it, the force that determines the ways of the world in general and, again apparently, of even helpless individuals like me. I certainly didn't go seeking another world. I didn't know there was another world, and yet suddenly there I was in the middle of it.

Which is to say, along the road I became a Wannabe, a non-Indian who ingratiated himself into Indian society, who was treated kindly (or perhaps even humored) by Indian communities, families, and individuals. They tolerated me within their society and took me as family within their lives and ways, even into the most sacred of secret and holy contexts. They shared their food with me, even letting me sit at their drums and learn their songs. They shared their jokes and prayers with me, gave me new names, and adopted me as kin.

My own experience seems to have been largely a matter of innocence, error, and good fortune, but having now been in this other world for almost sixty years I have seen many other non-Indians purposely working to gain that same access and experience. In some cases I get the impression they are like I was, not at all aware of what I was in for, while others know quite well what they are looking for . . . a way to avoid ignorance.

I suppose I should warn you: what I will offer you here is not a scholarly ethnography with references, footnotes, bibliography, and all the appropriate arcane language of the social sciences. This book is more than anything else a memoir. It is not strictly, logically, or even conveniently organized; it is a casual, straggling conversation in which I describe my own long pilgrimage through Native life (or perhaps more accurately, lives), which I hope will provide comfort and maybe even direction to others who might find themselves on the same journey. I would like to answer insofar as I can the question I have so often been asked: "How can I involve myself in Native culture?" I believe that if my experiences within the Native community are not unique, they are at least out of the ordinary. I do not suggest that mine is the usual pattern for the transition from outsider to Wannabe. The circumstances and experiences I relate here have been instructive to me, and I hope and believe they will be helpful to others. This is not a manual for interaction with Natives. It is not a systematic examination of Native culture, non-Native culture, or transcultural interaction. I have never worked as a professionally educated observer or researcher of Native culture. This book is not intended to be exhaustive, scientific, scholarly, or even enlightened. If anything it is biographic and anecdotal. I am only sharing here my experiences and impressions.

Obviously, my experiences are my own and almost certainly not the same as those of others. That is even more true of my impressions, which are those same experiences filtered through my eyes and mind and the matrix of other experiences, again uniquely my own. This book is not so much about those who have been attracted to Native culture and could legitimately be called Wannabes, or even those who may want to become Wannabes. It is not about Indians who are emulated by Wannabes. This book is about me, my experiences, my impressions, my thoughts, my conclusions, and my deep gratitude for the part Indians have played in my long and wonderfully surprising life. I can imagine that scholars will have had different experiences, impressions, thoughts, and conclusions; I have in fact already heard from some of them about their disagreements with me about some of the statements in this book. That's fine but it really is irrelevant. How can someone change the experiences and impressions of another? I do not care for tapioca; that is my personal opinion and I can't imagine anyone talking me out of it. Same with the opinions, impressions, and experiences I will tell you in these pages. I have already heard from academics—fine scholars and writers—who say they are not Wannabes, never have been Wannabes, and don't want to be Wannabes with an attraction for *any* other culture—Indian, Chinese, Basque, or the world of ultimate fighting. I can imagine that. I have worked with cultures other than Native American and have not been at all attracted to them; in fact, in a couple of cases I was repulsed by them. I do not intend to spend any energy debating such points of opinion and taste. If your opinions, impressions, or experiences differ from mine, don't try to change mine or argue with me about them. The thing for you to do is write your own book.

My exposure to Native culture has been unselective and serendipitous. I did not go to Indian communities as a scholar or researcher, so there was no plan, no schedule, no thesis to be tested. I have spent the most time with the Omaha people, and so most of my knowledge is about them. Recently I have spent more time with the Pawnees. Along the road I have dealt in a lesser degree with Otos, Poncas, Winnebagos, Inuit, Mayas, and Lakotas. What I have lost in focus by spreading my interest and associations so thinly and treating them so casually I feel I have gained in the breadth of my time and the intensity of my attention. I have watched anthropological scholars devote intense time and energy for a couple of years to one concentrated problem within one tribe and then move on to the next problem in their sights. I, on the other hand, have sat patiently with elders, listening, joking, taking no notes, no photos, no sound recordings—just sitting and listening.

3. *A Beginning*

There is a temptation when viewing another culture with a long history to imagine that what one sees is a relic of that past, a vestigial remnant. Again and again I have seen non-Indians dismiss a living, vital, dynamic Native culture as a curio from a lost past. Even sophisticated researchers can tend to think of an unfamiliar culture as a subject of an autopsy rather a vital, living organism.

That was certainly my feeling when I attended my first Omaha handgame about 1964. I had been working on linguistic problems with Mr. Clyde Sheridan as part of an undergraduate anthropology class and Mr. Sheridan invited me to attend a game in our community. I jumped at the chance, with no idea what a handgame was. I was a grown man but I was nonetheless uneasy as I launched off into this cultural experience; moving within an unfamiliar culture is not a usual experience for most Americans, and it is an experience that is only rarely welcomed or enjoyed. The game was in a seedy part of town and the address took me to the door of an even seedier clothing rummage shop. Even from the outside the store smelled pretty much like a rummage shop. But the venue of the game wasn't even the store proper, but through a side door and down in the building's basement. I found the side door and peered down a long, narrow stairway to the bowels of the dark basement, from where I could hear voices and the thundering throb of a large drum. High-pitched male voices sang not just unfamiliar songs but modes of music I had never heard before. I stepped past a half dozen dusty children playing in the dirt of the stairway and ventured uneasily down into the dark.

I emerged into a dank room in which the principal feature was a huge, octopus-like furnace. Off to one side of the old furnace in a cramped open area five men sat around a large drum. Two dozen people sat in chairs around the edge of the room. Off in one corner women worked at cooking food over a gas burner; steam and the smells of boiling soup and seething-hot lard filled the room. From his seat at the drum Mr. Sheridan saw me, signaled, and pointed me to a chair along the wall, beside, as it turned out, his wife, Lillian, who would help me learn the game during the evening.

I sat in this unfamiliar situation in stunned silence. I had no idea what was going on. The sounds, smells, sights, strangers . . . it was all new and confusing for me. It was a cultural wrenching I had never before experienced. For one thing, for the first time in my life I was not just a minority in a room of people but the only person of my race, an experience rare to mainstream, white Americans. The music was wonderful and again like nothing I had heard before. I heard in a living context a language that I had previously heard only one kinship term at a time in my linguistic work with Mr. Sheridan. I saw grace in dances that was not part of a performance but an inherent part of a cultural matrix—Native music, language, and dance in its own natural environment. I struggled at learning the complicated game and was struck and pleased when, even as an unknown intruder in this social but private activity, I was included in the game, invited to "hide the stones." When I was inept and failed at even a first deception of the other team's guesser, there was laughter, but not cruel laughter. There was instead obvious pleasure that I had indeed joined in the game and that I too laughed at my obvious lack of skill in the game.

That night I climbed the rummage store's cellar stairs and went into the clear night air with my mind spinning. Yes, the handgame and all that swirled around it was a confusing experience and I had been uncomfortable with the struggle to cope with the assault on my senses. But I had acquired many new friends and had actually come out of the experience exhilarated. It had been a wonderful adventure. I had gotten past my initial unease in a totally alien (although that adjective seems now remarkably inappropriate when associated with Native culture) cultural context. At the time, however, I wondered too if I hadn't seen a dying relic of a lost culture, a once-in-a-lifetime experience. I had read in Margaret Mead's work on the Omahas, *The Lost Culture of an Indian Tribe*, that activities like the handgame were dying when she was on the Omaha Reservation in the 1930s. So I presumed that I was seeing only a vestigial trace of what had once been. Perhaps, I remember thinking, I had just attended the last Omaha handgame. It was, after all, a small gathering, impossibly out of place in "modern" American life. Well, that would have been something of an honor, I supposed. I resolved to remember every detail I could of the evening because this might turn out to be something I would tell my grandchildren about: "Yes, I was there when the last Omaha handgame was played in 1964."

I quickly learned better. The handgame and Omaha culture in general may not have been what they were a century or two earlier, but they were far from dead. During the next forty-five years I attended scores, maybe hundreds of handgames. And not only within the Omaha Indian community. I have played the handgame (with some slight and interesting variations) with the Pawnees and Wichitas. The handgame is alive and well. And so is Native American culture.

4. *Beyond the Handgame*

Mr. Richard Fool Bull, a Brule holy man, taught me other lessons about the nature of history, especially history that is not within the mainstream—for example, that it lives on even when and where we do not see it, and in ways we cannot expect. I have trouble relating the story of one of the first times he did this for me not simply because it was a remarkable, unlikely event in itself but also because it occurred within a context that was equally complicated, and as a result it wound up being a memorable experience the meaning of which still leaves me mentally out of breath.

I had heard a lot about Mr. Fool Bull from a mutual friend but had not yet met him. About ten o'clock one evening my friend, with whom Mr. Fool Bull stayed when he was in our city, called. She began her conversation with an apology for bothering me, especially since the reason for her call was a bit peculiar, maybe even inappropriate. Mr. Fool Bull was at her home and had made a curious request, one that in fact made no sense at all to her. But she felt she owed it to her friend Mr. Fool Bull to do the simple assignment he had given her.

Mr. Fool Bull made beautiful Lakota love flutes but had been stymied in his efforts to obtain suitable material, the dark-red core wood of juniper, or red cedar as it is frequently called on the plains. He had tried to make flutes with redwood, but it proved to be too soft and did not have the resonance he needed for his instruments. Out of nowhere, having never met me, he told my friend Kay to call me because he felt I would be the person to obtain for him the wood he needed. Knowing that I lived at the time in a relatively new suburban house not far from her and quite aware that the only two trees on my property were soft silver maple trees no more than three or four years old, my friend knew I was about as unlikely a source of fifty- or sixty-year-old juniper heartwood as she could imagine. But she called me nonetheless. Because Mr. Fool Bull told her to.

As I listened to her apology and explanation of her errand I was as dumbstruck as she was apologetic, because I had spent that day at hard labor with several friends—felling and hauling red cedar trees.

An old building at the small college where I was teaching was to be razed, and I had asked the school's officials if I might have their permission to salvage twenty-five or thirty gigantic, ancient juniper trees that stood immediately around it. I was doing consulting work for a museum and we had been looking for juniper—red cedar—trees to use as roof beams for a sod house that was to be constructed as an exhibit. The school gave me permission to harvest the trees, so I borrowed a couple of chainsaws, rented a truck, and rounded up some friends to help me cut and trim the trees, load them, and haul the massive trunks to our suburban home for later transport to the museum.

Or at least, that's what I thought I was doing. It was a lot more work, to begin with, than was really necessary. I needed only five logs for the sod-house construction, but I figured I should take all the wood I could get while I had the help, equipment, and opportunity. I could figure out later what to do with the excess. As a result, I had thirty huge juniper logs stacked in my side yard, probably to the consternation of my long-suffering neighbors. I told my friend who telephoned that very evening that I couldn't explain how Mr. Fool Bull could have possibly known it but somehow he had had her call a man with probably the largest collection of raw juniper heartwood in the state of Nebraska! In his side yard. Piled up and ready for whatever it was intended for. I told my friend to bring Mr. Fool Bull over the next morning and we could cut from that pile of logs whatever he needed for his flutes. *All* he wanted.

When my friend and Mr. Fool Bull arrived the next morning my friend was as stunned by the sight of the huge pile of logs as I had been by her call of the previous night. It was an impossibly lucky coincidence. No wonder Mr. Fool Bull later and in another context told me that an unrelenting faith in coincidence is the white man's real religion. We have somehow convinced ourselves that things that are clearly not accidental are in fact random occurrences and that things obviously arrayed and occurring in patterns are instead unconnected. This moment was clearly not a coincidence. Somehow Mr. Fool Bull knew, precisely as he said, that I was the man to call about juniper heartwood.

After brief introductions, I waited for some sign of surprise from Mr. Fool Bull once he realized that he had somehow stumbled on the most unlikely possible accumulation of precisely what he had been looking for. But there was no surprise, so finally I asked him if, well, he wasn't just a little surprised that he had indeed stumbled on exactly the right person for what he needed. No, he said, surprised not at the abundance of red heartwood but at my apparent dimwittedness. The reason he had had our mutual friend call me, he explained, was precisely because I was the man to call. His logic was impeccable. It just wasn't the logic I expected.

He moved quickly around the yard, pointing out which pieces of wood he wanted cut to the appropriate lengths. He also felt no need to thank me because . . . well, the reason I had come into possession of all that juniper heartwood was because he needed juniper heartwood. So there was no more reason for gratitude than there had been for surprise. We cut the wood as he instructed and loaded it into my friend's car until the rear springs sagged under the weight.

To Mr. Fool Bull's way of thinking, we were all simply doing what we were supposed to do, fulfilling our roles in a logical, directed process of getting juniper heartwood so he could proceed to do what he was intended to do—make flutes.

But that remarkable twist in an alternate reality was only a beginning. At some point, perhaps when we were touching up the chains on the saws or taking a rest, Mr. Fool Bull talked. He told me that he wanted to make me one of his flutes for my trouble but laughingly warned me that one has to be careful with Lakota love flutes. Their sound does not speak of love to a woman who hears its tones and is somehow convinced. No, a woman who hears the flute's song has no option but to fall hopelessly in love with the man playing the love song. He said that for that reason he never played his flute when he was staying with our mutual friend, Kay. He laughed when he told us this, but I think he was also to some degree serious, even though he was well into his nineties at that time and our friend was perhaps thirty. The flute's magic, he explained, knows nothing of history and does not speak to the usual senses. Its power was beyond the white man's conventional understanding of love, the love song, and the flute.

At another point Mr. Fool Bull told us about his pride, at his advanced age, of having been asked to be a spiritual representative by the young, angry Indians of the American Indian Movement during their occupation of the Wounded Knee, South Dakota, village and church during the siege there in 1973. He spoke of the courage of the young Indians and the obscenity of federal marshals and troops besieging them in the lonely, beautiful little church at the top of Wounded Knee hill. Thousands and thousands of rounds of ammunition were fired during that sad event.

The direction of our conversation drifted to other topics, we cut and loaded more wood, and in passing Mr. Fool Bull talked to us about his vast knowledge of plants, medicines, and traditional foods and ways. And then in something of a conversational tangent he spoke of the gunfire again, clapping his hands to imitate the sound of the guns. I asked, "Were those the weapons of the federal agents surrounding the church or the weapons of the AIM warriors? I know some of them had AK-47s they had brought back from Vietnam. Is that the sound you heard?" There was an uncomfortable moment of confusion as we realized we had somehow jumped the track and were speaking in different directions,

Mr. Fool Bull and I. "No," he said, trying to bring our conversation back into synchrony. "Those were the soldiers' Hotchkiss guns."

Oh my God! I suddenly realized that plains history had just accordianed on me, collapsing into one crumpled wad between Mr. Fool Bull and me. This man in front of us had indeed been at the American Indian Movement occupation of Wounded Knee in 1973. But he had also been (as we learned in a moment) close enough to the events to hear the guns of the first massacre at Wounded Knee in 1890.

For a Wannabe the brevity and proximity of American history is a constant element. The white occupation of the plains is only minutes old. To Native Americans, immediate contact and conflict with non-Indian, mainstream American culture is only a blip in the larger historical timeline. Native culture in North America is ancient, at least as old as Roman culture on the European continent. Just as evidence remains in the twenty-first-century world of our Roman history, ancient elements of Native cultures can still be seen modern America. But just as surely as there are modern traffic jams in the shadow of the Roman Colosseum where gladiators died, modern Native Americans live in the world of computers and communications satellites while still holding traditional beliefs and practicing old customs, the juxtaposition unseen by practitioner and observer alike. A few weeks ago I was amused to find a reference in a scholarly study stating explicitly that we know little about the Skidis, a sub-band of the Pawnee Nation, because "the Skidi have been extinct for some time now." In my next conversation with Pat Leading Fox, elected chief of the Skidi band, I noted that for someone who is extinct, he sure does eat a lot. Similarly, when I mentioned to a scholarly anthropologist that I was about to travel to Pawnee, Oklahoma, to be given a Pipe Ceremony I was informed that the Pipe Ceremony has been dead for many generations. So I guess the moving ceremony I witnessed and participated in was imaginary. To be sure, the modern Pawnee Pipe Ceremony is rarely practiced today and is only a thin shadow of the classic Hako Pipe Ceremony that took Alice Fletcher et al. four hundred pages to describe; nonetheless, it is the Pipe Ceremony *as practiced today*.

Even when and if the Skidis and the Pipe Ceremony have disappeared, Mr. Fool Bull would insist, they may not really be *gone* in an absolute sense. As mentioned, Mr. Fool Bull was particularly knowledgeable about the ancient uses of medicine plants among Plains Indians. I once commented that I hoped he had a young apprentice on the Rosebud or perhaps someone who was recording his vast knowledge so it wouldn't be lost when he was gone. Mr. Fool Bull chuckled at that notion and explained that even if we should somehow forget that aspirin eases pain and headache, if that knowledge somehow were totally erased from human memory, that would not mean that aspirin (or the willow bark from which its almost magical salicylic acid was originally derived in the Native pharmacopoeia) would no longer ease pain and headache. It would still have its powers, even if for the moment we forgot those powers. As he summarized that wisdom, "Truth never dies."

5. *History, Long and Short*

I remember once being at a handgame in Lincoln at a time when I had acquired a solid knowledge of the game. Scoring seems simple enough, but it can be complicated, so I was proud that I was consulted now and then when there was confusion about a particular scoring problem. I knew the game and its rhythms, or so I thought, but on this occasion I realized that there was an irregularity in the sequences of handgame songs, Round Dance songs, and Gourd Dance songs. I expected one kind of song and its appropriate dance but was seeing something else. I knew better than to ask my aunt Lillian, who was sitting beside me, about the irregularity—asking direct questions was and within some traditional Native circles still is considered impolite—but I knew that it would be acceptable to comment on what appeared to be an irregularity, hoping she would then comment in turn. "Aunt Lillian, I was expecting another handgame song but I hear another kind of song instead."

"Yes," she said. "This is a song we sometimes sing when the score is tied three to three."

That night I had a lot to think about. If I had gone to only a few games and the score was never tied three to three, even if I had been there for years, I would never have heard that song or understood that possible feature of the game. On the other hand, if I had attended only games at which the score happened to tie at three to three, I might have concluded that at that place in the game sequence one *always* sang that song. Thus, in any Native cultural event I could never be sure of exactly what I was seeing—a constant in every observation of the ritual or an anomaly that took place only on those occasions when I happened to be there. The point is, the best course, the only course, toward understanding what I was seeing in Native culture was to be there often. And even then my conclusions would have to be tentative. There might be degrees of certainty, but absolute certitude is out of the question.

I decided at one point that I would sit at the handgame drum and learn the songs. I had been attending games for a number of years, so I had some idea of how things go and had even sung along to a few songs. So I asked my uncle Oliver Saunsoci to make me a drumstick. My friends and relatives welcomed me into the drum circle and I sang along and worked at learning songs. One night the games went quickly, and we had completed the last handgame, Round Dance, Gourd Dance sequence before the women had finished preparing the food that is an inevitable part of any Omaha gathering. One of the singers at the drum suggested that we sing a few . . . some kind of songs. I can't recall what the name of songs was but I did know I had never heard of them before.

Small wonder: another of the singers at the drum said he thought that was a good idea. He had always liked those songs. He said he couldn't even recall how long it had been since they had sung those songs. Others in the drum circle ventured guesses: Twenty years? Thirty? The elders sitting at the drum could not agree on a specific date when they had last heard those songs but yes, it had been at least twenty or thirty years. They began hitting the drum and singing while I sat there dumbstruck.

The men were singing songs they hadn't heard for twenty or thirty years. That made it pretty clear that there was no way I was ever going to master the repertoire, if parts surfaced only every few decades, especially since I was already struggling to sing songs I had heard only a week before. My experience is limited to the narrow scope of my lifetime within a culture that is practiced in a continuity of decades, generations, and lifetimes. The traditions of these societies are a process measured in centuries. At least. Every participant in that culture is only a step in the system, and my step was doomed to be limited because my time in it was short. I had started late, and however deeply I immersed myself in it my participation would never be more than periodic. I still believed (and believe) that a short-term researcher of Native culture (perhaps any culture) is forever limited to only the smallest conclusions about that culture, but now I also knew that even though my much longer and broader exposure to Omaha culture might give me more insight than that of most outsiders, I would forever be an outsider, too.

6. *Who Are We?*

I did not come to my long association with Native communities as an anthropologist. In fact, I carefully avoided any suggestion in that direction, an approach that became harder once I was given a position in a university anthropology department. I wasn't going to try to explain that I was a folklorist, not an anthropologist, a distinction not even folklorists and anthropologists are clear about. Anthropologists have often been regarded as pariahs by Indians, and with good reason. I took no notes or photographs, offered no credentials, published nothing serious about what I saw and heard in Native circles, presented no papers in academic settings. I was just there when I was at Native gatherings—ceremonial, social, or simply standing around.

So why *was* I there? I don't recall that anyone asked me, but I wondered in my own mind. All I could come up with was that I was there because I was among friends. I enjoyed their company. I came to love the music, dance, general behavior, and ways of my Indian friends. I notoriously loved their food; there were threats that I would be given the Indian name Fry Bread because I had become Indian by ingestion. I found peace and comfort with my Omaha friends.

But still, I must have had deeper motives. Perhaps being with Omaha friends fulfilled some emotional need. I'm not given to self-analysis, and so I didn't explore that possibility far. Perhaps I felt a need for family and association because I was an only child in a larger family that was not particularly close. Who knows? I don't feel that my motivations were or are particularly important. We all have our reasons. I had become a Wannabe. Not that everyone does. That's okay. But I was and am and that's okay, too.

I'm comfortable with the idea that I have somehow prepared a path during the past fifty-five years that would help others with similar opportunities. I can't even be sure other people have similar opportunities, having never objectively or systematically considered the experiences of others. But I know there *are* other Wannabes and in our casual conversations there are suggestions that many of us enjoy the same kind of good fortune in moving into and within Indian circles. To be honest, I think—I know—my good fortune was in large part like the rest of my life, a matter of incredibly dumb but equally incredibly good luck. Just plain old good fortune, a flat-out roll of the dice coming up with a hundred sevens in a row: meeting the right people, being in the right place, saying the right things (by accident, not design), not making fatal mistakes, and . . . who knows what else? No doubt about it, I have led a long and magical life filled with remarkable good fortune, in large part coming to me as my Indian associations, friends, and family.

That is in large part what this book is about. I hope I am sharing a few suggestions and hints here and there for others who perhaps feel the drive to associate with Native people, but I guarantee nothing without the gift of good fortune. I have as much reason to believe that my advice is bad advice as any assurance that it is good. I am sure that will be pointed out to me in the future by other people who do not enjoy the same good experiences and successes and by Indians who find plenty of reason to resent my presumptions, assertions, guesses, and goofs. As I have noted, I know that my experiences are not typical, much less universal, perhaps not even likely, if not unique. But here they are, for what they are. All I can say by way of excusing myself where I am misleading you is that this is all I know. It's all I have. I can only tell you what I have been given. This volume is not based on systematic research but rather on my own serendipitous wanderings and the fickle gaming of my little brother, Coyote the Trickster.

7. *The Call of Curiosity, Keep the Change*

The most recent theories about the survival of humankind as of this writing (winter 2009) posit that humans have survived and evolved not so much because they were particularly successful in dealing with any particular environment but because they are especially well equipped to change. That is, our talent lies not in dealing specifically with heat or cold, drought or flood but in adapting to, accepting, welcoming, and even seeking *change*. Our interest, like the mythic Coyote's, lies in trying to be what we are not, a constant probing and exploring, change and adaptation, seeking, trying, and even pretending. It is not in enduring that we find the very substance of our survival but in constant change. We are, it is argued, genetically inclined to prosper not in safety but in deliberate exposure to risk, even if only temporary and relatively slight.

In my story of Coyote and Big Bull Buffalo, for example, adapted from an Omaha trickster story, what are we to think about Coyote? As usual in American Native stories, it is not easy to pin down Coyote's character. Is he stupid or clever? Is he a cultural hero or a villain? Is he a demigod, a human being with the name Coyote, or simply that beautiful animal we sometimes see running across a road or field or hear singing those rococo cantatas on moonlit nights? He could be any one of those. The Coyote of fable frequently shifted forms, perhaps deflowering the most beautiful maiden of the village while disguised as a handsome young man. And then in the morning, disgracefully, he leaves her but only after changing back to his animal form, thus revealing to her entire family, lodge, and village that she lost her virginity to . . . a coyote!

Again, is Coyote the man, the animal, or the spirit? Perhaps he is not just one but a constant flux of all three. Who else do we know who is sometimes clever, sometimes stupid? Sometimes a hero, sometimes a scoundrel? An animal in one guise, a human in another, sometimes even believed to be endowed with a spark of divinity? Well, I would suggest that would be us. You and me. That's the way folktales work. They let us talk about ourselves and look at ourselves with some detachment, to understand our peculiarities, foibles, weaknesses, deepest fantasies, and dreams without having to find the courage to talk about them directly. Coyote is us.

Whatever we are, we all wish to be something else. That is the human character. Every serious actor wants to play the role of the clown and every comedian wants to be a tragedian. People who live in the city want to be farmers and farmers ache for the excitement of the city. Famous people struggle to find anonymity while the obscure dream of fame. Living in a world of complex technology, we throw sleeping bags into our cars and like Billy Danek and me strike out into the countryside to sleep on the ground and burn supper over a campfire.

Generally speaking, our results are the same as Coyote's. We probe and explore and, as often as not, retreat. Did Coyote fail in his adventures with Big Bull Buffalo? One might think so at first but his behavior on his return to his grandmother's lodge doesn't reflect failure. Coyote did not succeed as a buffalo bull, but he learned that maybe the life of a buffalo wasn't as idyllic as he had imagined; he concluded that his humble life with his grandmother wasn't quite as bad as he had thought. He simply learned something. For example, he learned that being what he was wasn't all that bad. That's a lesson a lot of us would enjoy. Upon reflection, perhaps we must conclude that the adventure was therefore a success. I think of life's lessons in terms of my own scoring system, and in my lifetime scoring calculations Coyote's return on his investment was more than a one-pointer. I believe that when you learn something new, you get one point. But if you learn something new while at the same time finding that something you had previously believed true is wrong, you get *two* points. I would suggest that Coyote earned double points with his adventure into the world of the buffalo.

Let's reprise my camping expedition with Billy Danek. And the insistence on a return to the wild by those with a comfortable life right where they are. In my lifetime of teaching in higher education and therefore within a community of people in their upper teens to lower and middle twenties I have encountered more than a lot of young enthusiasts eager to "get back in touch with nature," to "find the true nature of man," and—here it comes!—to "return to the simple life." As a teacher of folklore I think I have had more than the usual academic's number of students coming into my office dreaming of this "return to the plain and simple." I have wavered between an inclination to warn the naïfs outright that they are heading toward trouble or to wish them luck and send them out to learn that same lesson the hard way.

The second choice is best. Deduction is a better learning method than induction. It is better to learn for oneself than be told. The reality is that our modern lives are the simple ones. Yes, we are surrounded by manifold and manifest complexities—computers, power grids, hybrid engines, space travel, satellite communications, GPS, handheld communication devices, complicated human relationships (just what the heck *is* a family these days?), on and on. I've had the feeling myself: "Oh, to retreat to my nineteenth-century log house down by the river, to escape all the crushing complications of my life up here at the house—you know, in *civilization*."

While the world around us *is* complicated, our relationship with it, our role in it, is not. Zen-like, what seems complex is actually simple and what seems simple is actually complex. I have no idea how the computer on which I am writing these words works. None. I have no idea how the words end up on a USB drive or are sent by e-mail to the University of Nebraska Press or how the process works that then puts the words on paper. I have no idea what happens when I turn the key to start my modern automobile, even though, I'll admit, I have a good idea of what happens when I turn the crank to start my 1936 Allis Chalmers wc tractor. I don't even know what happens when I flick the switch to turn on the lights here in my office. I have an idea how the switch works, but electricity? It makes no sense to me at all, and I'm no dummy. Technological complexity is all around me, but I am not a part of it. I am only within it.

Consider again my comment about turning the crank to start my 1936 Allis Chalmers wc tractor. With my ancient tractors I *am* a part of the technology. I do more than turn a key. That is, my relationship with that old tractor is more intimate than is my relationship with my car. I am a part of that old tractor technology.

Therein, I believe, lies the attraction so many of us have for activities like camping. Why would anyone leave a perfectly comfortable house, bed, television, and automobile to sleep on the ground by a campfire? Not because it is simple, but because it is complex. And we have an involvement with that complexity. We have no understanding, much less control, in the high technology of our modern life. That is, it happens around us without our involvement. While the technology is complicated, our lives within it are simple. Distressingly, frustratingly, infuriatingly simple. If you doubt me, try to change it. The next time your computer provider's service or the gps locating system in your automobile fails, well, just go ahead and fix it. *Make* it work.

Now that you have tasted your powerlessness, let's go back to my cabin by the river. When I am there and I want more heat, all I have to do is throw another piece of wood into the stove. There's no wood? I can grab the saw and cut some. When it gets dark and I want light, I trim the wick on the lantern, fill it with kerosene, lift the chimney, light it, and adjust the wick so it doesn't smoke. Bathroom? Unlike my house, there's no plumbing to worry about at the cabin . . . the toilet is that little house over by the tree. I built it myself. It's over a hole I dug with a shovel. Entertainment? Let's tell a story, or sing a song. Your every need is taken care of. By you. You are in charge.

That's the secret. That's what you want when you come out here. Not the simple life, but the *complicated* life. We want to be in control. We want our lives complicated by all the details of survival, and we want those details to be within the reach of our capabilities. We're Wannabes. We want to be in another time, in another relationship with our environment. We are Coyote, and we sometimes long for the life of Big Bull Buffalo over on the other side of the hill.

8. *Enter the Wannabes*

My training was in modern languages and linguistics, and I learned early on that learning a second language like French or German is not primarily a matter of communication but a way of moving a step away from one's first language and thus acquiring some perspective from which one can look back and better understand one's own tongue. Two birds, one stone. One of those lifetime pluses on the scoreboard.

Another level of intellectual gain is added when the second language is historically important, even if it is a dead language—Latin or Old Norse, for example. Then the student learns another language *and* ventures into another historical context. Double profit. Put two points up on the scoreboard.

To be a Wannabe is not primarily, then, a slavish aping of another culture out of empty envy but a way to gain a better understanding of culture in general and one's own culture in particular. In addition, it is a possible way to obtain a new understanding about culture and cultures in general as well as in particular.

I was born and raised in a small city, Lincoln, Nebraska. I am careful to use that adjective "small"—you can imagine the guffaws I draw from people who live in truly metropolitan centers when I refer to Lincoln, Nebraska, as a "city." But Lincoln *is* a substantial population center when it is compared with Dannebrog, Nebraska—population 347 . . .

or 346—where I currently live. I had never been to Dannebrog before I bought a piece of exhausted pastureland near that village in 1974. The land was nothing but sand and cactus but with a quarter mile of river frontage on a very pretty, clean river, the Middle Loup—l-o-u-p, French for "wolf," a bit of trivia that will have some import later in my story. While I came here completely by chance and knew nothing of the ground I now owned or of the village with which it is associated, I was not disappointed as I came to know the ground and the nearby village. For one thing, I had no intention or need to find a profitable application for the land or any thought of making a living in the village. I wanted the land just as it was, a rugged, un-"improved," mistreated but salvageable piece of the plains where I could find some refuge from Lincoln and academe. I thought of it as a retreat, not a residence, and certainly not as farmland.

I quickly fell in love with these sixty acres that I have converted over the years to a tree farm, not with any commercial intent but wanting only to restore the land. Just over the hill and out of sight unless you are on the highest hill is Dannebrog; the curious name is the Danish term for its flag, the oldest flag in the world, handed down to the Danes in battle by God ... none of that Betsy Ross stuff for Vikings! The town was, as one might guess, established by Danish settlers in 1871; when they crossed the river within yards of where I sit writing this they found an encampment of three hundred Pawnees who turned out to be very helpful to them, which was comforting, since there were reports of less congenial Lakotas not far to the north. I found and moved in an 1872 walnut and oak log house that was only a month away from being pushed into its basement and burned, from near Lincoln. I loved the cabin, the land, and the town. I spent every moment I could there by the river. I wrote about the town, the river, and my land. I gushed. It was not long before I was reacting strongly to anyone's suggestion in the town that when I left my cabin and the river I would be heading back to "civilization" in Lincoln. I argued that in my mind civilization was the quiet by the river, the friends in town, the proximity with wildlife, the gentle pace of life in a small Nebraska town.

The town's reaction to my romantic enthusiasm for the bucolic life was not what I expected. I thought they'd be flattered by attention from an outsider, and from the Big City! Most of my Dannebrog friends, in fact, thought I was nuts. This place is a damned zoo, they said. Not the "Little Town with the Big Heart," as the mural by the post office says, but "the little town with the big hard-on," the mockers hooted. I learned the verb "to brog," as in "I was brogged," meaning dismissed as an ignorant meddler. I learned that I was an outsider . . . and always would be. Other newcomers scoffed at my affection for the town; it hadn't taken much time living there for them to come to see the shortcomings of small-town life and start throwing the participle "brogged" around with disdain and disappointment.

They had a point. I had been part of the town maybe fifteen years when I walked into the Chew 'n' Chat Café one day and Bumps Nielsen looked up and said, "Well, look here . . . the *tourists* are in town." I would always be an outsider, and the tombstones of my children will probably say something like "Here Lies the Child of an Outsider." I saw the village as charming, pretty, idyllic, and comfortably easy, but for the people who lived here it was restrictive, parochial, nasty, petty, and oppressive.

I gave that idea a lot of thought, and the next time I had a conversation with those same friends, we talked it over. My argument, which they accepted, was that as an outsider it might be true that I did not know the uglier parts of living in a small town, but that as an outsider I *could* see the assets those who did live here might have forgotten while dealing with the less pleasant aspects of life.

The same is true of being an outsider looking at any other culture. Our vision of that reality can never be the same as the viewpoint of those who are in it and looking out. That certainly is the case as I have entered Native American life, have come to know and appreciate it, and have found myself increasingly active within Indian culture and life, urban or on a reservation. Oh, I have seen and know the negative aspects of what goes on in those contexts, and some of what I see makes me thoroughly furious; but as an outsider I can also see what the insider might not see or may have forgotten along the line. Reality is only what one person sees at any one time.

A popular notion is that only an insider can know what a culture is and how it functions. That is, no one can understand a woman's life, or an orphan's life, or an Indian's life but a woman, an orphan, or an Indian. To be sure, someone embedded within and born to a culture does have a special point of view that the outsider cannot, but I would argue that precisely because that observer is embedded within the culture he or she has a restricted or at least skewed field of vision. If that insider's point of view is not smaller than that of the outsider, it is at least different. The outsider also has, after all, a unique view of what he has seen. Because, in turn, what he has seen may be not only viewed through his eyes and mind but unique to that one situation.

There are complaints from Indians about non-Indians writing about Indian life. Nonsense. I have as much to say from the outside as a Native has to say from the inside; the point is that we should both be offering up our perspectives. Ignorance of either point of view offers no benefit to anyone. A Native objecting to a non-Indian like me writing about my observations and impressions of Native culture, historically or contemporarily, should be saving her energy and time for writing her own observations and impressions, thus adding to the general body of information. Researching, studying, learning, and writing about another culture are as natural as breathing. To do otherwise would imply the death of a culture and a lack of curiosity. For Indians to protest non-Indians writing about Indians is an exercise in futility. What we do need and where those energies would be better spent is for Indians to write their observations and opinions or even express contempt for white culture. *That* would make sense and perhaps even do some good.

In fact, one could argue that someone who is not a Wannabe is in no position to understand or judge the Wannabe's Weltanschauung. It seems to me there is as much confusion about what a Wannabe is as about what exactly an Indian is!

So first Indians, *then* Wannabes.

9. *What's in a Name*

hat's the right word? Can we call people Indians if they are not from India? How about Native Americans? Wouldn't that include pretty much anyone born in America, including a German named Welsch? Natives? Indigenous peoples? Tribal people? Indigenes? Amerinds? Aboriginals? Artifacts, informants, resources, subjects . . . numbers, items, statistics? Bloods or Skins? Nah, those are terms permitted only to insiders and these days are so out of date that the young are offended. And there is always the esoteric-exoteric dichotomy of term usage that seems to me quite clear but remains utterly mysterious to many. Why can African Americans use the N-word but I can't? Why can an Indian call a tribal friend a Skin, but a white guy is headed for trouble using the same word? I don't find that process all that complicated, and frankly I don't think anyone else does either; it is a disingenuous linguistic game the mainstream uses in an effort to irk minorities, plain and simple. Call people what they want to be called. How complicated is *that*?

Many Native Americans don't like, understandably, the word "Indian." You know the story: Columbus or someone equally lost thought he was in India, so he labeled the locals "Indians." Personally, I like the word "Indian" precisely because it is a vestige of major and manifest ignorance. The word and its inherent error say a lot about our history.

On the other hand, sometimes I use the word "Indian" for the historical sense of American Natives of the past and the term "Native American" as a more modern designation for the Indians of today . . . again, I won't go through all the problems with that phrase, but problems there are. You have already heard them all, and there's no sense in rehashing them here.

At the same time, I am baffled by people who take personal offense at the idea of referring to people with a word or phrase they themselves prefer and request. That is simple civility, and I really do imagine therein lies the problem: ordinary civility has become a presumed insult to an entire layer of American society. Arrogance, ignorance, and incivility have become for some a Constitutional right; they quite cheerfully exercise their First Amendment right of free speech in the form of insult and illogic. For this segment of American society, the idea that they should abandon their mistakes, insults, and mockery in favor of pleasant conversation and accommodation is an unthinkable offense to *them*. They demand their right to be jerks.

The "right" term for those of Native blood remains a problem. And as strange as it may seem, in writing this I also have a problem coming up with a suitable term for . . . uh . . . er . . . well, white people. I mean, non-Indians. After all, there are people who are not Indians but also not white—Latinos, Asians, African Americans. (Or is it Hispanics and Afro-Americans?) That's why I sometimes use the word "mainstream" to designate the American cultural majority, whatever the race—the dominant population that in most cases would exclude the clear racial, religious, social, economic, and political minorities. Like Indians. And I have used the portmanteau word "whiteman" as a useful if obviously inaccurate term (and one I am having trouble getting past my computer program's spelling checker!) for those who are the majority of that mainstream. For variety I have thrown in now and again "non-Indian," hoping you will understand my dilemma. So much for all languages being "adequate." As much as I treasure American diversity, sometimes describing us in whole or part can get to be a real problem!

Equal in IQ—ignorance quotient—when it comes to what is "Indian" are questions like "What is the Indian word for this?" or "What is the Indian position on this issue?" or "Why do Indians do this?" There is no more a collective Indian than there is a universal whiteman. Each person of Native provenance and heritage is as individual as each white person. Just as a Catholic does not have the same opinions about many things as a Baptist or atheist, a Native who follows a medicine bundle tradition does not see things in the same light as an Indian who follows the Native American Church. Or who is a Catholic or Methodist. (I was a victim of my own stereotypical point of view when I once asked a close Pawnee friend and relative if the Native American Church among the Pawnees is the form called "Half Moon" or that labeled "Crossfire." My friend laughed and said, "Idadi, you're asking the wrong Indian! I'm a Southern Baptist!" Oops!)

As I deal with confusions about what one calls Indian, what Indians are, who Indians are, what Indians think, I do not intend to be acting superior. I like to feel that I have broad experience in such matters and have given more thought to the issues than most people might. So I am trying. Any lack of clarity may not simply be a matter of the complexity of the situation but also a matter of my own uncertainly and holes in that experience, as broad as it might be. We are all individuals, including the Indians among us. All of us in mainstream America have our own distinct personalities and must be judged as individuals no matter how diverse and distinct our different heritages might be. I know that. And I forget it. I was once having problems in negotiations with a tribe I know a bit about but not much and with whom I have had only rare and superficial contact. As I have repeated here, emphasizing its truth, knowing a Navajo or Mandan is not the same as knowing a Cherokee or Mayan. In fact, knowing a Navajo or Mandan is not like knowing anything but *that* Navajo or Mandan! Knowing a Navajo or Mandan cannot be understood as somehow understanding Indians as a whole. So, as I struggled to sort out why I was having difficulties with this particular tribe, I could only presume I was encountering some narrow tribal cultural misunderstanding that I simply knew nothing about and that I was perhaps violating completely without awareness on my part.

I contacted my Lakota brother, explained my problems, and asked him where he thought I was going wrong, what the problem could be, why I was having such trouble getting a problem sorted out that appeared so simple. He has had a much wider cultural experience than I have, having worked on a national level with many, many tribes, including the one I was having trouble with. I hoped he could help me understand where I was going wrong. He gave my problem some thought and then explained it to me in one of the very best lessons I have ever learned, one of those nuggets of Native wisdom that comes down like the words of the Oracle, except maybe not quite as enigmatic. "Roger," he said, pausing to make sure I was absorbing the wisdom he was about to impart. "Roger, some Indians . . . are just assholes."

Of course! There it is. Some Indians are just assholes.

10. *Who Is "The Indian"?*

Just as any mainstream American is a composite of his own personality, his religion, his family, and his education, so too is every Indian an individual. My Baptist friend mentioned previously is a college graduate, a retired schoolteacher, a veteran airplane pilot, and a sophisticated and experienced bureaucrat. When there was some concern in a small Nebraska town about the Pawnee Nation acquiring property in the area, I was asked by a local citizen what the community should expect. I told him that among my closest Pawnee friends were a schoolteacher, a policeman, a journalist, an artist, a lawyer, a professor, an office manager, and a graduate student in anthropology. I added that other than a slightly darker tint of skins in the village, the community probably wouldn't even notice the elevated social, economic, and mental level of the population.

Beyond what passes in the United States for "family," family relationships are very strong within most Indian communities. So family history and traditions affect the nature and vision of the individual. Beyond family are many Indian-specific relationships that tie the Native elements of American society together. There are clans, adopted relationships, societies (some secret, some open by invitation or application, some—like those recognizing military service—not just public but celebrated), and tribal customs and characteristics. Where intertribal marriages are involved an individual's attitudes may be strongly influenced by multiple tribal associations. The surviving culture, even today, of an Omaha or Pawnee, coming from a fundamentally agricultural society that dwelt in semipermanent villages, never actually battling with white invaders even though there were certainly disagreements, hostilities, and confrontations between them, differs substantially from the point of view of, say, an Oglala Lakota or Cheyenne-Arapaho, whose societies were primarily nomadic warrior-hunter tribes, initially, constantly, and still traditionally at odds with what they see as the very recent occupation of their lands by white invaders. Which again is not to say there is any standard personality within any tribal group that can be said to be a norm for all its members. I guess the only statement of a standard set of norms for "Indian" is, "no standard set of norms should ever be presumed."

My experiences have been largely within central plains tribes, so that is what I am most familiar with and draw on for my examples and descriptions. If I can't be honestly specific about the broader character of tribes within one region like the central plains, one can imagine how much more difficult it would be to find generalities for tribes separated by miles, mountains, rivers, and even seas. The culture of the Kwakiutl and Tlingits in what is now the northwestern United States would obviously be different from that of the southwestern Apaches, and the Apache culture different from the Eries' of what is now New York. And I don't mean just a little different but worlds different. At one end of the huge area represented by today's Nebraska were the Lakotas and at the other, four hundred miles to the east, the Omahas, also speaking a Siouan language, also hunting at least twice a year among the great bison herds, and yet completely different in more ways than Germans differ from their close relatives the Irish.

Of course nothing human is simple, including cultural separation. Within traditional Omaha culture, women and men spoke slightly different languages—really, men and women in the same tribe spoke slightly different languages. (One could argue that even in America today men and women speak different languages but . . . well . . .) So, while noting that Lakotas and Omahas spoke *similar* languages, we should also note that German and English are related and similar languages. But not the same. There were lingua francae among tribes, artificial languages used only for intertribal communication that allowed commerce, but still . . . their own languages were different. Tribal representatives traveled astonishing distances at what are today remarkable speeds (often and easily a hundred miles on foot in a day!) and doubtless other tribes were encountered and communicated with, perhaps with sign language, which is not simply a Hollywood-generated cliché after all. Representatives of various tribes and linguistic groups interacted regularly at neutral sites like the pipestone quarries in what is now Minnesota or flint quarries in Wyoming and Kansas or salt licks like the one northwest of what is now Lincoln, Nebraska. Captives and adoptees were regularly exchanged, as evidenced by diffused folktales, beliefs, customs, and songs. But fundamentally, the tribes were more different than they were the same, and those differences remain, despite the passage of time, new alliances, new forms of communications, and the common culture of mainstream America.

All of which is to say, there is no such thing as "Indian" any more than there is such a thing as "Caucasian." These are artificial concepts that may be convenient for labeling but that mislead anyone who is looking seriously for a community of united thought, custom, belief, language, tradition, song, dance, costume, or just about anything else. I am reminded of the time I was a guest on Dick Cavett's interview show to discuss my latest book. Dick is an old friend, a classmate (Lincoln High, not Yale), and a frequent visitor to my home village. He asked why I enjoyed life in a small town in the middle of Nebraska, and I said that even in Lincoln, the state capital, my neighbors, friends, and acquaintances had a certain stifling consistency—upper middle class, educated, academic—but in a town of 332 my compatriots were of every stripe and texture. When I sat down to breakfast at the Chew 'n' Chat Café on Main Street I would be in the company of a farmer, a carpenter, the bank president, the town drunk, and the village wit. Dick laughed because he knew what I was saying, something not obvious to his studio and broadcast audience but apparent only to Dick and my friends back home: I was talking about one man . . . farmer, carpenter, bank president, drunk, and village wit.

There is no "Indian," as such, only Indians, in as full a variety as human beings exhibit in any group. And yet here are cultural overlays that affect that group's behavior, from the way they shake hands to their belief about what God is. And layered on those larger templates are thousands upon thousands of other variables of tribe, family, clan, region, age, degree of transculturation, embrace of tradition, on and on and on. For fifty years I have cautioned against the whiteman (and especially the Wannabe) speaking for the Indian—"Indians believe that [fill in the blank]"—and yet that, in part, is what this book does. I have tried insofar as my own cultural straitjacket allows to speak not so much for the Indian as about what I have observed of Indians. Some broader generalizations are legitimate, as long as we constantly keep in mind that they are indeed generalizations and not reliable constants.

11. *Who Is the Wannabe?*

If Wannabes struggle with the snarl of operating within two cultural systems, that is scarcely a unique situation. We all do it. We even have different, distinctive languages for our various roles—one language for the office or classroom, another in a circle of friends, another in a personal relationship, another with our children, yet another with our dog, and so on. If the leap is large for a Wannabe, it is just as wide or wider an abyss for an Indian who cherishes tradition and grows up within an Indian home, community, or tribe and yet tries, *must* survive within or alongside the crushing and ever-present mainstream culture.

The process of Wannabeism depends, of course, only half, if that, on the nature of those who want to participate in another culture. A white, mainstream Wannabe is making a rather dramatic transition from being a member of a dominant, majority, overwhelming culture into participating in a much more fragile minority. While the Wannabe has an enormous chasm to bridge, a successful entry depends less on the attitude of the aspirant than it does on the members of the host culture. If such Wannabe adventurism is not welcome or is even firmly rejected by the Native community then any hope for deep cultural exchange is pretty much out of the question. There are any number of individuals, even in the warmest, most welcoming Indian community, who have no interest or desire to welcome Wannabes into the dance circle. Frankly, I think logic is in their favor. Why would they want to dilute their own highly prized culture with the ignorance and misunderstandings of outsiders? These newcomer strangers are the enemy, the very people who have tried too hard to destroy this culture in the first place and may pose a threat to it again now, even if unintentionally. The situation is all the worse when the outsider arrives uninvited, well intentioned perhaps but also unexpected. It's as if a stranger were to show up at your own family reunion; okay, he seems nice enough and has done his homework so he knows a lot of our names, but still . . . why is he here? Isn't it a bit uncomfortable practicing our family rituals and telling family stores with this newcomer sitting here at the table?

It's not as if Indians don't know the processes and complications of cross-cultural transaction. They know it well and from the inside. They are de facto anthropologists. They have to be. Most of us from the mainstream rarely if ever have to deal with Native culture; most Indian people, on the other hand, deal with white culture every day in a thousand ways. But within each Indian community, each tribe, each family there is a range of anthropological skills, depending on the intellectual skills of the individual members, their education and experience, and most importantly the inclination of individuals to change and adaptation. Same as with white folks in general and Wannabes in particular. There are non-Indians who do not find cross-cultural adaptation easy, and there are also those who simply want nothing to do with cultural change. Same with Indians. It may be that they place a high value on their own Native culture and don't care to vary from it or have a particular contempt or even hostility for what they see around them in white, mainstream culture. Similarly, some tribes with great determination and an inclination toward traditional tribal life erect walls to protect their traditional ways, while others have no problem accepting outsiders—as long as those outsiders demonstrate at least minimal civility and respect for traditional ways and the people who embrace and practice them.

Arguments about this and many other things rage within any Native government. Dissension, sometimes ferocious, is a common condition within tribes, communities, and families. Tribes tend to exercise a more perfect form of democracy than the mainstream—individuals do have equal voice and they are not reluctant to express opinions. There is tension between reservation Indians and urban Indians, full-bloods and mixed-race individuals, between families, between traditionalists and modernists. A Wannabe is well advised to steer clear of tribal politics, because there is little to be gained from meddling in them, as frustrating as tribal disagreements and their consequences may seem. Yes, things could move more smoothly and more profitably in many ways for a tribe if everyone could "just get along," but in my experience that isn't going to happen. Unless the families, tribes, clans, or individuals find a common enemy—perhaps in the form of a meddling outsider—and that just might be you, the Wannabe.

A curious experience for me centers precisely on my own adoption of the term "Wannabe." I'm used to that kind of thing, adopting a pejorative by way of a banner of pride. It's an old social device. When you are called a Mick, Wop, Polack, Nigger, or Redskin, Geronimo, Chief, or Tonto, or any of the other insult terms that go in and out of favor in this country, you can get into a fight every time you hear an insult or you can adopt it as your own term of defiance and affix it to your battle banner. My parents were dismayed when I started identifying myself as a "Rooshen," the derogatory term used on the plains for a German from the Russian colonies. They worked all their lives to be rid of that word, to prove it an unworthy term for a good and virtuous people. That's not my style. I'd just as soon adopt the term as mine and wear it as a badge of honor.

That's how I have approached this role that has dominated my life for well over fifty-five years. Detractors have called me a Wannabe. Okay, I'm willing to wear that mantle not with shame but with pride. I'm a Wannabe and damn proud of it. There are worse things. For example, a prejudiced, cruel hate-monger. For me the choice has been easy and actually something of a joy.

I use the word Wannabe in this book in mocking humor and to make it clear that that's what I am. I am not a "blood," or enrolled

Indian, and I am not entitled to any (or at least most) of the rights and obligations of the truly hereditary, genetic Native. On a few occasions when I have been asked to participate in ceremonial activities in roles usually reserved for "genuine" Natives, I have done so only with enormous humility, respect, and gratitude. The obligation and trust I am given in such situations weighs heavy on me, and I never bear the duties lightly. Moreover, I try to be aware at every turn that I am where I am, doing what I am doing, only by the grace of a delicate balance between those who approve and those who are not so certain about including an outsider in a role usually restricted to insiders. Moreover, one can never express disapproval or discontent about being excluded from what are essentially closed activities, where your presence is inappropriate or might make others uncomfortable who do have every right and perhaps obligation to be there. You *are* an outsider, no matter how well meant your intentions, no matter how little a distraction you think you are, no matter how helpful you want to be. There are ceremonies that are restricted to men in a tribe, or to a clan, or to veterans. There's no sense in being offended by that; it is simply the way things are. Women having a menstrual period are excluded from some rituals, religious ceremonies, and contexts. Forget women's rights. This is about tradition. Believe me, there are situations where such traditions are painful for tribal members, visitors, or women and their kin but there is no variance allowed for the old ways. They are what they are. And the strength of tradition is astonishingly strong. It has momentum and inertia, heft and dynamics. We like to think that we move steadily onward, shedding the obsolete cultural holdings of the past. That is not true. We carry the baggage of the past with us far beyond where we think, often hidden in the deepest recesses of our minds and behavior.

So what to do with terms for those of us who are not Indians but wind up involved in Native culture? I use Wannabe in the subtitle of this book. Is that appropriate? I can imagine some admirers of Native culture being offended by that word, and I will admit that it has a pejorative zing to it. How about Gottabes? Oughtabes? Apples, sycamores ...?

Joking, I refer to myself as a Wannabe to my Pawnee or Lakota brothers, and I am scolded. My Pawnee brother Francis Morris sternly says, "Don't call yourself that, Idadi. You are more Pawnee than most of the Pawnee here on the Reserve." But you can imagine the firestorm that would erupt should I make a habit of calling myself Pawnee. I'm telling you, it's not easy being a Wannabe. Dear friends and family have told me the same thing about my position within the Omaha Nation. At prayer meetings I have been told that I should embrace the honor of full rights of the worship ceremonies because I am "more Omaha than many of the other people sitting in this circle who are accepted as Omaha without question."

A good part of the problem is the complexity of what a Wannabe is. No kidding, it really is complicated. It is not my intention here (or anywhere) to use the word as a pejorative. At least not when I apply it to myself or others like me. Yet I can imagine a situation where I might see yet another white man trying to inveigle himself into Native culture for less than noble purposes and snarl, "He's a Wannabe. Nothing but a Wannabe." Maybe I would qualify the usage by adding, "And some Wannabes are just assholes." The use of the word as a pejorative is clearly the most common application, describing someone who wants to be an Indian, maybe someone who builds a Grass Dance outfit and dances at powwows but performs only at gatherings where other Wannabes are doing the same thing, never actually being involved in or understanding Native cultural life, never making real Native friends, always taking, never giving. I have seen it all dozens of times at Boy Scout jamborees, muzzle-loader gatherings, "historical" reenactments, and even a gathering of the Karl May Society in a Bavarian meadow.

I'm not ready to condemn that sort of thing. In a well-funded and highly respected historical museum such activities might be called "experimental archaeology" or "didactic historical recreation" and be held in considerable scholarly regard. You just have to respect someone who learns enough about flint-knapping and any particular tribe or historical period's methods and forms to reproduce a flint projectile point that is virtually indistinguishable from the real thing. We *can* learn something from historical reconstruction and reenactment, but it must be done with careful research and immaculate craftsmanship. Wearing funny clothes is not enough. The person who acquires such traditional skills in a scholarly way learns something, and that in no way diminishes the art and skill of people who made the originals. Indeed, it provides new reasons to respect those skills. Within just the last few months I had to gently argue with to a wonderful young woman at a museum who was performing magnificent services in pedagogy and research and going way beyond the limits of necessity to serve the interests of the Pawnees. I urged her to reconsider labeling things like traditional beadwork, rawhide parfleche painting, pottery, and buffalo-hide tanning as "primitive crafts." It is clear to me that those skills are not "primitive." In fact, those primitive crafts look sophisticated beyond my abilities. They are a highly developed, demanding, alternate technology and should be presented, admired, respected, and identified as such. Now *that* is education!

There are do-gooder, bleeding-heart Wannabes. There's almost a paradigm for their progression. They discover Indians. And wow . . . what they see is impressive, even on the surface. And then comes the sympathy for the wretched treatment of Native peoples historically and the current conditions of many today in cities and on reservations. And then there is the gathering of carloads of used clothing, winter coats, and canned goods for reservation food pantries. It isn't easy to dismiss that kind of compassion as a bad thing, even if it is insulting, paternalistic, and demeaning. Yes, I know what road is paved with good intentions, but good intentions are still better than bad intentions and good intentions may be a place to start. I suppose I am sympathetic with this process because it is the course I followed in my own development. Every step.

Sometimes good comes of all this. I like to think it did in my case. I went through all the do-gooder stages, and while I'm embarrassed now when I see others doing the same things, I remember that perhaps that's where the good stuff gets launched. At some point—and fortunately it wasn't that long after 1957, when I started spending time with the Omaha communities in Lincoln and on the reservation at Macy, Nebraska, on the Missouri River about fifty miles north of Omaha—I realized that my relationship with my Omaha friends was not what I had always thought. In fact, it was almost completely the opposite of how I had seen it. I wasn't doing anything for the Omahas; they were the ones who were nurturing me. They were the givers and I was the recipient. I was the one who needed to be grateful, because I was the one who was being treated graciously and profiting from every association, every contact, and every lesson. They were rich and I was needy.

Moreover, I couldn't even offer much by way of good advice or information; the wisdom was all in their hands. I sensibly decided it was time for me to sit down, shut up, and listen. And that's what I have tried to do for more than fifty years now. Not easy for a white man. Not easy for a German. Not easy for a man who made his living talking and teaching. Not easy for a man whose great-aunt once said of him, leaving him no room for rebuttal, "Dar Rodger, dar hat iver di Rache uf." That Roger, he always has his big mouth open.

12. *The Contrary Lesson of the Prime Directive*

The television series *Star Trek* was basically made up of tales of cross-cultural confrontation and tension, the misunderstandings that are an inevitable part of dealing with cultures other than one's own and of struggles to mitigate differences. We are told that these explorations of space are under the rules of the Prime Directive, a set of rules like one might see in an undergraduate anthropology class on the day they discuss field ethics. The idea was that the observer—in this case the crew of the starship *Enterprise*—was not to interfere with the cultures it encountered in its galactic travels. There was a time when a lot of Americans could recite at least parts of the Prime Directive from memory, and all true Trekkies presumed it to be the Gospel according to Captain Kirk:

> As the right of each sentient species to live in accordance with its normal cultural evolution is considered sacred, no Starfleet personnel may interfere with the normal and healthy development of alien life and culture. Such interference includes introducing superior knowledge, strength, or technology to a world whose society is incapable of handling such advantages wisely. Starfleet personnel may not violate this Prime Directive, even to save their lives and/

or their ship, unless they are acting to right an earlier violation or an accidental contamination of said culture. This directive takes precedence over any and all other considerations. . . .

Starfleet allows scientific missions to investigate and secretly move amongst pre-warp civilizations as long as no advanced technology is left behind, and there is no interference with events or no revelation of their identity. This can usually be accomplished with hidden observation posts, but Federation personnel may disguise themselves as local sentient life and interact with them.

This philosophical basis for cultural interaction may have seemed like good theory for the science fiction writers, but they needed to have some actual exposure to other cultures right here on earth in the present before they put forth the assumptions behind the Prime Directive, because it sure doesn't seem to work this way. They may have known the future, but they didn't know folklore or anthropology. At least not in my experience, nor in the experience of most Wannabes, casual or scholarly, I know and respect.

Rarely does the serious observer of another culture come away from the experience without the explicit impression that if the material he or she happens to be looking at is not indeed a superior alternative technology then it is at least an equivalent alternate technology, which is a direct contradiction of the Prime Directive's presumption that the visiting technology—that would be us, on the *Enterprise*—is almost inevitably superior. It has been my experience in my own life and from what I have learned in conversations with other ethnologists that the flow of information and change is not from the visitor toward the other culture but exactly the reverse. It is the visitor who comes away changed. If the visitor finds it possible, in the end, to come away at all.

13. *First Steps*

My conclusion, then, is that it is not the visited society that needs protection from outside pollution, improvement, interference, distortion, agitation, meddling, or whatever you chose to call it, but the *visiting* culture—that is to say yet again, us. We who visit another culture are the ones who are vulnerable to change . . . life-shattering change. Or at least we should be. However, those who come to another way of seeing the world are not simply changed but changed in ways they cannot have imagined. Approaching another culture, we are the innocents who have no idea what we are about to subject ourselves too, if anything.

There are people who experience the very same encounters that those of us who are Wannabes deal with and come out of them utterly unchanged. Or even more content with their original condition than they were before. There are those who see other ways and simply turn away contemptuously, dismissing the notion that they need any improvement or that the culture before them has anything worth learning. Those who are moved and changed by exposure to another culture, whether it is French, Thai, Inuit, or Mayan, are few, actually; busloads of tourists clearly attest that the norm is to look at other cultures through a pane of glass and a frame of arrogance and see nothing there worth anything more than a snapshot to be pasted in a scrapbook labeled MY FOREIGN VACATION.

I don't know if cultural travelers' exposure to another way of life necessarily does anything for those they visit, but I can tell you for sure that it does the Wannabe a world of good. It doesn't take much for some—say, a visit to a public tribal powwow. For others it takes years of apprenticeship to take on the mantle of being a Wannabe.

We enter another culture for many reasons. The evil agents in cultural encounters have unfortunately and far too often dominated our history—slavery, exploitation, greed, religious domination, just plain evil. And if the road to hell is paved with good intentions, we can be sure that the road to the reservation is, too, rarely with better outcomes than those resulting from overtly evil intentions. My interest lies in why I and others like me have become involved in Native issues, have become Wannabes. I imagine that my motivations might explain the directions of others and help them understand their own behavior. But now that I have reached this point in my life I cannot in all honesty say I have much to offer by way of analysis about a Wannabe's personal motivations. Not even *this* Wannabe's personal motivations.

The most important conclusion has to be, however, that we seek entry into and acceptance from other cultures (in my life and this book, that of modern Native Americans) for our own personal reasons. That is, it is about us, not the Indians. For one thing—a certainty—we cannot approach Native culture with the idea that we can and will "fix" it, helping Indians to be more like us, presuming that *we* are somehow the ideal for anything. If there will be change, it will be we who change, not the Indians. They have no reason to change, while simply by our presence we admit and suggest that we do.

Why did I become so completely immersed in Native culture? In all honesty, I simply do not know. What could be the reasons that I have spent fifty-five years now involved in Native culture? As I noted above, perhaps it was the instant acceptance into a larger family with no lack of new uncles, aunts, grandparents, children, nephews, and nieces, with regular social gatherings and open affection, that I found in Indian circles. Perhaps it was the drama and thrill of attending gatherings, hearing music and language, and eating foods that no one else of my acquaintance had. Maybe it was just plain old James Fennimore Cooper romanticism. It could have simply been a part of my intellectual interests at the time—linguistics and ethnomusicology. Maybe it was deeper than that. I can't deny but don't want to make too much of the issue that there was clearly a gap in the religious dimensions of my life, because I spent years looking for a spiritual direction and the moment I experienced Native religion it was like a dramatic revelation: I had found the truth. There was no question in my mind then and there hasn't been any since. Here was a spirituality I was immediately at home with. All that *is* guesswork. There is no sense in pretending otherwise.

A small, perhaps practical, immediate, undeniable rationale for my initial contact with Indians was my interest in wild foods. While I am not and never have been a so-called survivalist, I was (and am) interested in wild foods. One of the ideas I encountered while spending time at handgames and in casual conversations with Omaha friends was wild foods: plants most people in the mainstream consider to be useless "weeds" that are accepted and even relished by Omahas not only as food but as delicacies—milkweed, chokecherries, and corn smut, for example. This information fed easily into my opinion that the best survival kit in the world isn't an inventory of things you tuck into your basement, automobile trunk, or backpack but what you carry in your head.

14. *The Fix Is Out*

There was a time when I believed I could easily survive on what I could find in the wild, and I demonstrated that to my own satisfaction on several occasions. But practical or not, that motivation for spending time with my Omaha friends quickly faded as other motivations captured me. Forty years into my Native associations I was approached by a friend who was not, like me, an accidental novitiate into the Wannabe Tribe but was consciously striving to be accepted into Native culture, working deliberately to find his way into a tribal relationship. To my unease he wanted openly to be dubbed "brother" by a man who had served as a fishing guide for him and his family for many years.

This friend, I want to make clear, was innocent enough, well intentioned, and not at all working from ulterior or malevolent motives, but inevitably he started his efforts with some major hurdles between him and acceptance by his target society ... and I use the term "target" intentionally because his determination was anything but casual. First, he had been the employer of his prospective "brother" and believed that working with him on this basis could serve as an entry to the man's culture. I suggested this was not an auspicious beginning. Furthermore, he insisted to me again and again, privately and indirectly, that he intended to "fix" his friend's personal and cultural failings.

And perhaps the inadequacies of the man's entire tribe. That would be his contribution to the tribe—explaining and demonstrating the importance of the white man's understandings of time, work, saving, acquiring, social climbing, economic progress, all of those virtues he was sure had brought the white man to the exalted position he himself enjoyed. He came startlingly close to declaring that he intended to fix the entire tribe by rescuing it from its history and culture.

I was shocked and appalled and tried to explain to him the difference between concepts of generosity within mainstream and Native cultures. I told him to give up his efforts, relax, and hope the respect would come to him from his friend and his friend's people, once he demonstrated his respect for them and their ways. I suggested that this was a situation where he could and should learn rather than instruct. The situation seemed to get worse: by way of following my suggestion of generosity, he paid his Indian friend and fishing guide a season's pay in advance, furthermore requiring him to sign a contract obligating him to work in accordance with the advance payment. When I tried to point out that this was scarcely generosity but simply a business arrangement, my friend insisted that trusting an Indian with a year's advance pay was indeed generosity. I countered by saying that the way things work, at least in the Native cultures I know (I am not familiar with the specific customs of the people he was attempting to charm), one expresses brotherhood by acting like a true brother: if your brother is in financial trouble and needs help, you don't pay him in advance and require him to sign a contract to work for the money. If you have money and he does not, as was the case here, you simply help your brother by giving him money. (Remember, I am speaking here of Native, not white mainstream, ideas of brotherhood.)

Again and again my friend felt he was indicating generosity by buying things from his Indian friend, paying him for work, working at fixing his deficient understandings of work, time, and property. I despaired. I pretty much gave up. I had suggested things for my friend to read, I had spent far more time than I could afford explaining to him that he was in this relationship to change *his* ways, not to reform his friend or yet an entire tribe's traditional ways.

Somewhere along the line things did change for my friend. For one thing, he may have been difficult to educate about cultural matters, even argumentative although I had no intention, time, or energy to debate with him, but he is also good-hearted and accepted my frustration. He would not quit trying to understand and follow my suggestions. Remarkably, slowly but surely, I sensed a turn in his relationship with his tribal contact, who also seemed to have enormous generosity of spirit in dealing with my friend and his persistent, almost deliberate misunderstanding of cultural differences. As time went on I began to get letters from my non-Indian friend describing genuinely cooperative interaction—not work for pay, not commercial interaction, not efforts to fix the Indian's "problems," but actual indications of . . . well . . . brotherhood. That is one of the more convoluted paths I have seen to cross-cultural acceptance and Wannabeism, but with the generosity of both of these good men, it was coming along.

In the dynamics of my friend's association with his Indian employee-cum-friend-cum-brother lies one of the most curious factors of Wannabeism: the generosity of the besieged Native. I can understand from my own experience why a white man wants to associate, be accepted, be a "brother." It is harder for me to explain why an Indian would have anything to do with the process. And the more difficult the approach seems to be, the less I understand the Native's patience. I have been blessed by three men asking me to be their brother—not just ordinary men, although that certainly would have been flattering enough—but intellectual and cultural giants. Not just within their own tribes and cultures but also on the larger scale of mankind, accepted by the mainstream as men of integrity and wisdom. I remember vividly the first time each of these men called me "friend." I was proud just to be able to say I knew them, but when they said "friend" it was like pinning a medal of honor on my chest. These were precisely the kind of people I would want to call a friend, or in my most vain fantasies "brother," but now they had called me "friend" and then "brother." Later, two of them asked me to accept the term "brother" formally and participate in kin-making ceremonies that would make us brothers in fact and not just in practice. Throughout all of this I was welcomed warmly into families and tribes, generously, genuinely.

Why? These are not just people, other people, fellow Americans, neighbors, acquaintances, colleagues, fellow warriors. These are people who were crushed by people who looked, talked, and acted a lot like me, by anthropologists who treated them as artifacts and resources, subjects and relics, by neighbors and politicians, merchants, and the ignorant who saw them as enemies, inferior to themselves. My people destroyed their people historically and were in many arenas still doing it. Where was their hate? Resentment? Suspicion? Oh, I knew there were those who had that anger and unease, and I certainly could understand it. But what about the others, the clear majority who expressed, of all things, real affection? That is the miracle at the basis of Wannabeism: not that outsiders want to come in but that the door is opened again and again by those inside.

Who are these people? Again, with the understanding that all generalizations are dangerous and largely inaccurate, I'm still going to venture some wild guesses about the nature of Indians in modern America. If nothing else, I will try to consider some of the things that make the Indians of modern America what they are, in all their varying forms, without suggesting any inevitable results at all.

15. *Indian Wannabes*

There are anthropologists, especially archaeologists in my experience, who seem to be attracted to Native American culture, art, technology, history, whatever, but make a point of never having anything to do with *living* Indians, often dismissing them as somehow culturally diminished because they aren't the same people being disinterred at dig sites or who made the items that are the subjects of their studies. Now, *there* are Wannabes I feel comfortable dismissing as offensive—and believe me, I've dealt with my share of them so I know they are out there. No, the Omahas of today are not the Omahas of the past. My Omaha son Jeff has retired as a nationally acknowledged and respected expert in the area of submersible pumps in nuclear energy plants . . . and as a roadman within the Native American Church. My Omaha daughter Jennifer is a highly respected employee on a factory assembly line making mufflers for Harley Davidson motorcycles. (Who would have guessed there were mufflers on Harley Davidson motorcycles?) They deserve respect as human beings. That's all. They don't ask for anything more, anything special. Jeff, in my opinion, deserves further respect as a tribal authority, religious leader, singer, and elder, known to many Omahas much older than he as "Grandfather" because his wisdom and knowledge are well beyond his actual age in years. That deserves respect, too. But aren't they in a sense Wannabes, too?

A couple of years ago a young Pawnee living just fifteen miles from us contacted me and said he had heard there was a gathering of Pawnees at our rural tree farm. His name is clearly Pawnee, and he is physically obviously Native American. He grew up within an hour's drive of the Pawnee Reserve but his family had broken completely from any tribal or family matters. He had never so much as been to a powwow or eaten pumpkin soup. As I talked with him I found that he was utterly ignorant of anything Pawnee. I told him what I could, put together a package of references, and like any good professor organized a reading program in Pawnee ethnology for him, and I have made sure that he knows about Pawnee events happening in this area (something I will explain a bit better below). Talk about Wannabes! Here is a Pawnee who wants to be . . . a Pawnee.

What is to be said about the most visible, vocal Wannabes? Ward Churchill of recent academic controversy comes to mind. I don't know where to start with Ward Churchill. Is everyone who claims Indian blood going to have to answer birthers? Do Indians have to prove themselves by carrying identification papers? Family trees? Tribal enrollment certification? God, as if genealogists weren't annoying enough as it is. And what would be worse in today's world than to find solid proof that your great-great-grandfather actually *did* marry a Cherokee princess? Can there have been a more prolific, miscegenational subgroup in all of mankind than Cherokee princesses? Does a white family exist in America that does not have a Cherokee princess lurking in the branches of the family tree? Did no white man ever take a Flathead or Digger princess for a wife? And what of my Winnebago brother Louie LaRose, who (when he is visiting us in Dannebrog) makes a point of being sure all the Jensens, Hansens, Larsens, and Nielsens know that *his* great-great-grandfather married a *Danish* princess? There are so many questionable claims to Cherokee royalty in family trees that even a legitimate claim would almost certainly be dismissed out of hand. In fact, I wonder if ever a white man actually did marry a Cherokee princess.

Sometime check out any of dozens of Native American–specific blogs—for example, that of my Lakota brother Charles Trimble—and follow just a few pages of the squabbling about who is actually Indian and who is not. Who is Lakota and who is not? "I am truly Lakota," posts read, "because I spent the first fifteen years of my life on the Pine Ridge and my enrollment file reads that I am eleven-sixteenths Lakota." "Well," comes the snippy retort, "I *still* live only fifty miles from the Pine Ridge, and I am thirteen-sixteenths Lakota!" I can't help but wonder if the occasional claims on these sites of total, 100 percent Lakota blood doesn't suggest that this guy's ancestors never managed to bring home a single Pawnee, Ponca, or Crow captive. Wouldn't that suggest total failure in a warrior society? Again, my brother Louie LaRose, who has worked professionally as a stand-up comedian, sometimes brings a thoughtful audience to a befuddled silence when he notes that his father was two-thirds Hochunk.

16. *Gottabes*

U p to this point in my story, the Wannabes I have discussed really are Wannabes—people who Wannabe Indians. Even though some are Indians who want to be *more* Indian. But my real and most recent interest and the subject that I want to bring into this conversation at this point is another sort of Wannabe. Not really a WANT-to-be but a GOT-to-be, a term I got from a man I respect enormously, admire, and appreciate as a dear friend, my buddy Mick "The Brick" Maun. He quite correctly feels this word better describes the process by which he was pulled in the cultural vortex of Indian culture. As a result of being my friend, Mick, a brick mason, tile setter, and good guy, passed too close to a body of greater cultural gravity and found himself inexorably sucked into the black hole at the center of the Wannabe spiral galaxy. I needed help, sometimes a ride, sometimes a delivery, sometimes hard labor preparing for Indian ceremonies, and so I called Mick. He came as a helpful friend, a completely disinterested outsider, and then slowly but surely found himself up to his ears in Native activities, ideas, culture . . . and friends.

No matter what our mothers tell us, we do not determine our own fates. Not even close. I learned that long ago from the Omahas and watched it, sometimes with horror, in the epicycles of my own life, but I also saw it during the past thirty years as I watched Mick's helpless, increasing involvement in matters Indian. I have never seen the intensification of my own Indian associations coming, no matter what they happened to be, and neither has Mick. I suspect that any of us who are honest have to admit pretty much the same thing about any major changes and developments in our lives. My life has been nothing but blind corners. I come to an intersection, quite innocently turn the corner, and run smack into a life-changing collision I couldn't have imagined in my best or worst dreams. But there I am, and by then it's too late to do anything different. There is a long list of such events in my life, but I am only going to tell you about a couple of the biggies because they are central to my interest in the Wannabe phenomenon.

My point in telling you the following anecdote is to stress that no matter how detached I might have wanted to be in regard to Omaha culture, or even just my pleasure in Omaha company and society, in one simple event I was without my knowledge or understanding drawn into a situation where objectivity and distance were impossible, not only on this one occasion but for the rest of my life.

I had been attending handgames, camping at powwows, keeping company, just sitting around with my Omaha friends for some years, feeling comfortable, sharing songs, laughing at what I was coming to appreciate as the remarkable Indian sense of humor, listening to stories, eating . . . just being there. In 1967 the Omahas extended the time of their usual three- or four-day powwow on their home reservation on the Missouri River to a ten-day event in observance of Nebraska's centennial year. The Omaha powwow is held on the August weekend during the waxing moon just before the full moon on the ancient powwow grounds in the village of Macy (a contraction of MAha agency). A friend, Francis LaFlesche (descendant of the famous Francis LaFlesche), invited me to pitch a tent on the crowded campground on a site that was historically his family's. I was already learning. I had been to many powwows before and had always just put my tent where I found an opening, not knowing until that moment that campsites were considered to be hereditary. My Omaha friends had been too kind to inform me that I was, in effect, trespassing!

The weather was good all week and it was an idyllic time. I sat at campfires, shared food, listened to stories, and laughed at jokes. I felt that I had found a home. But I had no idea what was going on behind the scenes. A few days into the week my old friend Clyde Sheridan took me aside and said he needed to talk with me about something very serious. Uh-oh. He told me that the tribal chairman, Alfred Gilpin Jr., wanted to speak with me. Mr. Sheridan said that we would go to Mr. Gilpin's home directly across from the powwow grounds entrance that afternoon. He would accompany me. It was about a serious matter.

Of course I knew who Buddy Gilpin was. He was an imposing figure, tall and lean, dignified and obviously respected. He was a prominent announcer at the powwow, so I knew his voice. I had read a series of articles about him and his leadership in the Native American Church in the Lincoln newspapers some years earlier. I had probably shaken his hand, perhaps even greeted him, so I knew who Buddy Gilpin was. I could not, however, say that I *knew* in the sense that I would have engaged him in casual conversation on the powwow grounds. I'll admit that I was uneasy about this command audience and even intimidated. But when Mr. Sheridan came to my tent, I was ready and we walked the couple of hundred yards to Mr. Gilpin's home. He and his beautiful and elegant wife, Naomi, greeted me. They offered me a glass of iced tea. Mr. Gilpin spoke words of introduction, a long, almost prayer-like invocation about the Omaha tribe and kinship and Wakonda (God), about friends and relationships between the Indian and the whiteman. Well into Mr. Gilpin's speech—perhaps an hour—I still had no idea where we were going in the one-sided conversation. I sat. I listened. And then Buddy stated his intention: he wanted to take me as his brother. He wanted to give me a name. He wanted to have an open ceremony with his people to announce this intention. He wasn't giving me an invitation or an order. It was simply a statement: he was taking me as his brother. It was a given. And Clyde Sheridan and all my Omaha friends who already knew about this or would come to know it soon would help me prepare for the event, which would be held there in Macy in about a month.

There was a lot to be done. We needed to prepare a large feast because there would be hundreds of people attending the ceremony. Naïvely I later asked Mr. Sheridan how much food I should get for the feast, because before that moment I had never hosted a meal for more than a handful of people, much less hundreds. Mr. Sheridan was baffled by my question because it was a whiteman's question that no Indian would ever ask. He took a moment to consider it, to grasp how I could ask such a thing, and then answered, "All you can." No whiteman ever spends all he can, no matter how big the celebration. That was an Indian idea. It is a feast; provide all the food you can.

I got hundreds of chickens from the University of Nebraska poultry building, which was being emptied; I went to box stores and carted out what seemed like barrels of baked beans, crates of cookies, huge cans of ground coffee, bags of sugar, cases of bread. But that was only *my* part. My Omaha friends accumulated and pledged more food to help me present the best feast I could. They saw this as an effort not by me as an individual but by the Lincoln Indian community in general, in support of one of their own. I was already humbled by the friendship of this circle of friends I had accumulated over the years.

On the appointed day a parade of trucks and cars went north to Macy from Lincoln. Not long after dawn fire pits were started up and women began boiling chickens in large, copper wash boilers and heating huge tubs of lard to make fry bread. More and more people came into the yard, bringing more and more food. It was going to be quite a party that evening!

In the middle of this fury of activity I began getting the first hints of how little I understood about what was to happen to me later that day. I saw a serious conversation develop between Buddy, his brothers, and some other elders, three of whom were to serve with Buddy as assistants, taking me about the drum circle to receive my new name. The conversation started with just a couple of these honored elders but grew one by one until a sizeable crowd had gathered around Buddy. The discussion was serious but not heated. It was not for my benefit, but I was not excluded. As I listened I tried desperately to follow the logic and implications of what these men were saying: they were trying to convince Buddy that he was making a serious mistake in his plans for that evening, and the men were deadly serious … not a metaphor, as it turned out.

It took me some time to figure out what the problem was, but eventually I realized that these elders were concerned that Buddy was not just planning to give me a name, he intended to give me *his* name—Tenugagahi, Big Bull Buffalo. And his brothers and friends were warning him that that would be a violation of tradition that was sure to bring him major problems, perhaps even death. One, it turns out, does not give the name of a living person to another living person, most assuredly not your *own* name. Buddy's friends and family recommended instead that he make a list of perhaps four or seven good names and let me select one, by choice or chance, thus avoiding adverse, probably inevitable, consequences.

Buddy did not follow their advice that night and wound up spending a good part of the next year in the hospital, problems of course attributed to his defiance of powerful forces in giving me his name. I was already honored by Buddy's invitation to be his brother—an honored elder, the holder of a respected fireplace, a roadman, tribal council chairman—who wouldn't be honored? But now I also learned that he was willing to risk his life to take me as his brother. And give me his very name. A sacrifice like that can't be taken lightly.

The ceremony that evening was moving. Buddy and three of my closest Omaha friends (Clyde Sheridan, Oliver Saunsoci, and John Turner) took me around the great circle, throwing cedar smoke in all the four directions and to the Omahas who were there to witness the ceremony. Moving prayers were said and more statements were made about brotherhood, friendship, and family.

Even though I had begun my contact with the Omahas years before while studying kinship terms I found that evening that I hadn't yet started to understand what family and kinship really meant to the Omahas. I had never attended a kin-making occasion, nor had I heard about it, but I doubt that I would have understood its nature even if I had. I knew that the Omahas use mainstream kinship terms with the same meanings as within our larger society: father, mother, aunt, uncle, nephew, all that. And I knew that imposed on that there is a system of honorifics, so that I showed respect to elders by referring to them as Grandmother Saunsoci, Uncle Oliver, and Aunt Lillian. I knew of the old system that reflected traditional Omaha family structure, that all of one's father's brothers are referred to as "Father" and all one's mother's sisters are called "Mother." But I quickly learned that even knowing those terms and concepts I did not grasp the depth of those relationships: they are not honorifics or obsolete niceties. I didn't know it yet, but I was being changed. I wasn't just getting a new name, and even the word "identity" doesn't cover it. I wasn't having my opinions changed or my position within the tribe. I had, before I knew it, without knowing it, still not knowing it, become a different person.

That night, when everything was done and I had a new name, I had the good fortune to walk out of the community building into the cold September night to find I had a flat tire on my truck. And no spare, or even a working jack. So Buddy and I decided to wait until sunup, when we could get some help and send me on my way back to Lincoln. We sat on the curb and talked. And I learned even more about the gravity-dense cultural black hole that I had brushed too closely. The misfortune of a flat tire gave me the chance to learn what had actually happened that evening. Buddy and I talked. I did not simply get a new name, he explained; I had gotten a name within a clan. Within which I now belonged. I was now a part of the Kontha Clan (as in Kansas). Another example of Native wisdom—I had been given a name that placed me in the Wind Clan. I know—funny, funny—Welsch ... Wind Clan ...

It wasn't so funny when, several years later, I was confronted by an angry Wind Clan member who objected to me suggesting I was indeed a clan member, because clan membership is open only to full-blood Omahas. It took some of my Gilpin relatives explaining to him that I was now a full-blood. Not enrolled, of course, but in the spirit of the Omaha Nation, a full-blood. I was uncomfortable with all this. I had no pretensions to Indianness, or Indianhood, or whatever. But I had had no choice in the matter. I could not take back what had been done, nor would I. I honored my brother Buddy and was not about to reject his gifts. I had no choice, I explained, but would do what I could to bring honor to that name, to the Omaha Nation, and to the Wind Clan.

That night on the curb Buddy had made this clear to me. I had no choice. And probably neither did he. We had simply moved in directions defined for us by greater powers. My name was now my name, and all of the implications of that were on my shoulders. He explained that I could no longer eat our totemic kin, shellfish—no more lobster, shrimp, oysters, mussels, clams, the children of wind and rain. I had to put my left footwear on first, always. I could not wear green or blue face paint. (I like to joke that that is why I am never seen wearing blue or green eyeliner!)

I asked Buddy about the nature of these prohibitions: are they like the old days when Catholics didn't eat meat on Friday, or perhaps like Lent when one gives something up as a voluntary sacrifice, or like Jews and pork, or . . . what? Buddy gave long thought to my question. I don't think it was something he had considered before. He had always simply obeyed the prohibitions of his clan as everyone else did theirs. Finally he spoke and said something that drove even deeper the realization of what transformation had happened to me that night. He said, "Brother, it's like when you touch the fire. It doesn't matter why you touch fire, you are burned. By accident or on purpose, to protect someone else, it doesn't matter. When you touch the fire, you touch the fire. What I am telling you is as much a fact of your new life and world as it has always been up to now for you to touch the fire."

Gulp.

For a decade it had been a standard joke for my Omaha friends to make sure I got up and danced when the Half Breed Dance was sung because, the jests always went, I had become half Indian through association. But the next time I rose to do the Half Breed Dance at a handgame, Aunt Lillian reached out and grabbed my arm—something a proper Omaha woman would, in those more traditional days, never think of doing if it hadn't been so important—and she pulled me back to my seat, saying, "Roger, you can't do the Half Breed Dance any more. You are full-blood."

Now there was a new bottom line, it seemed. And a new reality far deeper than I had imagined, even as seriously as I had always taken this gift of a new name. And that was the problem in my perception: this was not simply a matter of getting a new name. I had, in the moments of the adoption ceremonies, taken on a new person. I was no longer what I had been just hours before. My new name offered only small, if visible, evidence of the transformations that I had undergone. I had become a different being. Things that had been perfectly ordinary for me hours before were now potentially fatal for me and dangerous to those I knew and loved. I was no longer what I had been all of my life up to that point. It was not a matter of being honored and given a title, a kind of nickname. That night I was not just changed, I was transfused.

Double gulp.

17. *Becoming New*

And so it was. In the intervening forty-five years I have not broken those Wind Clan prohibitions. I came close once and, even though I violated the prohibition inadvertently, the obvious consequences were such that I have been doubly careful never to do it again.

Once you assume the identity of an alien culture or even a deep association with it, it is not easy to remove yourself again because you are trusted. You are obligated by that trust if you have any principles at all, and most importantly and finally, you find that you are no longer making decisions but having decisions made for you. You are forced to abandon any sense of cultural superiority, realizing that the ultimate arrogance was thinking that you were the one in charge. And then, all at once, you have been transmuted from observer to Wannabe, or more precisely, Gottabe.

How did I become a Wannabe? Why me? Believe me, I've given those questions a lot of thought. Things for damned sure haven't gotten any simpler or easier over the years, as I will tell you shortly.

18. *How It Goes, How It Went*

The development and consequences of my association with Omaha culture blindsided me September 1967, and the past twenty-five years with the Pawnees have been an equally stunning turn of events, coming not simply out of nowhere but in a form I would never have suspected and with results I would have dismissed as a joke up until five years ago, or maybe even listened to with the conclusion that, mister, you need professional help because you are crazier than hell.

In 1986 I achieved one of the major goals of my life: I was elected to the board of directors of the Nebraska State Historical Society, the principal resource for most of my work since 1960. The board was composed of major figures of power and wealth in Nebraska, from the publisher of a major state newspaper to wealthy investors and corporate leaders. I was, in short, out of my league. But not in ways I anticipated. Early in my tenure on the board an item appeared on a meeting agenda, buried and below, as I recall, most other, much more important business. Some Indians—mostly Pawnees—wanted to petition the society for the return of human remains excavated from gravesites. I remembered being taken aback in a freshman anthropology class in 1954 when our professor, the chair of the department, passed around, just before lunch (which is probably one of the reasons it had an impact on me), a cigar box of fingers and ears that had been disinterred in a recent dig south of Sioux City. The burials were fairly recent, in historic times, we were told, and copper ornaments on the remains had worked to preserve the flesh. Those were cavalier times in academia and especially in the field of anthropology.

What the Pawnees wanted from the state historical society were centuries-old remains . . . and burial goods. And their express intent was to rebury these Elders, as they referred to them. The Indians' presentation to the board was serious, respectful, well written, and hardly unreasonable, although I certainly came to the matter with skepticism. I mean, jeez, losing items of enormous historical, scientific, and artistic value? I didn't see *that* happening very soon, even though the Native delegation did have a point—archeologists, in the end, do not *create* sites, any more than oil drillers "produce" oil. They destroy them. Archeologists destroy sites even as they study them, even within salvage archeology. The sites are there, the archeologists come with their shovels, and the sites are gone. Yes, information is salvaged, but the sites themselves are gone.

No, the historical society board and staff were not likely to move quickly on a proposal like this. What did happen soon, in fact at the very moment in the meeting immediately following the presentation of the Omaha, Winnebago, and Pawnee delegation, was disgraceful. I was shocked, and take it from me, I am not easily shocked. The arrogant, insulting behavior of my colleagues in the society, both the staff and the board, and in a formal meeting of that body of leaders of the society, threw me for a real loop. The Indians' reasonable and civil petition was met with naked contempt from the historical society board and staff. I seethed. Whatever the facts of scholarly dispute, the incivility of the historical society board and staff was not acceptable.

And thus ensued a years-long debate about the issue of repatriation of Indian remains and burial goods. It was not a discussion, it was an argument. Which escalated very quickly into a war. My concern was not so much for the remains and burial goods in question but the unacceptable disrespect being shown toward those who did have that concern. The misbehavior of the director and board became ever more egregious and the behavior of the Native governments and representatives all the more restrained and powerful. I was the lone person on the board speaking for the Native perspective. I was insulted in public and in print by society staff, members of the society board, representatives of our state legislature, academic colleagues, and people I had considered to be my friends. I was deliberately excluded from board meetings, given misinformation about the time and location of meetings. The society launched a "shock and awe" bombardment against the Indians and, not incidentally—at least for me—against *me*. I resigned from the board in high dudgeon and fired a broadside salvo that caught the attention of the legislature, the governor's office, and even our state supreme court justices.

To make the story short, we—the Indians—won. Out of this came the national system known as NAGPRA, the Native American Graves Protection and Repatriation Act. The Pawnees invited me to be a part of the processes of repatriation of their remains, from the tense—as you can imagine—transfer of the remains from one hand to another, from the historical society to the Pawnees, to the reburial itself. I had never been a pallbearer for a funeral, and then in one day I was pallbearer for almost five hundred people. Genoa, Nebraska, the site of the old Pawnee mission, school, and agency was uneasy about the return of the Indians to their community, even for a day, but for many reasons, some altruistic, some venal, the community eventually did welcome the Pawnees back and donated a large plot of land in the city cemetery, at the very site of the old Pawnee village, for the reburial.

19. *The Plot Thickens*

F or me and a lot of people around me, this story was as much about what didn't happen as what did. When the Pawnees were first looking for a site for reburial of the remains they were regaining from museum shelves, my wife, Linda, and I invited them to consider our home and land near Dannebrog. Pawnees were camped right here in 1871 when the first Danes crossed the river that runs a quarter mile along our bottom ground, the Loup River—the wolf river, named for the Wolf Pawnees (a redundancy). A contingent of Pawnee elders and spiritual and political leaders came to visit us from Oklahoma, where most of the tribe had relocated in the nineteenth century. While they eventually decided instead to accept the village of Genoa's offer of space at that community's cemetery because of the historical mean-ing of the location for the Pawnees, the ultimate impact of their visit was profound for Linda and me. When the Pawnees came to look at our land for the proposed reburials, we watched as distinguished elders walked crying into the river—their river, which most of them had never seen before—to drink from it, speak to it, pull it over their hair, asking Linda for jars so they could take some of this water—their water—back south to the red dirt country of Oklahoma. And we, Linda and I, arrived independently at the very same conclusion, which we shared with each other that evening when the Pawnees had gone:

during those moments at the river we both felt that the Pawnees had not been our guests on our land, but without question we were guests on theirs. We immediately set about the process of changing our wills, leaving our home and land to the Pawnee Nation.

The situation grew more complicated later when the Pawnees asked me for information about constructing a large vault for a second repatriation and reburial in the Genoa cemetery. I know nothing about construction, so I turned to my friend Mick and asked him some questions about construction and costs. Even then, in this brief and very ordinary moment, I got the feeling Mick's life orbit was tweaked out of round, and he began his long spiral into the center of the galaxy of Wannabes. And my involvement was growing deeper, too. Mick and I, with some help from others, wound up building the burial vault, and I again served as a pallbearer for another four hundred repatriated remains. We made more Pawnee friends, accepted more responsibilities, and felt our lives slowly but surely change. As our relationship with the Pawnees deepened, our contacts with them became more frequent.

Then, only four or five years ago, the situation between the Pawnees, Mick, and Linda and me became even more complicated and much more personal. The Pawnees were in the process of repatriating another thousand remains but had no more ground in the Genoa cemetery. The asked if they could take another look at our tree farm as a possible reburial site. We said of course, that our original offer still stood, and we began planning for a meeting at our home with a committee from the Pawnee Nation, people who had by now become good friends. The problem facing us was, how would we arrange for some sort of property arrangement that would allow the tribe to rebury its dead here on our land? Should we lease them a couple of acres? Sell or give them a couple of acres? Or, since the land would eventually be theirs anyway in keeping with the provisions of our will, should we do nothing at all and just go ahead and rebury the remains in our soil? Would that be legal? (Not that I cared, frankly, but the Pawnees and Native American Rights Fund [NARF] attorney Walter "Bunky" Echo-Hawk Jr. didn't want to take any steps that might generate later snags. The Pawnees were determined to do things "right," which is to say in keeping with Nebraska state law regarding burial of human remains.)

For hours we worked at finding a solution to these problems with the help of some Indians and a local attorney friend. Then out of the blue Linda came up with the obvious solution: why not give the place to the Pawnees now? That would solve almost all the problems. They would be able to rebury their remains in Pawnee soil, on the banks of the Pawnee river, in the heart of their traditional landholdings. And we'd continue living here by their grace until our departure—one way or the other—and yet in our lifetime be graced by inclusion in all the things that go along with living on sovereign Native land.

There were still problems. We needed a state attorney general's opinion about reburying the remains. The key to our argument was that we weren't *burying* people, we were *re*burying people. We were proposing the reburial of desecrated remains, not "the dead" as such. The site was not to be a public or ultimately even a marked burial ground. It was not only on private land, but on land held by deed by a sovereign nation, the Pawnee Nation. No Nebraska cemetery laws applied. Besides, after the wars between the Pawnees and the historical society, with every battle having been decisively won by the Pawnees, no one in state government wanted to touch any further controversy about Indian remains. Walter Echo-Hawk and NARF worked long hours sorting out the details, because they could find no precedent for private persons returning land to a Native tribe. As Bunky Echo-Hawk put it, we were throwing a monkey wrench into the enormous, five-hundred-year-long pattern of Indian–non-Indian land dealings. But eventually the issues were resolved, all favorably for Linda and me and the Pawnees, and so we deeded our beloved land and home over to the Pawnees, one of the most moving moments of my life, and one of the best.

20. *Why?*

F or years after the word got out that Linda and I had deeded our
land to the Pawnees—we have come to insist that the appropriate verb is that we "returned" the land to them, not "gave" it to
them—the single most common question we have gotten from friends
and strangers alike is, Why? I had to do a lot of thinking about that
because neither Linda nor I had an easy answer. Detractors guessed
"white man's guilt." Well, I can tell you for a fact that that wasn't it: my
people didn't even come to this country until 1912, 40 years after the
Pawnees had been removed, so I carry no guilt for the misdeeds of 150
years ago. For tax benefits? No, Linda and I are continuing to cover all
expenses on the place, including maintenance, improvements, and taxes,
until we die or leave and the Pawnees take actual possession. Pity? I
think I've made it clear: I'm a Wannabe. If anything, my feeling about
my Native friends is envy, although I see no reason for pride or shame,
envy or pity resulting from accidental circumstances of birth. None. An
effort to regain justice? Well, as noble as that sounds, no . . . the return
of these pitiful sixty acres of mine, a modest frame house, and a clutch
of ragged outbuildings scarcely serves to balance the Pawnee loss of
all of northern Kansas and southern Nebraska. Publicity? Quite the
opposite. We worked hard to avoid even having our names associated
with the transfer, and it was only through an accidental leak from a

newspaper report that the information came out at all. Since it now has, we have sought to give out information about it only because it is clearly generating interest in many more and much larger property returns to the Pawnees and other Native tribes.

So ... why did we return our life's property to the Pawnee Nation? Again, because we had no choice. We did not *decide* to return our home and land to the Pawnees, we only somehow came to recognize that the place was to be returned to the Pawnees. We decided nothing, any more than we could take a vote tonight and decide whether the sun will rise tomorrow on the eastern or western horizon.

21. *Gottabes Again*

With the return of our home to the Pawnees, the black hole of Wannabeism was increasing its gravitational pull on us to a level that distorted all reality. We certainly wondered what Nebraskans would think about the return of the Pawnees, but more precisely, we wondered what the people of Howard County and Dannebrog would think when they learned that their old neighbors were going to be their new neighbors. As it turned out, there has not been a single wrinkle. At least not that we have seen. A question I hadn't thought about but one that was quickly brought up by the executive director of the Nebraska Commission on Indian Affairs, Judi gaiashkibos, was, How would this new actor on the stage (the Pawnee Nation) be greeted by the already established and official four Nebraska tribes? Would they see the return of the Pawnees as a step that cut the already inadequate power of and financial support for Native citizens into more and smaller pieces? Or would they consider an increase in their number from four to five to be to their advantage? To our great relief, the Omahas, Santees, Poncas, and Winnebagos enthusiastically chose the second option and went well out of their way to welcome their old neighbors (and sometimes enemies!) back to their ancestral home.

Temporarily the Pawnee seat at the Indian commission table would be ex officio, but that pattern had led to permanent status for other tribes, so this was a start. The Pawnee tribal Business Council and Nasharo (or Chiefs Council, with two representatives from each of the Pawnee tribe's four sub-bands) were asked by the Indian commission to name an official delegate. Both bodies said I would be their representative on the commission. The director explained that any representative from the Pawnee Nation would have to be Pawnee. Both tribal bodies said the same thing: Roger *is* Pawnee.

How could anyone turn his or her back on that kind of trust and responsibility? It was increasingly clear that I was not a Wannabe Pawnee, I was a Gottabe Pawnee. I have been asked dozens of times, "How can I get into the Indian world?" and I always answer the same: "I haven't the faintest notion." It was certainly nothing I *decided* to do. At every step my involvement in Native issues came to me more as a surprise than a choice. I have gotten the same question with a different tone from some Natives: "What the hell makes you think you have any business hanging around Indians?" It wasn't my idea. I can't even explain how it happened. It's a mystery and a blur. It doesn't matter what anyone thinks, anthropologists or 150 percent Indians. It wasn't my plan. But I am blessed by all that has happened. I am content being a Wannabe, or a Gottabe. In fact I don't think you can be much of a folklorist without eventually being a Wannabe of some flavor or another.

Nebraska author Wright Morris wrote about the relationship between rural people of Nebraska and "outside" visitors in *The Home Place*: "I'll tell you what it is I can't stand," a lady from New York complains. "It's *all right* for you to share their lives. That's fine. But they don't give a dam [*sic*] about yours." And that is generally true. So the Prime Directive of *Star Trek* is not only nonfunctional, impractical, maybe even impossible, it is also not applicable. Research problems we take up as a matter of interest or importance may wind up being, literally, life changing. For us. I don't know how to avoid that or encourage it, but I think it is worth keeping in mind and passing along as a kind of caveat to those contemplating a life dedicated to folklore. It is possible if not probable that you will come out of your work with an epiphany rather than the publishable paper for which you thought you were bargaining. That may be true, too, of astrophysicists; I don't know, I've never been an astrophysicist. But I can tell you from the point of view of a folklorist that you may go in to be a scientist and scholar but you may come out a Wannabe. Without having changed so much as the slightest jot or tittle of the Native culture in which you have embedded yourself.

22. The Ways of Foodways

I love food. Much of my research and writing has been about food. I like eating and I like new food experiences. I love Indian foods and have made the most of that in my role as a Wannabe. Food says a lot about a culture. It is usually the first interface where we encounter an immigrant population. We all have to eat, we all have our foods, we all identify with our foods. The term "soul food" is not a metaphor but a reality. It turns out we are indeed what we eat—but in more than physiological or even cultural ways. Food is where we demonstrate our willingness, or in the case of the Wannabe, our eagerness to be a part of another culture.

There's a reason why, when a new tide of immigration hits the beach, one of the first waves is food—fast-food stands, small family cafés, and most certainly new items on the shelves of even the smallest neighborhood grocery stores. Think about the most popular "American" foods: hamburger (German), French fries (French?), gyros (Greek), frankfurters (German), wieners (Austrian?), pizza (Italian), tacos (Mexican). Moreover, food is not only our first contact with another culture but also the quickest and most durable cultural element to then become "American." Everyone eats, and so food is obviously a common medium for interaction, but its content beyond nutrition is almost always more complicated. Courtship often begins with and revolves around food because it is a sharing of vulnerability: "I'm willing to let you see me dribble salad dressing and gravy down the front of my shirt if you are willing to do the same." It is a small but significant lowering of a bit of each individual's social armor.

The same is true of food in a larger cultural context: offering an outsider food is a meaningful and dramatic gesture of welcome and acceptance. The rejection of that offer is a profound insult. The first time I made a self-invited appearance at an Omaha social event, a traditional handgame, I had no idea what to expect or how to behave. Most Plains Indian cultures are deductive rather than inductive, so one learns by observing and imitating, not by being instructed. In fact, a common Omaha joke is to suggest that someone who is not rising and dancing at some appropriate point in an event should take dance lessons. The idea that one would take *lessons* to learn Omaha dance is considered utterly hilarious. Same with every other facet of Omaha culture. No one tells anyone else what to do; nor does one ask what one should do. Those are severe restrictions when one is starting from scratch. If I struggled with the completely strange and complex rules of the handgame, for example, what of the appropriate manners for the Omaha feast that inevitably follows?

Later in the year I attended my first handgame (1964), for example, I learned that no Omaha goes to any gathering without "dishes"—a bowl, spoon, tea towel, cup, small shaker of salt, and perhaps another closeable container for the inevitable leftovers, all carried in a peck fruit basket or cloth bag. On the occasion of my first handgame, I had nothing with me. So my first lesson was, if an innocent guest doesn't bring his dishes, some generous soul will quickly assemble enough spare items to equip that guest for the inevitable postgame "feast" (which, no matter how humble, is always a "feast"). This particular handgame, as I noted previously, was a small gathering—perhaps thirty people—in a dank basement under a tawdry rummage store in an unsavory part of town. I knew some of the people at the game from my previous contacts, and I knew that they were from the bottom of the economic ladder. The food gathered on a tarpaulin in the middle of the room made, to say the least, a meager feast. And as the traditionally long blessing was made for that "feast" I had deep doubts about my presence there: I was about to eat the food of people far less fortunate than I, people who had little extra food to spare. I decided that the polite thing to do would be to thank my hosts for the wonderful time—the music, dance, game, their kindness and hospitality—and to excuse myself with some lame excuse about needing to be somewhere else that night, thus not unnecessarily taking food from these poorer people's mouths. And that's what I did. It was not long before I realized how profoundly I had insulted my friends and hosts.

Food is even more important among the poor than the rich; more than that, food and hospitality are central to Omaha culture. I might as well have stood and given a speech to them about how wretched they are and how miserable their food was and how insufficient their hospitality was for an important person like me. I had behaved like a boor and it took some time—and a lot of enthusiastic eating at later Omaha social occasions—to redeem myself.

Even that redemption had its complications: I so enjoyed my first handgame that those occasions became a regular weekend activity for me. As I became closer to the Indian community in Lincoln, made more friends, learned more protocol, my new friends also came to know me. From my previous linguistic work with one of the community leaders, they knew, for example, that I was a university professor, and that carried some prestige.

It also carried some onus, however: even this small-town Indian community had had more than its share of exposure to and abuse from the anthropologists who inevitably drifted in and out of Indian culture, observing briefly and then leaving, taking much, leaving nothing. I took some pains to make it clear that I was *not* an anthropologist—I was teaching modern languages at the time—and I was there only because I enjoyed the gatherings, not because I was gathering data from them as "informants" or "resources," and had no intention of publishing whatever I learned from them.

As a "distinguished guest" in those early days among them, I was given special hospitality, especially when the time came for the inevitable feast. I was always seated at the head of the game room, at the side of the scoring table, and when food was distributed I was served as the first guest, right after the circle of singers in the center of the room and those elders and officials at the scoring table, who by tradition are always served first. So for months I gratefully accepted a couple of slices of white, pasty, sodden Wonder bread from those passing out the food and then watched as down the line, among the ordinary game players, bushel baskets of brown, richly redolent breads (which I later came to learn was fry bread) were passed out to those of lesser distinction.

And I lusted. As a child I was known in my German family as a "Brotfresser" (bread eater), but with the word for eater, *Fresser*, that implies I ate like an animal. But my new Indian friends wanted to make sure I had the best—grocery-store white bread—settling themselves for the more humble fry bread made in their own kitchens. Eventually I screwed up my courage and asked one of the servers if—I feel shame for my rude behavior even now, forty-five years later—I could have one of those round, brown breads from the bushel basket rather than the Wonder bread from the plastic sack. The servers were startled, as well they should have been: one never—*never*—asks for food. One never eats until the announcer at the game (the crier) says "Walate!" (Let us eat!). But now here was this white guy again violating all the rules and actually asking for food. Not just for food, but also for the lesser food, thus rejecting the best they had to offer—commercial white bread—and asking instead for the most humble thing they had to offer at their feast, fry bread.

Well, that first taste of fry bread settled the issue. Then a curious thing happened, and even I could see it in my innocence: while I had indeed violated protocol by asking for a food of lesser quality than they intended for me to have, my enthusiasm for that lowly Indian fry bread was an absolute delight to them, an acceptance on my part of their culture that swept away the stain of a lot of my previous gaffes.

Not a year goes by when someone doesn't ask me how one acquires access to Native culture. My first and perfectly honest response is that frankly, as I have already noted, I just don't know because as far as I can tell my own situation was visited again and again by the grace of sheer, stupid, good luck. Second, however, I recommend that people interested in Native culture start where it is easiest—at occasions where outsiders are invited and welcome, powwows, for example—and that a critical part of gaining acceptance is accepting the sharing of food when it is offered, even if it is only for sale at food booths operated by Indians. That is, given a choice between burgers and fries sold by the Methodist Church ladies from a town outside the reservation lands and something being served up by Indian cooks, one should always opt for the latter, whether at the common public and open feeding of guests or at booths where Indian dishes are being prepared—fry bread, Indian "tacos," corn soup, pumpkin soup, roasting ears, whatever . . . doesn't matter. I am always and fundamentally enthusiastic about trying new foods, especially in appropriate contexts. I would most assuredly and most enthusiastically recommend eating Indian foods when offered Native hospitality.

I understand that it is possible for one's own food customs to complicate the interaction, but it's not going to kill you to eat what your hosts eat. Even if it is dog. I am not joking. I was once at a Sun Dance on the Pine Ridge Reservation and a kind new friend, Edgar Red Cloud, invited me to join him for the big meal of the day being served to all guests, Indian and non-Indian. There were two rows of people lined up with their dishes in hand, and Mr. Red Cloud steered me to a shorter one, which he said was for distinguished guests like me and elders like him. Great! Nothing but the best for ol' Rog!

When we reached the head of the line I could see that squares of meat were being fished out and served up from steaming metal garbage cans . . . as Mr. Red Cloud then explained, bison intestine. No bones. No fat. Easy for us "elders" to chew. Just good meat. And who would I be to argue with the people who became great warriors and a powerful nation on buffalo meat? I ate it, enjoyed it, appreciated the consideration, and have tried since then to obtain bison intestine myself for cooking, being now an elder myself. I suppose I could have gagged, choked, refused Mr. Red Cloud's generosity—that is, behaved like a common whiteman—but I have never for a moment regretted rejecting that provincial behavior and joining Mr. Red Cloud instead for a meal suited to our elevated status. And dog? Yes, I have eaten dog. It's meat, plain and simple.

23. *Carnivores Forever*

I have argued elsewhere in print that it is haute cuisine that is suspect and boring. How can one go wrong when cooking with the most elegant, rare, expensive, and quality ingredients? How does one screw up prime rib or fresh salmon? Not easily. On the other hand, imagine for a moment the inventiveness and knowledge it takes to convert a pig's nose and stale bread into the Czech delicacy jaternice? Is a liver mush from a diseased goose really better than bison liver quickly braised over an open fire? Not to this peasant's and Wannabe's taste! What is better trusted—mass-produced beef cuts from an industrial slaughterhouse in some city several hundred miles away? Or raw ground beef mixed with spices and onions, served as a wedding specialty by a German family in Wisconsin—who raised the beef especially for the occasion—to guests at their youngest daughter's wedding? Who cares more about who is going to eat that product and if it is going to kill someone?

When I taught folklore in higher education I was an infamously easy grader. Folklore is so interesting that most students who passed through my classes not only got As but earned them. So it was an unusual occasion when I had to take aside an advanced student who had taken many folklore courses and for whom I had found employment in a nearby state program and suggest that he find another line of work. If he was surprised, it was nothing compared to my own amazement. He was working on wedding lore among the prominent ethnic population of that state and was telling me about what he had recorded by way of music and customs. I asked him what he had found out about wedding foods, a main interest of mine being folk foodways. He reported that he couldn't really give me much information on that because whenever food was served, he left and went out to find a meal elsewhere. I can only imagine the look on my face. "You don't eat their food, even when they offer it to you?" I asked in absolute horror.

"No, I only eat hamburgers and French fries."

"Only . . . hamburgers . . ."

"And French fries. I've always been like that. I don't like anything but hamburgers and French fries, so that's all I eat. Ever."

On the spot I advised him to get the hell out of folklore and work at acquiring a burger franchise. The last I heard, he had gotten an appointment in folklore work (you can be sure his employers never checked with me, and I'm betting he never mentioned that he had studied and worked under me!) somewhere in the East, where I can only presume he never indulges in ambrosial local seafood but instead eats . . . hamburgers and French fries. A wasted life, a squandered education, a plum of a job thrown away. It makes me weep.

There is no shortage of examples, even in my own limited experience, of the importance of respecting, by sharing, another culture's food. At Thule and Qaanaaq in northern Greenland I was invited to take a meal with an Inuit woman and her friends, which I gladly and eagerly accepted. My hostess asked what I would like to eat, because American and Danish groceries and prepared foods were easily available, especially at Thule Air Force Base. By now you know what I asked for: Inuit food! The woman glowed with pride. The food of her people is the nature of her people, and she was pleased that I was willing to dip my toe into that life. The meal was excellent, as I knew it would be. As I recall, there was caribou, perhaps some seal. I do recall there was an excellent dried fish and a bit of Beluga whale meat. This was not simply an interesting meal, it was an excellent meal, and as I said my thank-yous and left for my own quarters late that evening I told her the meal was especially important to me because it was unique and *her* food.

She paused in her farewells and seemed to want to say something more but was uneasy about continuing. I waited. Finally she said what she had on her mind: "Did you really like the food, Roger? Or are you just being polite?"

"Oh, no, Astrid, I thought it was wonderfully good and I was only worried that I might make a hog of myself by eating too much!"

Again she paused, apparently not wanting to expose herself to a rejection she almost certainly had received before from other Americans who had sat at her table. "Okay, then, I'll believe you. So . . . would you be interested in coming back tomorrow evening for a *real* Inuit meal? Tonight we had Inuit food but the kind of Inuit food we figure non-Inuit people might like. If you are being honest with me, Roger, come back tomorrow, okay?"

I gushed with enthusiasm! Of course I would be back. Because I really had enjoyed the food, without considering that the entire meal was also a culinary and ethnological experience. And the next evening there I was at Astrid's door again. With genuine glee she put dish after dish on the table in front of me, foods of her life and her people, foods she had been reluctant to share because she had found that most Americans and perhaps even some Danes were not enthusiastic about it. I was. Despite my fervent support of the Sea Shepherd Conservation Society's actions against industrial whaling, I do not share the fervor of some activists and do not extend my contempt for reckless killing to the taking of food by Inuit, Aleuts, and some other aboriginal peoples. As a non-Inuit military friend noted one morning in Qaanaaq while we watched Native hunters head out of the village with their dogs and sleds, "For all the weaponry we have at Thule, there go the *real* men, out onto the sea ice to kill whales with sticks." So Astrid, some of her friends, and I had whale prepared a dozen different ways, walrus, Arctic hare, and a dozen different kinds of fresh and dried fish. And we parted as friends we never could have been without the shared communion of food. (Can we for even a moment pretend that it is coincidence that Communion is in fact a food ritual?)

24. *Another World*

world away from northern Greenland, on the Yucatan peninsula
of Mexico, I pursued the same happy strategy in a similar situation. (I am not comfortable with the word "strategy," which
sounds as if I contrive to gain entrée to cultures by pretending to be
interested in their foods, when the truth is I love new and interesting foods, I am interested in diverse foodways, and I enjoy sharing
culinary experiences with people of cultures other than mine. It's the
most natural thing in the world for me, so it's not so much a strategy
as a way of life.) I have stayed on occasion with friends who have a
home on a beach not far from Cancun on the southeast coast of the
Yucatan. The Mexican couple who care for their home in their absence,
help them out when they are there, and cook many of their meals are
Mayan. (Probably the dumbest question floating around these days
is, Whatever happened to the Mayans? Answer: They are doing just
fine, thank you, flourishing, speaking their ancient native language,
both in the Yucatan and for that matter in places like Grand Island,
Nebraska, where a common insult from nativists is the suggestion that
Latino immigrants should learn "American" when in fact the Mayans
in our midst are already bilingual.)

After I visited and stayed at the home of my friends four or five
times, Artemia and Dino had become old friends of mine, but we

still go through the same ritual at each visit. Through my friend Terri, Artemia asks what I would like to eat during my visit. And I respond, again through Terri, that I would like to eat—what else?—Mayan food! Again there is that glow of pride that I have seen among the Omahas, Pawnees, Lakotas, Germans, Czechs, Inuit, and now Mayans, the pride of presenting one's own cuisine. And again I am treated to menus of food so good that then I too glow, but with a gourmet's delight rather than any sort of pride. And the food is inevitably exquisite.

My respect for Mayan food and friendship with Artemia and Dino eventually resulted in a benefit I could never have imagined or wished for in my wildest fantasies. One day, through Terri, the question came from my Mayan friends if I would like to visit their pueblo in the Yucatan interior. Would I? I was excited by the prospect, but the realization was so much more than my hopes that I could never have predicted what that trip would present. We scheduled a day for our trip and headed down the shore toward Belize, where we stopped at a small town to meet Artemia's family at their small bodega and buy some items Artemia said we would need—candy and that kind of thing—probably for the children of the pueblo. From there we turned away from the tourist-clogged area immediately adjacent to the ocean and steered our car into the interior. The roads grew ever narrower and rougher, on and on into the jungle closing in around us. We finally arrived at a small clearing in which there were a dozen huts, little more than rows of poles set in the ground with thatch roofs. Artemia took us into her family home, where I felt we had stepped back five hundred years, except for the television set on a shelf on one wall, playing a soccer game, watched by her father reclining in a hammock. He sprang to his feet to greet us, as did his wife, from her cooking fire in a hole in the ground inside the shelter, a pot boiling on a rack made of salvaged truck springs, a rack hanging from the roof on which perishables were out of the reach of dogs, pigs, children, and various pests and protected by the smoke of the cooking fire. We were offered food from the large pot over the fire, which was superb . . . pork, as I recall.

Then Artemia's father took us to his garden immediately behind the shelter, fenced with sticks, branches, and stakes. He explained as best he could through layers of interpreters (Mayan to Artemia, Spanish to Terri, English to me) what he was growing there, his pride in his gardening skills obvious in his enthusiasm and smile. Peppers, tomatillos, herbs, plants I had never seen and for which no one could find the English words. Again food was proving the ultimate medium of human interaction. And it was my respect for their food that had given me this incredible opportunity to see a way of life many think has been dead for centuries.

But the experience in living archeology in Artemia's pueblo was far from over. Artemia, again through Terri, asked if we would like to see "a church where some white men tried to burrow in and steal a treasure but it caved in and killed them." Well, uh, okay. If Artemia thought it might be of interest, perhaps it would be. So we set off again, but this time on foot away from the village, down a narrow path into the dense jungle. It was like a movie set, but more dramatic. We walked for perhaps half an hour, maybe a bit longer, until I took a break from staring straight forward at the back of Artemia's head in front of me, hoping I did not lose track of her in this maze of green. I paused and looked around. I blinked my eyes and tried to refocus. I leaned forward into the jungle to our right, unable to believe what I saw: obscured but dimly visible through the jungle about fifty feet from us was some sort of structure—ancient, vine covered with bits of color showing through, naked stone veiled in the centuries. I was looking at a Mayan temple. My mind simply could not accept the reality before me. "It's a Mayan temple!" I blurted. Artemia apparently understood enough English to realize what I had said, or she read the astonishment on my face. She smiled and nodded. I asked Terri to ask Artemia, "When did the Mayans worship here?" and once again I was set back hard on my heels when she gave my question a moment's thought and answered, "Tuesday." She pointed ahead a few yards into the jungle and to our left, where there was a pit under a thin shelter of fronds and signs of recent cooking. We continued on the path but with considerably more stumbling because we could not take our eyes off the massive stone temple we were flanking.

We approached the temple and a small *palapa*, or thatched shelter built against the wall. Small, melting candles burned on an altar. Food gifts lay about. Artemia indicated that she was about to speak to the gods, and she took out the candy we had purchased in her mother's bodega and placed it on the altar with the other gifts. And she spoke to ancient gods in her (and their) ancient language. Again, food as an intermediary, this time between us humble beings on the floor of the jungle and the powerful gods that still reigned in the stone edifice before us. Artemia took us around the corner of the temple, where there had clearly been excavating and a collapse of the structure. There were still large sections of plaster and painted frescoes on the temple's exterior walls. This was the church she had mentioned; the Spanish had been the white men attempting to loot the treasure, and here was the place they had died for their greed and desecration. We all swallowed deep. History had just collapsed in on our heads like a Mayan temple falling on the heads of conquistadors.

See the magic to which food can lead the curious and fearless—or foolhardy—Wannabe? Food, respect, and honest interest can lead one to an education no tuition paid to a university can offer, culinary experiences not found in the finest and most exotic dining rooms, and personal exploration and spiritual revelation that jars the soul and changes one's life.

25. The Consequences of Incuriosity

Conversely, an unwillingness to explore other cultures can potentially be self-destructive. I live in the very center of our country, among one of the least intellectually curious populations I can imagine. Commercials currently running on local television stations state, "Nebraska football—it's not a game . . . it's a way of life." What sadder confession could a person or society make than that their soul lives in a game played by boys with a ball, and yet here it is, stated as a matter of pride. It's like waving a banner that says, HERE WE HAVE NO LIFE! Letters regularly appear in the letters to the editor columns of newspapers around Nebraska angrily resisting any change, any introduction of new cultural elements, any linguistic exploration, the appearance of any new foodstuffs in local grocery stores. Young and old alike complain of being bored. *Bored!* How, in this world with millions of mysteries and wonders, can anyone possibly, ever, be bored?

In a way, the resistance to new cultural experiences is itself a tradition of middle America. Plains pioneers, travelers on the Oregon and Mormon Trails, and homesteaders alike starved to death within sight of villages and camps where Natives ate well. Even today benighted commentators speak of the pre-homesteading plains as a barren wilderness, ignoring the fact that Indians prospered on this same landscape for centuries and saw the plains not as a landscape to be fought and conquered but as a benevolent garden land. White invaders ate rotten, maggot-infested bacon, leathery hams, wormy flour, and rock-hard biscuits and died of vitamin deficiencies while Indians all around them prospered and ate dried and smoked buffalo, wild turnips and potatoes, and a glorious variety of berries, beans, tubers, and greens, easily available for casual harvesting. This is not a story confined to the American frontier; Vikings faced with starvation at their settlements in Greenland refused to adopt the hunting methods (for example, the harpoon with a detachable point that is still used today) of the Greenland Inuit (contemptuously referred to by the Vikings as "Skraelings"), even though it was clearly superior, as hunting successes and failures showed, to the Viking spear. So the Skraelings prospered. And the Vikings buried their dead.

While investigating pioneer and Native foodways forty years ago I interviewed many people who had either lived on the sod-house frontier or remembered tales from those who had. Again and again I was told that in times of severe famine white settlers or travelers might find themselves reduced to the indignity of eating "Indian food," and they almost universally stated that to their surprise they found foods like dried beef and buffalo, dried chokecherry soup, and ground nuts to be quite tasty, even delectable. And yet inevitably when times improved, if times did improve, the newcomers reverted to their old foodways, not simply because they preferred the old foods but because they were embarrassed about eating something as lowly as Indian foods and feared someone might discover that they were eating it, a shame they were not prepared to accept. One has to wonder how often frontiersmen starved to death because of their unwillingness to cross cultural culinary boundaries.

How wonderfully ironic, then, that today many of those very foods that were shunned as beneath white people's dignity are considered delicacies or at least premium foods. If you have any doubts about this, go into any tavern and ask the price of a small strip of jerky in the jar sitting behind the bar! In my own case, foods that I once thought curious or peculiar—bison intestine, corn soup, fry bread, milkweed soup, dried and powdered beef, soup from dried chokecherries—are now favorites, and I eat them not only with relish but also with reverence.

Wannabes deal with at least two foodways systems, their own and the culture into which they venture. Even when we overcome our own doubts about another foodways system we must consider the nature, prohibitions, and customs of the foodways complex into which we are going. It was only after a year of regularly attending Omaha handgames, for example, that I observed that I was the only one who carried a fork and knife as part of my handgame dishes. When I mentioned this to an Omaha friend I was told that everyone had wondered when I would figure this out, a knife and fork being seen as weapons and scarcely the thing one would carry to a friendly social gathering. I quickly learned that food is considered a gift of special import among the Omahas, and years later I found that at a Pawnee feast one never turns down food as it is passed out around the powwow or handgame circle. And there is the issue of the Kontha Clan's totemic prohibitions against shellfish. A hard lesson indeed for a Wannabe!

Long ago I learned that food has little to do with nutrition, taste, availability, economy, or logic. A lot of mainstream American foods are considered nauseating to many people of the world. Much of what we consider distasteful is elsewhere a delicacy. Americans especially, because of our language and marketing methods, have no idea what they are eating and might be sickened if they found out. American children grow up eating pork, beef, veal, or mutton without the slightest notion of what animals those terms of French origin refer to. Most of us prefer not to know what is in those snack sausages we eat along with a beer in the local tavern!

On the other hand, some foods take on emotional or cultural baggage that is just as arcane, and we wind up relishing foods that really do not deserve the honor. Fry bread, for example, has become a symbol of Indianness, the very heart of Native cuisine, and yet historically in the regions where fry bread is now most prevalent no Indians had baking powder or flour, lard, or the iron pots necessary to make it. Fry bread was an introduction from, irony of ironies, the military, the enemy of most Native tribes. Soldiers couldn't carry ovens or easily maintain a yeast culture, so they did not bake bread except in permanent sites like forts. On the trails and campaigns, it was quick and easy fry bread that was the military staple and that became favored by the Natives who shared it, too.

Other foods like *wasna* (dried and powdered beef or buffalo), choke-cherry and milkweed soup, corn soup among the Omahas, and pumpkin soup among the Pawnees have become symbolic, too, powerful and meaningful relics of the past, of the buffalo times. When they are served, it is with special reverence. They may be served first and perhaps only to honored guests and elders. *Wasna* is placed first in the eater's hand, to be eaten in small bits, in an attitude of prayer. Such foods often play central roles in religious rites, too, and must therefore be eaten with appropriate respect. Like the Communion host and wine, these are not merely *food*—that is, a means of nutrition—but symbols with far more and deeper meaning.

26. *Symbols and Realities*

On the other hand, something that is only symbolic in our culture may be more substantive in other cultures. I am uneasy in writing that because I certainly don't want to diminish the importance and value of symbols. But symbols are first and foremost metaphors. To hit someone with a brick is one thing; to say someone is a real brick may be a significant statement, but it is not a statement of reality. A major confusion among some in mainstream American society is that our flag is a sacred thing when in reality it is a symbol for what one might consider a sacred thing—our nation, our Constitution, and in the case of many Native peoples, the land itself. Showing disrespect for a symbol is not the same as showing disrespect for the entity it represents and is in itself symbolic. Burning a flag is a symbolic action . . . infuriating, perhaps, but not actually harmful to the reality that it represents.

Sometimes non-Natives misunderstand such differences within Native culture. The Sacred Pole of the Omahas is not a symbol of something; it *is* something. It is a He. He is in and of itself—Himself—a sacred object. He is in fact a *living* object, spoken of as being the "ultimate" or "proto-Omaha," not symbolic at all but an actual human-spirit. He—the Sacred Pole—needs to be fed, craves the company of his kinsmen, communicates with us just as He did hundreds of years ago, mourns loss, celebrates success, and enjoys laughter.

Within many Native cultures the drum is a sacred object, as is to-bacco. Imitation or adoption of even highly respected symbols might be acceptable within some cultures; so while there are laws against wearing the American flag as clothing, super-patriots do it all the time and argue that they are honoring the flag when they make a shirt out of it, while of course they are "wrapping themselves in the flag," trying to transfer the honor of that cloth symbol to themselves. Wearing a beaded Pawnee star as a pendant when one is not a Pawnee, for example, may be a bit touchier an issue and yet still not outside the bounds of accepted propriety. Same with the Water Bird or Thunder Bird symbolic of the Native American Church: some church members might be uncomfortable with someone who does not understand that symbolism wearing a pin or beaded tie depicting it, but more often than not it is shrugged off as a misunderstanding, not a disrespectful blasphemy. What may seem a symbolic action, like going clockwise around the drum within Omaha culture (counterclockwise among the Pawnees), a custom sometimes explained as being symbolic (the path of the sun), is not in and of itself an absolute, violation of which is an offense. Yet going against the custom is considered a way of bringing very bad fortune to an individual, if not the entire group gathering around that drum.

27. *Indian Humor*

Despite the long-established stereotypes, Indians do have a sense of humor. Oh boy, do they ever! As one who thoroughly appreciates humor and laughter I cherish my relationships with Indian kin and friends as I love my wife, Linda—in large part because of their remarkable and unique wit.

However, despite the prevailing belief, now a cliché as mistaken as that of the humorless Indian, humor is not a universal language. "That is something everybody everywhere does in the same language . . . ," as the song goes. No, not really. One cannot say categorically even within one's own society that the young and old or even men and women share the same sense of humor. Oh, I know, there are women who have exactly the same sense of humor that men have and vice versa, but just pick a good joke and tell it to fifty people and see if you don't detect certain patterns suggesting that various social levels and compartments have different ideas about what is funny. In folklore scholarship there is a well-known and very useful theory (posited by an old friend, William Hugh Jansen) called the Es-Ex Factor, shorthand for esoteric-exoteric. The idea is that there are things that can be said, done, understood, whatever, esoterically (that is, within a culture of any size) that are not comfortably said, done, or understood exoterically (that is, outside that same culture or across a cultural divide). We all know—and some people grouse about it—that minorities, whether they be racial, religious, sexual, or age-related, can say certain words or tell certain jokes to each other, but the minute someone outside that group does the same thing there is bristling, posturing, perhaps even violent reaction. You know what I'm talking about.

Well, the Es-Ex Factor operates within Native American culture too. Sometimes Indian humor is simply so culture-specific, so peculiarly Indian that outsiders aren't likely to understand it. At Omaha handgames sometimes a poor guesser will be taunted with a splashing of water or shaking of water bottles. What's *that* about? Well, it is a long, arbitrary understanding that someone who is having bad luck guessing where the stones are hidden in a handgame needs a bath! Of course it doesn't make sense, but it is something that has come to be believed over the years—or people pretend they believe it—so it has become the stuff of jokes and joking. One needs to know history, culture, and tribal relationships to understand many of these esoteric ways. A researcher once said to an Oglala friend of mine, "I have information about Omaha, Winnebago, Cherokee, and Pawnee harvest festivals but can't find anything about when the Lakota had theirs." The Oglala responded, "The Lakota usually had their harvest festivals about two weeks after the Pawnee had *their* harvest festival!"

Sometimes the jokes are more obvious but would be considered insults if told by anyone except an Indian, because the Es-Ex Factor dictates that one can laugh at oneself but the same laughter will not result when that same comment comes from someone outside the closed social circle. Thus within one of my Native adoptive families my Lakota brother can tell the following joke about our Winnebago brother, when the same story would be considered deeply offensive if told by anyone not within our family and especially by a non-Indian:

"Back in his drinking days Louie was once walking back to Winnebago from Sioux City when he spotted a half-filled wine bottle lying in the ditch alongside the highway. Of course he picked the bottle up and opened it, but to his amazement a genie sprang out and announced that Louie had two wishes. Yeah, I know . . . white guys get three wishes but Indians only get two. Louie thought about it a second and said, 'I'd like to be rich like a white guy, drive a big fancy car like a white guy, and have a real pretty girlfriend like a white guy.' The genie went POOF! And there sat Louie in a big fancy car, wearing a new silk suit, with a gorgeous movie star woman sitting right there next to him. 'And what do you want for your second wish?' the genie said, and Louie said, 'I never want to work another day the rest of my life,' and POOF! He was a 'Bago again."

As I caution elsewhere in these pages, one cannot surmise a universal character for Indians (any more than we can for any other group of people), but certainly within my narrow and nonprofessional (but long-term and deeply interested) experience it seems that humor is a powerful and widespread element within broader Native American culture. Laughter is not universal from one Native people to another, but it is never altogether absent from Native circles. This is perhaps all the more notable in view of the stereotype within popular culture and within the wider American population of Hollywood's emotionless Tonto-Cochise character. Perhaps I am struck by it more than most might be because of my long interest in the nature of humor.

Most attractive to me is the self-effacing nature of the Native humor I have seen over the past fifty years. When the laughter is not directed inward at one's self, it is pointed at a member of the in-group, thus assuring that the laughter is good-natured and not insulting. I have seen some unpleasant and outright hostile arguments and debates among Indians and Indian groups, but in situations like that there is rarely humor. Native humor, it seems to me, is largely used to elicit laughter, not as snide insult. My Winnebago brother Louie sometimes notes that he is "brown with envy," for example. Gag lines about the plight of life on the reservation are endless—such as someone having a new set of tires on his "Indian car," all four of which have NO TRESPASSING written on them. Perhaps only an Indian accustomed to the condition of most Indian automobiles can detect the irony in a comment made while passing by a salvage lot or junkyard: "Oh, it's a junkyard. For a second there I thought someone was having a [prayer] meeting."

During my first contact with the Pawnees almost twenty-five years ago, for example, a contingent of distinguished elders and political and religious leaders were in our home for a meal. My wife, Linda, was nervous about serving a meal to such a notable group, and as she often does, a sparkling wit being one of her many strengths, she said at the end of the meal, "Where I come from, whoever does the cooking doesn't have to do the dishes." I usually respond to that comment by saying, "Where I come from, we just put the dishes on the floor and let the dogs clean them up." But with Indians at the table, that was not the end of the story; Vance Spotted Horse Chief then said with a truth and humor only an Indian could bring to the table, "Where we come from, we didn't have any dishes. And we *ate* the dogs!"

Linda and I recently watched a television presentation showing the opening of British Parliament and the queen's annual speech. Linda noted that the queen was carrying a purse and wondered aloud what the heck she might be carrying in that purse. I mentioned our curiosity the next time I corresponded with my Hunkapi Indian family and posed the same question to them. My Hochunk brother Louie speculated that she was probably carrying her "Bingo dauber," the large felt marker Indian women often carry in their purses to mark bingo cards, thus bringing the queen of England down to the level of the women of his tribe (or *up* to the level of the women of his tribe, if you share my opinion of royalty, or of Indian women).

The closest I have come to seeing tribal humor aimed directly at mainstream non-Indians has come from this same Hochunk relative, who has spoken of his plans to develop a "Great Plains White Guy Museum." He notes that a lot of Indian people come through Nebraska when traveling to powwows or conferences, and they naturally wonder what life is like in all those double-wide manufactured houses they see along plains highways. So he plans to furnish his museum exhibit just the way a white guy would, so Indians can do a walk-through and witness for themselves the typical whiteman's life. He says he would have a fat guy—when saying this he usually then looks in my direction—sitting in a recliner watching a football game, a Budweiser balanced on his belly and a bowl of potato chips close at hand, and a wife busily cooking up a typical white guy meal in the kitchen: lime Jell-O with mandarin oranges suspended in the neon green, or maybe tiny colored marshmallows floating in an orange Jell-O base, coleslaw, maybe an arugula and cress salad with a balsamic vinaigrette or bleu cheese dressing ready to be tossed and croutoned. Near the exit Louie proposes to place a gift shop where visiting Indians could buy the ingredients in kit form to make these same foods in their own home.

Louie often speaks of "white tape" rather than "red tape," since the source of most bureaucratic snarls in the Indian world are certainly not Indian-generated. One of his truly ethnographic observations is that during deer-hunting season on the Winnebago Reservation in Nebraska he is always struck by "all those Indians driving around in pickup trucks with .30-.30s and all those white guys perched up in trees with bows and arrows."

Is it really an insult to show us what we in reality are? Even if mockingly? I have always relished the increasingly rare appearances of the traditional clown dancer at powwows and other dance occasions. The clown has long been a part of Plains Native tradition, from the Pawnee clown society to the Lakota Heyoka, or Contraries, who provided a sacred distraction with their obverse behavior, doing everything wrong, everything backward. The clown dancers I have seen at Lakota and Omaha events appear from nowhere and are never identified. He—or is it a she?—is dressed in what looks like an ancient Goodwill Industries reject suit—too large, double-breasted, as drab as the Indian dancers in feathers, paint, and bells are colorful. The clown dancer has a white flour sack covering his or her entire head, so not even a hairstyle can be identified. However, a grotesque blond wig may flow out from beneath his or her battered fedora. Red lips and blue eyes are painted on the flour-sack face. (Do you see a pattern emerging?) In the clown dancer's hands, rather than a dance ax or totemic staff, is a mirror, into which the dancer frequently peers while preening. At his or her waist hangs an alarm clock on a great chain, which again is referred to with distracting frequency.

The clown dancer's actions are as incongruous, as incorrect, as his or her appearance. The dancer goes the wrong way around the drum (the right way among the Omahas being clockwise), other dancers are touched inappropriately, he or she interferes with the ceremonial duties of the whip man and tail dancers. His or her dancing is clumsy, perhaps exaggerated, and always out of beat. Worst of all, when the song ends, instead of matching the last dramatic step of the dance precisely with the last drumbeat, the clown dancer continues on another five steps. Or ten. Or twenty. Obviously, the clown dancer is a mockery of the whiteman, always doing everything wrong, ever intruding into Indian life but never getting it right. But the depiction is so funny and so gentle that even those non-Indians present have to laugh. How can they be offended, after all, when the joke is based precisely on the nature of the whiteman as seen from within Native society?

Humor is an important indicator for a Wannabe. The subtle shift when one finds that she is "in on the joke," as we phrase it, when she not only shares a joke that would only be told within a close and closed circle but now understands it as a silent but important rite of passage. Particularly telling is humor directed from the group toward the outside but not at a Wannabe outsider; the point being that now she is an insider and presumed to be sympathetic with the humor and its intent. The stereotype of Indians eating dog, for example, while historically based (and even contemporaneous in ritual circumstances—I have eaten dog at Native events in my lifetime) is often considered offensive to Natives when it comes from outside Native culture. Yet jokes about a new Chinese restaurant named "Wok the Dog" opening on the reservation are common within Native circles. So when my book about my love of dogs (*A Life with Dogs*) was published in 2004, my Indian friends received it with predictable jokes ("Why didn't you ask me for *my* recipe?"), reconfirming my status as an insider.

Indians tend to be on the bottom rung of the American economic ladder, for reasons I won't explore here but that are manifold and manifest. If that is true for Indians living directly within the mainstream of American culture, it is all the more painfully evident on reservations.

As anyone, Wannabe or not, can imagine, that is not a happy topic for Indians and most assuredly is not something for an outsider to make jokes about. Therefore, it is precisely the kind of thing the Indian in-group *does* use as a point of humor, whether the topic is commodity foods, government housing, or simply the inadequate services on reservations, usually the very poorest areas of any state's population.

My Hochunk brother Louie's story is well understood when he tells it in any Indian company but may border on the obscure within non-Indian circles. Allegedly, he was at an Indian conference in Las Vegas and hit a generous slot machine jackpot. Of course, then the noise was immediately raised that he should buy a round of drinks for everyone to celebrate, but he demurred, saying that he planned to take the money home instead so he could buy his wife the much-needed washing machine that she had wanted for many years. All the Indians in the group admired his dedication to his wife and applauded him for being so unselfish. At the next gathering, however, he was asked how his wife liked that new washing machine, and he replied, "You know how Indian women are. Now she wants *electricity!*"

Indian humor is often directed intertribally, between historical rivals: "The Lakotas started their campfires by rubbing two Omahas together." Or, "I always thought the Omaha Nation flag was a white rag tied to the top of a stick." In an e-mail from a Lakota friend to a Winnebago friend: "What has ten eyes, five mouths, and no teeth?" "A 'Bago drum [that is, the circle of singers around a Winnebago drum]."

"What's a mile long and four feet high?" "A Hopi Grand Entry."

"What do you call a Lakota walking his dog?" "A vegetarian."

"Two Cheyenne guys on relocation spied a sign in a café window that said HOT DOGS. Thinking they were some other kind of dogs, they ordered two to go and went to a park to have lunch. The first Cheyenne guy looked inside his sack and threw it down in disgust. 'What part did you get?' he asked his buddy."

"Three Indian commandos were out in the Iraqi desert. 'I understand you Indians brought your own indigenous survival equipment,' ventured their white captain. 'Sir, I brought an entire barrel cactus,' said the Pima guy proudly. 'When I get too hot I just cut off the top and take a drink.' The captain was impressed. Not to be outdone, the Pueblo guy said, 'Sir, I brought the sacred corn pollen. When I get too hot I pray with it and then it rains.' The captain looked even more impressed. Not to be outdone, the Pawnee guy said, 'I brought a door off a 1959 Chevy Impala.' 'Why would you do that?' the captain asked. 'Well,' said the Pawnee, 'when I get too hot I just roll down the window.'"

Or, as is the case within mainstream American humor between genders:

"Three Indian women died and came into the presence of the Creator at the same time. The first one was a Diné [Navajo] woman. Creator said, 'Tell me what you think. What is important?' And the Diné woman said, 'I think we need to take better care of the earth, the waters, and all the things that are of it.' Creator said, 'That is a very good thought. Come and sit down next to me.'

The Creator then said to the second woman, an Ojibwa, 'Tell me what you think. What is important?' And the Ojibwa woman said, 'I think we need to take better care of our People, of the young ones and the very old.' Creator said, 'That is a very good thought too. Come and sit down here next to me on the other side.'

Then Creator said to the third woman, who was Lakota, 'Tell me what you think.' She looked Creator up and down and said, 'I think you're sitting in my seat.'"

When it is a Wannabe's turn to be the butt of the joking, his only defense is to be prepared to laugh along. And then be deeply moved and grateful to be so honored. The next joke will be directed at someone else down the line, and then the Wannabe can feel genuinely included because he is now seen as one who is allowed to laugh, even at the expense of a Native.

I remember with genuine pleasure the first time I was included in Pawnee tribal humor. I had long been a part of Pawnee efforts to regain the remains of their eldest from museum shelves, but I was obviously an outsider, a white man, and the occasions were serious enough that humor might have been out of place. (Although during those solemn educations I was often at the side of my Winnebago brother Louie, and his humor never lets up. As we were covering the remains, a process that was serious not simply because it was a funeral but because the dead we were reburying had been desecrated, Louie paused at his shovel and turned to me, saying, "Rog, don't try to keep up with me. Just set yourself a pace and stick with it." Now, twenty years later, that line is still a tradition within our family.)

It was at the reburial funeral feast in Pawnee, Oklahoma, in the Pawnee tribal roundhouse, that I was called out into the center ring to receive a beautiful beaded "medicine" container. When I returned to my seat at the side of the building, the Pawnee next to me on my left said in a whisper, "Roger, it is Pawnee tradition that when you get a nice gift like that, you are supposed to pass it over to the person sitting on your left." I paused, I looked at the gift, I looked at him . . . and then everyone around us chuckled and mumbled, "Roger, don't listen to him. He tries that routine on every white guy who comes here." Suddenly I felt I had been brought in closer to the Pawnee circle—now they could joke with me.

When you are included—that is, when you become part of the esoteric community—your inclusion is broadened all the way around the circle, not just on the sector that deals with humor but also the one that deals with serious personal and spiritual issues. The laughter is only a step in becoming more than a Wannabe . . . a Gottabe.

28. *Names and Naming*

A notable feature of contemporary Native culture is the importance of one's name. Naming and names don't seem to be particularly important within mainstream American culture. While names once honored admired historical, cultural, or religious figures or continued a family naming tradition, today the tendency appears to be the opposite—that is, to give children names that have nothing to do with the past or family tradition. Does anyone name a new baby after a grandfather or honored elder today? Not likely! Perhaps that is because families no longer exist in the sense of a closely connected, continuing unit or because there are no honored elders. What is the attraction of arcane, silly, even grotesque spellings? I'd attempt to offer examples so grotesque that they wouldn't offend anyone because they are well outside the possibility of being actual names. But frankly I don't think I am inventive enough to come up with anything so goofy that it would fall outside today's naming processes in America. Scharry, as in Cherie—a curious name to begin with? I bet I have hereby offended a dozen Scharrys in Nebraska alone. Marryloo? There have to be a few of them around. Kazhoo? Xzyphyzl? Somewhere there is one. No name is too bizarre to stick on a child.

Not to mention the clerk who has to ask to have the name Chandra-Leveetra repeated twelve times to get the name written onto a registry form. Or the person waiting in line behind ChandraLeveetra, whose name is almost certainly Roger. That is apparently not a consideration of other American parents today.

Please don't accuse me of elitism with this observation. Roger is a name picked out of the air by my parents. As was my middle name, Lee. My beloved Linda Catherine Angela … arbitrary generic labeling. Linda and I did what we could to make our daughter's name meaningful: Antonia Emily Celestine Welsch. Two cultures, four generations, two nationalities, four grandparents, and one literary giant heaped up within eleven syllables. Even as we spent days working on her name we said, "She's going to hate us when she grows up."

The average American male today is stuck with one name. My best friends are Mick, Dennis, John, Dick, and Verne. But they are all over fifty years of age. Younger friends are named as if their parents had no aspiration for them to ever amount to anything important—Fustler, Plummer, Colander, Carburetor, Inkubator, whatever. No more meaning in their names than there is in their Social Security numbers. (And again, please, don't complain to me about my suggesting that these names are meaningless. They are. ChandraLeveetra, ask your parents where they came up with a name like that. You can bet they gave more thought to naming their boat or favorite dog!)

I have been formally given Native names in adoption ceremonies within two tribes, an informal third within another. That is understandably an important life event for a Wannabe, especially a non-Native Wannabe who has been stuck with one name that he presumed he would be stuck with forever. (An obvious exception to the "eternal name" syndrome being the notable exception of the increasingly rare American woman who marries and chooses the option of taking on her mate's name.)

I described previously the nature of name giving within Omaha culture and the deadly seriousness of the process. Much later, in a Lakota kin-making ceremony, a Hunkapi, I was given another name, one so powerful that I was cautioned to use it or tell it only with great care, because it is likely to induce fear or discomfort in anyone who hears it. (Curiously, in both the Omaha and Lakota experiences my new name carried with it "lightning medicine," which gives the new bearer kinship with wind, storm, and lightning but, as is the case in many world religions, the kinship carries with it certain perils and should not be abused or used in vain.) When a Native has an "Indian" name in addition to his or her name used in general daily life, that name is sometimes, within some tribes, clans, or perhaps in the case of one person's personal preference, not exactly secret or sacred but treated with special deference. It may be known by close friends or relatives (in some cases the name is known only to its bearer), but it is not used in casual discourse. It is known but not used, a holding so personal that it is held closely and quietly. I have made the mistake myself, even recently, of being too cavalier about a friend's personal tribal name and have had to be reminded that it was not to be used freely. I am not aware that a similar practice prevails anywhere in the American mainstream, so a Wannabe should use special caution in using a private name that has been given through tribal custom or ritual.

As I have mentioned elsewhere, one of the distinctive features of American culture is an immediate and off-hand use of a person's first name: "Rog, I want you to meet my friend Clyde Sheridan." "Glad to know you, Clyde." Very poor style in most parts of the world, especially with American minorities, where it has long and unfortunately been the custom for minorities to address the white mainstream by a formal last name—"Glad to meet you, Mr. Welsch"—while the majority mainstream person in the exchange instantly goes to an informal address: "Glad to meet you, Clyde."

The practice of Natives having an "Indian name," perhaps earned or given but in some cases a name held within a family or clan, is common. The name may be used with outsiders only rarely or not at all, and yet considerable importance is put on a person's knowing his or her name. It is standard ritual within many Native cultures when encountering a kinsman to ask him if he still knows his name, whereupon he is expected to say that name. That name is essentially who you are or have become, as opposed to your "white man's name," which historically may have been imposed casually, mistakenly, ironically, or even as an insult.

29. *The Crazy Horse Surrender Ledger of 1877*

On the Astonisher.com website one finds a remarkable roster of Lakota names that seems to fly in the face of my assertion that names and naming are profoundly serious within Indian history and culture (http://www.astonisher.com/archives/museum/crazy_horse_surrender.html). If you are of tender sensibilities, brace yourself before opening this file! It is sometimes seen as an example of obscene naming, but other explanations seem, from the Native perspective, more likely. The site explains:

> An amusing sidelight of the *Crazy Horse Surrender Ledger* is the presence of many scatological names like Shits On His Hand, Pisses In The Horn, Soft Prick, Snatch Stealer, Makes Widows Cry, Tanned Nuts, and the woman, Bull Proof. These names may reflect the Sioux habit of enlisting a *winkte* (a male transvestite, whom the Sioux believed had the power of prophesy) to give children "joke names."

> It has also been suggested that members of Crazy Horse's band may have used these names when they surrendered as a tacit, passive form of disrespect for the surrender process. Another obvious possibility is that these scatological Sioux names were intended to disguise the true identity of the individuals. Who were the last

three members of Crazy Horse's band to surrender—really? We'll never know for sure, but I'll bet they were better known by names other than the ones they gave the gullible Americans: Singing Prick, Stinking Tie, Dog Nothing.

Another common interpretation of the remarkably obscene names appearing on the Crazy Horse list is that they result from the sense of humor of the white men who compiled the list. However, a close Lakota friend tells me it seems more like Native humor. His theory is that in the making of such lists a white military interpreter would ask a cooperative Indian what the names were, for example, of "those people over there." "Those people" being unfriendly with the person asked to provide names, he might say something like, "That is Mr. Shit For Brains, Mrs. Lard Ass, and their girls Loose As A Rabbit In Heat and Ugly As A Mud Fence." And those names were then written on the census and officially assigned with the inertia common to official practices. Credence is lent this interpretation because my friend has identified two of his own relatives to me as Uncle Shit and his cousin Prestone (from his drink of choice). And yet, while these names seem incredibly insulting, one must admit they are nonetheless significant, and that is my point. One could, after all, say the same of Roger, related if not in fact derived from the verb "to roger." Look it up. My name with its etymological root might as well have been included in the Crazy Horse Surrender ledger!

30. *Names . . . and Names*

The Omaha example may explain why at least that Native nation puts great importance on tribal or "Indian" names. An outsider might say that the names of Omaha tribal members are not particularly noteworthy, not dramatically Indian like those of my Pawnee friends Pat Leading Fox, Adrian Spotted Horse Chief, Karla Knife Chief, James Riding In, or John Only A Chief. Common Omaha names are Sheridan, Canby, Philips, Grant, or Turner. Do those names have anything in common? Do they strike you as somehow significant? Perhaps incongruous? They should. They are the names of notable white, primarily military leaders, and they were assigned to the Omahas, especially children in the mission schools, as substitutes for their "uncivilized" (or in some cases admittedly unpronounceable for mission teachers) names. I have no evidence that this horrendous naming practice was malicious rather than simply stupid, but it most assuredly demonstrates a cultural contempt of the highest degree. No wonder that the Omahas still bear their "white" names officially but take particular pride in their Native names.

For the Omahas, the whiteman came in three distinct guises: "black robes" (missionaries), "long knives" (soldiers), and "one of us" (the French traders and trappers who came as visitors to Omaha land, learned the language and ways of the people, married into the tribes, and generally became . . . one of them). Thus, those Omahas who do not have military leaders' names often have French names with much more genial meaning, like my own daughter Jennifer Saunsoci, from the French *sans souci* (without a care). A people's history can be seen in the Omaha Reservation telephone index.

On the other hand, it is possible for too much to be made of an Indian name. Nicknames often result not from deep spiritual considerations but simply from Native humor. A few Lakota friends call me Pisko, or the Night Hawk. That might seem to be a flattering, mysterious name, right up there with my favorite Lakota name, Neither Man Nor Wolf, but my friends and I and others also know the reputation and nature of the nighthawk, as shown in its nickname, which describes the sounds it makes as it spirals high overhead on summer evenings—The Bird That Farts.

Among the Pawnees I am known as Panitaka—White Wolf—or White Pani, either of which is, indeed, flattering. But my closest Pawnee friends, inveterate jokers, sometimes call me Kuteese. They translate the word as Afraid Of His Woman, but I turn the joke and insist that my own, more accurate translation is Ever Attentive To His Woman's Every Emotional And Physical Need. Even Linda laughs at that.

Sometimes, of course, names are just names. Pat Leading Fox, chief of the Skidi band and head chief of the Nasharo, or Chiefs Council, was once interviewed by a television reporter who, obviously awestruck, asked, "Mr. Leading Fox, what does your Indian name mean?"

A bit startled himself by the remarkable question, Pat thought a moment and then said, "Well, I guess it means 'the fox that's out in front.'"

"Oh my," the woman fluttered. "And what are your children's names?"

By now Pat was ready for her and turned on the subtlest degree of his Indian humor, while simply stating the truth. "Let's see . . . there's Jennifer, and Elizabeth, and the boy . . . he's Junior!"

31. *Matters of Faith*

Religion is a sensitive topic, anywhere, any time. And complicated. A Wannabe entering into a Native context is entering another world—literally. The same, in fact, is true of anyone coming into contact with another religion, because that is what religion is—a distinctive, dearly held worldview, usually seen as a unique and separate truth. When I taught folklore in higher education I sometimes included Carlos Castaneda's *The Teachings of Don Juan: A Yaqui Way of Knowledge* a reading assignment. To this day, some fifty years after the first publication of the book, there is controversy about how accurate the book is ethnographically. Is Castaneda's account even close to truth or is it simply an imaginative bit of fiction, possibly drug induced? Did Castaneda really experience what he said he did and in the way he described? For example, if the experiences described did happen, did they indeed happen within the Yaqui Tribe, or was Castaneda perhaps disguising his resources to protect the real people from whom he sought to learn an alternative truth?

When I assigned the book, none of that mattered to me; perhaps it didn't matter to Castaneda, either. I suspect that a lot of my students were confused by this: Why would I have them read something that might not be true at all? And why something so utterly crazy? Precisely for those reasons. I taught primarily in Nebraska. I love Nebraska, but it is the hinterland in the very real sense of that word—the backwoods. People here often send their children to a state college or university with the intent of having the prevailing attitudes and opinions reinforced. (Or merely to cheer for the football team, which many Nebraskans see as the primary function of the university.) That's what *my* father thought he was doing when he sent me to the University of Nebraska!

That, of course, is not what education is about. Higher education especially is an opportunity for students to experience new ideas that confront, oppose, or confuse old ideas held only as a matter of habit. (And a university is most assuredly not mandated to provide weekend entertainment for people who otherwise have little concern or knowledge about what goes on in campus buildings other than the stadium!) I wanted my provincial—okay, "innocent," if you prefer—students to be wrenched from their Nebraska understanding of reality and just for a moment imagine a totally different reality. Not a false reality, please note, but a reality no more real or unreal than the mainstream's, simply different.

That one, simple concept is perhaps the most difficult cultural idea there is, and yet it is central to all culture. We live in different worlds. It is as simple as that. What we see is not what others see, as utterly crazy as that may seem. There is not one world of the obvious and others that are distortions of that one; there are different worlds, each true in its own way but not at all based on the same truth. No two witnesses to the same event, perhaps something as simple and everyday as an automobile accident, see the same thing and issue identical reports, even if they experienced it from the same visual perspective within the same hour. Obviously, then, something as subjective, elusive, and uncertain as religion offers even more opportunity for divergence of interpretation.

32. *Deduction/Induction*

One of the first realizations I had when establishing my residency within Omaha culture was that Omaha society is a passive, deductive culture (although less so now than it was fifty years ago, when I first began my cross-cultural adventures). One didn't ask questions in Omaha society; one observed and learned. Questions, in fact, were seen as a kind of confrontation, and thus Western-style education, based on instruction and questioning, was incredibly intimidating for young Omahas, as the entire cultural interface was for adults. Mainstream Americans are erroneously taught that they can be anything they want to be, go anywhere in life they want to go, become whatever they aspire to be. Why, if you want, you can become president of these United States! Is that true? Of course it isn't. We all know better than that. We may want that to be the case, or not, as I often suspect, but it isn't actually true. The traditional Omahas, then and to some lesser degree now, saw the world happening to them rather than their own activity moving within the world. It makes historical sense: only a century before I was making Omaha friends the tribe planted their corn and beans and hoped for rain. And prayed there'd be no raids from the Lakotas or crops trampled by herds of wild animals. It either rained or it didn't. The women hoed the crops and carried bits of water, but there's only so much of that they could do to manipulate the future in an eighteenth-century or even twentieth-century Omaha village.

Men went on the hunt twice a year. And they found buffalo. Or they didn't. Who could predict what the buffalo would do, especially once the whiteman came into the equation, split the continental herd with trails and railroads, slaughtered animals just to see them drop, and put up fences and planted their own crops? People lived or they died. The Lakotas raided or they didn't. You died in battle or you didn't. It was a matter of fate, of the world happening to you. Crazy Horse dismounted in battle and, with a light peg tethered to his ankle, anchored himself in place on the battlefield. The statement was plain: this was as good a day as any to die. And if he died, he died. If he didn't, he didn't. His survival or success, he was declaring, wasn't up to him. It was a matter for Wakan Tanka, the Great Mysterious, to decide.

That worldview continued within the Omaha Indian community well into my lifetime and to some degree persists today. And it remains as true as anything taught or learned in mainstream American culture. We die or we don't. We prosper or we don't. We just don't admit it. Or perhaps we purposely or accidentally just don't know it.

It took me a while, then, to understand some events—for example, a time when I got a call from some Omaha friends who wondered if I was headed up to the reservation for some important event. As it turned out, I was going to the same gathering they had planned to attend. They needed a ride, and so I picked them up at the bus depot and we headed north. Along the way they talked about what had happened that day. It was not what I saw as happening that day. They had arrived at the depot late and had therefore missed their scheduled bus. But that's not how they expressed it. They told me, "The bus left without us." Well, yes, that's true. The bus did leave without them—but because they were late. And I was not doing them a special favor by giving them a ride. I was going anyway, right? So . . . there you are. It's not a matter of them doing anything wrong or everything right; the world had simply worked the way it is supposed to work.

I have written elsewhere about a remarkable epiphany I once had in an Omaha experience, so forgive me if you have read this elsewhere. It is so important in my life and to an understanding of Native culture, and in particular Omaha culture, and even in terms of implications for mainstream culture, that it deserves constant iteration, in my opinion. I got a phone call one day from my old friend and tribal uncle Clyde Sheridan. He told me that he and some other Omahas in Lincoln were organizing a Tiapiah Society Gourd Dance. He said they would like me to be the head dancer. Now, that is quite an honor, especially for a Wannabe, but what's important here is to note that Clyde didn't ask me, he simply stated the facts: there was going to be a Gourd Dance and my friends wanted me to be the head dancer.

Okay, fine. I was indeed honored. But Clyde also didn't tell me when or where the dance was to be. Nor did I ask. I'd been around long enough to know better than commit a social gaffe like that. I waited and listened and hoped to *deduce* that information. But the day before the dance, I still had no information about the location or time of the dance for which *I was to be the head dancer!*

Uncle Clyde was a traditional man, and I was therefore careful to observe tribal tradition when dealing with him. So I couldn't just call him and ask for the information. On the other hand, his brother Frank dealt more easily with mainstream traditions and anxieties, as well as question-asking, so I called him and asked if he could tell me when and where the dance was to be held. He said no, he hadn't heard, but the next morning—the morning of the dance!—he was going over to Clyde and Aunt Lillian's house for breakfast and so I should call him again about noon. The day of the dance . . .

I did. I was getting nervous at this point. Frank said, well, he'd been over at Clyde's all morning but no one had said when and where the dance would be. Sorry. I was stunned, but then I did what I should have done in the first place and started to think like an Omaha. There were, after all, only a handful of places in Lincoln such a dance would be held: the Malone Community Center, the municipal swimming pool bathhouse, the Antelope Park Pavilion, the National Guard Armory, or the Pioneer Park picnic area. So I did what an Omaha would do—I got in my car and started down the line, first driving out toward Pioneer Park. On the road there, I met a car full of my Indian friends. They waved cheerfully. Okay, obviously the dance was not going to be at Pioneer Park because they were coming back from there. I went to the Antelope Park Pavilion. The parking lot was empty. Not there.

It was only a short distance to the swimming pool bathhouse, so that was my next stop. It was locked and quiet but—aha!—there was Clyde's car parked near the bleachers of a nearby softball field. So I parked beside him and ambled over to the stands. I spotted Clyde, so I went up the stands, greeted him, and sat beside him to watch the game. As long as I had Clyde, I was on the right path to the dance. The game ended. Clyde stood up, dusted off his pants, turned halfway around, and made some remark of realization. I turned too and looked in the same direction. There by the bathhouse door were maybe fifty Omahas, and the parking lot was full of their cars. They all waved. They had done the same thing I had—the Indian thing to do—and had found Clyde and me and had therefore arrived at the site for the dance. At the right time.

Clyde then said something that jarred me to my whiteman, middle-class, mainstream roots: "It looks like everyone is here. So we might as well have the dance here. Now." The only conclusion I could reach, the only one that was true, was that I had spent weeks of time and immense amounts of energy trying to learn facts that didn't exist. There was no place or time for that Gourd Dance until Clyde stood up, turned around, saw his community and tribal compatriots, and said, "It looks like everyone is here. So we might as well have the dance here. Now." And I couldn't help but wonder how often in my life I had done that before, how much this seeking of nonexistent facts went on in mainstream white culture. The Omahas had a completely different understanding from us about how the world works, and in this case they were right.

I have watched the government definition of "on or near a reservation" change from year to year. When it came to eligibility for educational grants or scholarships, fifty miles was considered "near" one year, so young Omahas and Winnebagos in the city of Omaha were eligible for the awards. On the whim of some bureaucrat or politician, the next year "near" meant within twenty-five miles. Little wonder that the Indian term for arbitrary paperwork snarls is not "*red* tape" but "*white* tape."

33. *What Is Indian Religion?*

What could, or should, be more representative or formative in the development of a worldview than religion, essentially a codified worldview? On the other hand, what is more difficult to understand from the point of view of one's own religion and worldview than someone else's vision? But if we must use caution in discussing Native culture without considering individual, regional, clan, family, and tribal associations—that is, if dance, music, foodways, taboos, language, or even physical characteristics vary widely from one group to another—imagine the variation in something as strongly held, as personal and yet also cultural, as a belief system. What is the religion of the American Indian? One might just as well ask what is non-Indian religion? What does the whiteman believe? Not what is *said* to be the whiteman's beliefs or, more abstractly, what the whiteman believes are the whiteman's beliefs, but his *real* beliefs? Does any whiteman honestly believe that it is more difficult for a rich man to go to heaven than for a camel to pass through the eye of a needle? Is it truly better to give than receive? That is the word of God as they insist was handed down to them by God himself, but clearly it is not a genuine belief or even a superficially followed practice.

The whiteman's religion has confronted Native religions from many directions—Catholic schools, Mormon missionaries, television evangelists, at the point of a sword, in the words of martyrs, in courts, and in battles. Imagine the Omaha Tribe first hearing about Christianity, perhaps from missionaries, in the early nineteenth century. A good deal of it must have seemed perfectly logical and reasonable. Among the Omahas even today prestige and respect is accrued through generosity. Food is shared. Those who have food share it; those who are hungry eat. While Omaha culture is inevitably if slowly changing and has changed since I first encountered it a half century ago, when there were still monolingual Omahas, there remains a strong sense of open hospitality; guests are welcomed and treated as guests, not intruders. And isn't that what the Bible says is the way of the righteous?

The problem is, it is the rare Western Christian who actually believes that. Even fewer practice it. Sharing is charity, not an assumption. Among the Omahas it is a way of life; within white mainstream culture it is a favor doled out to the pathetic. At the bottom of it, Christianity is an Eastern religion and it has never fit comfortably, even after two millennia, within Western culture. Christianity's ideals may still be a hope or aspiration for many, but they are far from realized or even seriously held as truths. I can imagine many readers bristling at that assertion; as I said and as we all know, religion is a sensitive topic and there are vast gulfs between what we believe, what we want to believe, what we say we believe, and what we believe we believe. Moreover, Native religions have experienced such abuse from mainstream America—violation of sacred rituals, distortion, mockery and shallow imitation, outright banning of practices and beliefs even well into my own lifetime, misunderstanding, blatant ignorance of profoundly important and dearly held prohibitions—that Native people (and I think here a wide generalization is legitimate) get a little nervous when non-Indians, non-tribal members, any outsiders, start asking too many questions, imposing on confidential if not secret ceremonials, or eyeing sacred sites and mapping them with tape measures and surveying transits. In these pages I will therefore avoid describing or even alluding to many specific Native religious practices, to protect them from such desecration or misunderstanding.

For fifty years I have been invited to and have participated in some Native religious practices. I have carefully avoided interfering insofar as I have been able. (Anytime an outsider becomes involved in a private or secret religious practice, there is by definition a compromise of that ritual. I have been aware of that, however, and have made every effort to minimize my impact on such practices.) I was first included in a Native prayer service in 1967 and through the years have attended when I could and when I knew I was welcome. On the other hand, during a couple of periods when these Native practices have been under various official or unofficial pressures from the outside, I've been asked by friends and Native kin if I could perhaps not participate, at least for a while, to help them protect their religion from false accusations ranging from Satanism to drug abuse. When they have asked me this, they have inevitably spoken with tears in their eyes because, after all, they were asking me to absent myself from something that over the years has become my own central religious practice.

I have never been offended by these heartfelt and painful requests. I love the religion too, after all, and if the least I can do to protect it is abstain from participating in its most visible practice for a while, I can do that. And I do. As I have explained to my friends, "The perfume of the cedar and tobacco is forever in my nose. The taste of the sacraments is in my mouth. The sound of the sacred songs is forever in my ears. The warmth of the fire in the heart of the tipi is on my face whether I am actually there in the prayer circle or not. Those things cannot be taken from me and I hold them dear and respect them enough to know them from afar as long as that needs to be my relationship with it."

34. *The Sun Dance*

Imagine being invited by a traditionally oriented Brule Sioux to attend a private (actually, secret) Sun Dance deep in the back hills of the Rosebud Reservation. I once was. I was told I would be the only white man present for this sacred ceremony, which was made a punishable offense under the Courts of Indian Offenses in 1883 and outlawed by the federal government of the United States in 1904, remaining illegal until John Collier issued Circular 2970 on religious freedom in 1934. (This information comes to me from the Native American Rights Fund legal office, but there is considerable uncertainty about precise dates for both the initiation and the cessation of the ban on the Sun Dance.) I didn't have to be told that the invitation was for me alone, that the information about the ceremony's location was told to me in confidence, that I would be expected to observe a respectful silence and distance, and that I shouldn't violate this confidence by photographing or making recordings of anything taking place during those four days.

I was moved by the trust given me by my friends and felt especially privileged the day I drove to the site of the Sun Dance. I turned off the narrow highway and constantly referred to the directions I had been given as I wove and bobbed down dusty, two-rut paths back into the remote hills of the Rosebud Reservation. As I had been instructed, I eventually reached a small, clear stream. I turned off the road, directly into the narrow streambed—not across the streambed but *into* and along it, in the water. I followed the stream's narrow canyon until I came to a large clearing, where I saw other automobiles gathered and people scrambling about making preparations—women cooking, men working on a shade arbor, young women gathering sage, tents and tipis being erected, a sweat lodge being dug into the rocky ground and covered with robes and blankets.

I'm sure some of the participants wondered why this outsider was here and who had invited him, but my friend had prepared the gathering for my appearance so I was welcomed, shown to a site where I could pitch my own small tent, and as always with Native gatherings on the plains, told to bring my dishes to the cooking pits because food was about to be served. I have been to many Sun Dances during the past fifty years, but none was as deeply moving as this small, rigidly traditional, private one. As you can perhaps read in my words here, every moment I was there, everything I saw and heard, is etched in my mind as if in stone. If I never attend another Sun Dance, I will forever have that one.

I am not violating any confidences by telling you this now; most of the elders, including my friend, have long ago died. Sun Dances are held today and, as I said about religious practices in general, are widely varied in how they are conducted and the degree to which they are kept apart from the outside world. I have seen Sun Dances that were virtual tribal fairs, with fast-food stands, missionaries circulating through the crowds, large campgrounds, and even non-Native participants in the ceremony itself. I attended one Sun Dance where, on the Sunday morning of the four-day ritual, a Catholic priest celebrated the Holy Sacrament at the base of the Sun Dance pole in the center of the dance arena! There are still adamant traditionalists who are deeply offended by such compromises and therefore still hold quiet, private Sun Dances deep back in the hills, perhaps with only one trusted whiteman attending, or more likely with none at all.

What other Native practices are never witnessed by outsiders? Many. I know of many, sometimes only because I have been told or gently urged to avoid a particular place at a particular time. Some rituals are even closed to other Natives or open only to a few. Women who are having their period may be excluded. No offense, that's just the way it is. Some activities are open only to those who have served with the military or who have seen combat or been wounded in battle. Some rites can be attended only by certain elders or clan members. What has surprised me over the years is the remarkable durability of many ceremonies, some of which have been declared dead and gone even by ethnographers who consider themselves close to the culture in question.

For example, I once mentioned the long-dead Ghost Dance to a Brule elder and spiritual leader, Richard Fool Bull. He laughed at my suggestion that it was dead. But, I noted, it was still outlawed by the federal government. Mr. Fool Bull said that not only was the Ghost Dance still practiced, at no time had it ever *not* been practiced, outlawed or not. He recalled that I had mentioned I had been to Sun Dances on the Pine Ridge and Rosebud Reservations. He said, "When you see the women dancing like this"—and then, already in his nineties, he nonetheless did a few steps by way of demonstration—"when you see the women dancing like that, they are doing the Ghost Dance. There's just no sense in announcing it to everyone who is not Lakota. There's no need to make trouble, after all, or confuse people who don't know what the Ghost Dance is or who, like you, believe it has been outlawed and is long gone. Nor is there any reason to announce it to the Lakota because they already know it is the Ghost Dance."

Officially banned by law, regularly practiced without regard to the ban. How many other religious practices are followed in the same way? There is justifiable fear and suspicion of outsiders. The religions are themselves private, so there is no need to call attention to them. The religions are more often than not a fundamental part of life, not something separate and discrete from everything else in life, so they may even be of no particular note. The Ghost Dance is a part of Native life as much as breathing or eating. So it is done. Without fanfare.

My Omaha brother Buddy Gilpin once commented to me in a private conversation that he was curious, maybe even confused, by the loud noises being made at that time about the need (at least as perceived by some) for prayer in public schools. He wondered why anyone would want that. I was taken aback by the question but said that, well, some people felt that a minute or two should be spent at the beginning of each school day for prayer. He thought about that a moment and then, by way of explaining his question, I imagine, told me that that wouldn't make much sense among the Omahas. I have never forgotten his next words, because they say so much about Native religion, about religion, about prayer: "Among my Omaha people, every moment of life is a prayer of gratitude." I have never heard a more eloquent sermon, and in only thirteen words.

35. *The Native Church*

It may have been on this same occasion that I was not only struck by Buddy's own understanding of prayer and faith but was given a new understanding of my own. At the time I was in my early thirties and had spent ten years exploring religions and trying to find a meaningful path for myself. As I remember, I had asked Buddy about the status of the Native American Church on the Omaha Reservation. How many Omaha people followed the Native American Church? I knew that some within the tribe were Catholics, that because of a long history with the Presbyterian and Congregationalist Churches there were many of those (although the first Christian missionaries of note to work among the Omahas were Baptists). The Mormon and Methodist Churches were active, too. Again Buddy's response surprised and informed me: "I'd say maybe 30 percent of my Omaha people follow the ways of the Native American Church. And I suppose 50 percent are with the Presbyterians."

Thank goodness, by that time I had learned not to speak too quickly in conversations with Indians but to wait for what more might be said, so I gave my brother, a spiritual leader and honored elder, time to finish what he had to say. Native debates and discussions, at least traditionally, are interesting in that way. Everyone has a chance to speak, but more importantly, to speak without interruption. I was once privy to a discussion about whether the Omaha Tribe should accept a proposed gift from the Kiowa Tribe, the Tiapiah Gourd Dance Society. It was as serious as any debate I ever heard within a university faculty meeting, graduate seminar, or session of a professional society meeting. One woman noted that several of the positions within the Tiapiah Society are hereditary, and the Omahas would therefore be accepting this dance and society not just for themselves and their own use but with obligations for their descendants for all time to come. Wow. That is serious talk! Following that woman's comments there was a long silence as those in the meeting considered her words. Not just a moment's pause, but perhaps fifteen minutes of studied silence.

Another speaker signaled the presiding elder that he would like to say some words; his comments were that the regalia for the Gourd Dance could be rather pricey and he wasn't too happy about the idea of spending a lot of money on it since it might not last in the traditions of the Omahas and he wasn't sure yet whether he was really interested in the society. It was clear even to me that his observations were trivial and scarcely worth consideration. No one said as much, but almost immediately someone else at the gathering signaled and was given permission to pursue a more serious line of thought with almost no pause at all. Watch any television talk show, especially about politics, with all the usual shouting, speaking past and over each other, noise, and tumult of the typical non-Native debate, and then consider what I have told you about the serious, deliberate, civil manner of Omaha debate.

But back to my story about religions among the Omahas: Buddy was telling me about the distribution of church followings with the Omaha Tribe. He had estimated that 30 percent followed the Native American Church and perhaps 50 percent the Presbyterian Church. But after a brief moment of thought, he continued, "I suppose there are 15 percent of the people who are Baptists, 15 percent call themselves Methodists, 20 percent Catholic, more and more Mormons . . . maybe 10 percent, 5 or 10 percent drive over to the Lutheran Church over in

West Point, there are quite a few . . . 20 percent? . . . who attend the Church of God in Sioux City . . ." We were already up to something like 160 percent of the Omaha people! Buddy sensed my confusion and explained the logical conflict without my having to ask about it. "Brother, we don't see any conflict in our faith, so a lot of our people belong to two, three, maybe even four churches. The various forms simply express different sides of the same thing." And once again I wished that the whiteman had slowed down, shut up, listened, and learned through our long and tortured history with Native peoples. What a different world it could be if no one insisted that he or she had an exclusive ownership of the truth.

At about this same time in my relationship with Buddy Gilpin and the Omaha Nation I was invited to my first prayer meeting on the reservation. I had been curious about the Native American Church for many years and had asked, impolitely, about meetings, my chance of attending one, and when and where I might find one. The Native American Church is in no way a proselytizing religion; there is, in fact, as I have mentioned several times, a reluctance to share much information about the church with non-Indians because meetings are generally not open to non-Indians. It is, after all, the *Native American* Church. There is constant and legitimate worry about persecution of the church, as there have been many and substantial efforts to suppress it since its introduction to the Omaha people around 1912. Adherents worry that the "instruments," songs, procedures, and rituals of the church might be misappropriated by non-Indian people and abused, as we have seen with the sweat lodge, vision quest, dance, drum, tobacco, cedar, sweet grass, and powwow rituals, for example, in recent years. Many Natives are understandably and particularly offended when a fragment of their religion is stolen and marketed for profit by non-Indians. Special offense is taken when sacred gifts, processes, and words are performed or shared for money. As I once heard it expressed by indignant Natives resisting and protesting the theft of Native religious practices, "The white man is like the raccoon: what he can't eat or tear up, he shits on."

No one refused to give me information about the church or upcoming meetings, and yet the information was never quite there. No one had said *no* to me, but no one had given me solid information about the church, either. There is a profound dignity and courtesy with such things as non-Indian intrusion into Omaha matters, or for that matter, Omaha misbehavior. I was once sitting at the drum at a handgame with six or seven other singers when a very intoxicated member of the Indian community (this was off the reservation, in Lincoln, Nebraska) came in and joined us in the singers' circle. Because of his condition, this old friend missed the beat, especially the crucial last beat of every song. His singing was slurred and inexact. He was not doing at all well. The handgame is not sacred, but it is culturally respected and the drum is treated with respect and even reverence; this man's inappropriate behavior obviously bothered everyone in the gathering. At some point he got up from the drum and staggered from the room to relieve himself outside the game circle.

One of the respected elders in the gathering quietly came to the drum, took the empty chair, and placed it along the wall, away from the drum. When the man returned he reeled to the drum only to find there was no chair for him. He stood there a moment gathering his wits, struggling to figure out what had happened. No one said a word to him. The singing continued. No one had to explain things to him; eventually he surmised what he was being told and he quietly left the room. In a way, that is what happened to me for about a decade while I was aggressively trying to find out about the church. No one told me to stop asking or mind my own business, but the information I sought—like when and where the next prayer meeting might be held and if I might attend—was never available, somehow. It was as if my chair simply disappeared from the information drum circle.

The night of my adoption in 1967, when I was sitting on the curb with Buddy waiting for the dawn so we could get some help in changing my truck tire, I said something to Buddy, this time without asking, something like, "I have wondered about prayer meetings, Buddy. You say a lot of people here are followers of the church but I never hear much about it or when the meetings take place." He said only, "Listen." And once I focused on the night sounds, I could hear far off in a direction south of the village the sound of a drum. And then the high-pitched single voice I would come to recognize later as the songs distinctive to the Native American Church. About the same time another drum's sound came to me from another direction, with its accompanying song. For the next couple of hours we heard drums and singing from around the village. Oh yes, Buddy was telling me, the Native American Church is alive, all right, and well. It just wasn't obvious to an outsider. Or perhaps better said, wasn't *made* obvious to an outsider.

Buddy then said that he would be leading a meeting a couple of months later and that I should come and be welcomed into the circle of worshipers now that I was Omaha. That would be the first night I heard the drum and singing from inside the tipi, and I could hear the drums and singing from other tipis around the reservation community, too. My life was never the same.

During that long night sitting on a reservation street staring at a flat tire on my truck, Buddy made a comment that suggested he would like to know about my spiritual inclinations. I explained that I had been exploring various paths for many years and had settled most recently on Unitarianism. He expressed an interest in what that meant. I briefly stated the tenets of Unitarianism, that we were a community of seekers rather than believers, that we joined our minds and thinking, our learning, reading, and experiences in an attempt to come to an understanding of the nature of God.

I thought I did a pretty good job of explaining a church based on reason, curiosity, and an admission of my (and our) collective innocence about life and its meaning. Buddy chuckled. Not exactly the reaction I expected for my extemporaneous but fairly erudite presentation, sitting there on the curb in a darkened reservation town. As always, I didn't need to ask about his reaction. I waited and listened. And in a bit, Buddy explained. He was amazed that I would think for even a moment that with my puny mind, our assembled puny minds, humankind's collective and pathetically puny minds—even if focused through all time and around the world—could possibly come up with any understanding of something as vast as Wakan Tanka … Wakonda … the Great Mysterious (two adjectives, no noun—a remarkably sophisticated understanding of the powers and mysteries that swirl around us). Buddy said he felt that we would be lucky, any one of us or all of us in concert in a humanity-wide effort, to get so much as even the slightest glimpse of the nature of God. And if we were so lucky as to have that, perhaps through a revelation in a Native American Church prayer meeting where that gift would be given but not achieved through any effort of our own, we would almost certainly not understand it. For one thing, we are too small to see more than a glimpse, and then we are not mentally up to understanding the gigantic whole from this slightest sliver of insight.

Just like that, my cherished confidence in reason, logic, honesty, reality, and collective philosophies disappeared like a puff of smoke into the reservation night. Suddenly what I had thought of as a clever and even learned philosophical statement turned out to be just plain silly. Of course I would never understand the nature of God, at least not through my own labors. But I could experience enough through the revealed power of that Great Mysterious to tell me that something enormous and probably beyond my ability to comprehend is indeed going on. And that would and should be enough. That may be all we can ever know. But as Buddy noted that evening, very few people come to grasp even that much, so we who do are well ahead of the game.

And again, he was right.

Now, imagine taking your religion that seriously and then seeing it mocked by yahoos at a football game, trivializing the sanctity of head-dresses, dance, drum, and eagle feathers. (Yes, those are not real eagle feathers in the phony headdresses, but the imitation itself is a cruel mockery.) Imagine holy sites destroyed, houses and businesses plopped down on sites considered sacred. The single most sacred Pawnee site, Pahuka, a loess cliff on the Platte River south of Fremont, Nebraska, had been commonly used as a dumpsite before it was recently put into trust. Imagine your term for the central mystery of your religion, the very name of God itself, being applied to something like Wakonda Golf Course, Lake Wakonda Estates, or, worse yet, Wakonda Brewing Company! Why not the Jehovah Casino? Why not God Acres? Why not the Jesus Christ Our Lord Saloon?

I know of no effort by Indians to muscle non-Natives into Native religious beliefs or practices; in fact, as I have pointed out repeatedly, Native people try hard in most cases to exclude outside visitors, participants, and observers, to keep intruders *out* of Native religious practices, ceremonies, and beliefs. The constant request I have heard from Native people during my fifty-year relationship with them is simply for their ways to be respected, for the freedom to believe what they will and to worship as they wish. Nothing more. One could add to the list that Native peoples would appreciate a recognition that Native religions are not a thing of the past, nor are they heretical belief systems that disrespect majority religions simply by their existence. Native religions are a dynamic of the present and, I hope, the future, not just an echo or relic of the past. Because non-Indians rarely hear of them or see them does not mean they don't exist. Nor is symbolic respect for Indians and their history, culture, and religion enough. Again and again during the past half century I have been approached by people who want to honor and show respect for Native tradition and practice by erecting a statue or establishing a fanciful prayer garden or developing an exhibit or, worst of all, reenacting sacred Native practices. What we—Natives and whites alike—need is not symbols of respect but respect itself.

36. *Inside Native Religion*

Native-based religions (as opposed to mainstream church systems, where there are externally imposed political or hierarchical frameworks) may be basically and theoretically Christian, like the Native American Church, or not Christian except for small gestures toward those worshipers who embrace both (Yuwipi, sacred bundle religions, or the Sun Dance, for example, may include mention or even significant inclusion of Christian elements). Yet they all share a simplicity and humility, an immediacy (as opposed to a remote god that spoke to mankind in an ancient time), and a theistic or even pantheistic spirit. While they are in all likelihood as complex, profound, majestic, inspiring, symbolic, dramatic, steeped in pageantry, and ornamented as any religion, including Hinduism or Roman Catholicism, there is nonetheless a dramatic contrast between Native religions and other, more strictly structured theologies. While the complexity and ornamentation of Native religion frequently—in fact, persistently—lies in its thought and process, the physical expressions and settings are humble in the extreme. The Native American Church, for example holds its ceremonies in a simple room whenever a plain tipi, the usual church shelter, is not available. In either case the supplicants sit flat on the floor or ground, perhaps on a few blankets or robes. At a meeting I attended on the Omaha Reservation, Elmer Blackbird, an elder, Church leader, and dear friend, sat beside me, steering me through the complications of the dusk-to-dawn ceremony and gently helping me avoid as many errors as he could in the quiet but active context of the meeting. At one point when participants could openly speak, he half apologized (and yet spoke with obvious pride) about how he had recently been invited to participate in a conventional, mainstream Christian protestant church service a town near but not on the Omaha Reservation.

He quietly outlined to all of us sitting in the humble tipi circle what he had seen, heard, and done in the whiteman's religious service. No doubt he had attended such services before in his long life, and almost certainly so had everyone else in the dimly lit tipi; my impression was that he wanted to remind us of two things: how other people serve their spiritual needs, and that we had chosen the more difficult, more humble—and yet also the most satisfying—way to find our connections with Wakonda. Mr. Blackbird talked about the beautiful oak pews in the whiteman's church, with soft pads and backs fitted for easy resting. For one full hour, he said, the white people spoke to their religion, while here we sat, flat on Mother Earth all night in growing discomfort, from the time the sun set in the evening until the morning star first showed in the east-facing tipi door. He compared the gloriously robed whiteman's church choir and its harmonious singing, accompanied by a huge and powerful organ, with our pitiful efforts in the tipi that night with nothing but a simple, small iron drum and a lone singer. He spoke with praise of the beautiful interior of the whiteman's church; the stained glass windows, elaborate sculptures, and rich painting; the minister's elegant robes; the books of song and prayer. And again he turned our attention to our circumstances there in a plain canvas tipi with only the light and shadows of the sacred fire in the center of us, throwing its light on the canvas walls and us. He spoke approvingly of the fine clothes everyone wore to come into the whiteman's church and the dignity of all who were there to worship. And he commented on us in our humble clothing, old men barely able to walk, women in their best and yet still humble Indian-style clothing. He described the pulpit and the preacher's stentorian voice, made all the stronger with the assistance of a microphone and amplifier. We all knew he was thinking, too, of our roadman's simple place at the west of the tipi, his voice raspy from the smoke of the tobacco, the strain of praying, and the effort of speaking and singing throughout the night.

When Mr. Blackbird finished his detailed comparison of the two churches, not one of us sitting in the circle in the tipi that night had a scintilla of envy for those who had instead sat an hour on soft cushions on finely carved pews, listing to elegant choirs and organ music, dressed in fine clothes, surrounded by beauty and wealth. No, without having to say a word, we all knew we had just heard validation that the very simplicity of "our humble church," as Mr. Blackbird again and again described it, was closer to genuine reverence and meaningful worship, without show, with no motives other than worship. At another meeting years later I heard Mr. Blackbird give much the same recitation. It was clear that he was not only reminding us about our church but also making comments about the whiteman's ways, all the while sounding almost as if he envied those ways, when he clearly did not. Mr. Blackbird expressed no criticism or disdain for the whiteman's church; he was only offering us honest comparisons and letting us draw our own conclusions. Not one person in that tipi that night doubted which course brought one closer to Wakonda.

37. *Knowing What We Don't Know*

A very real problem in any cross-cultural adventure is that we are not only seeing another culture and trying to understand it but also trapped in our own culture and trying to get beyond it. That's not nearly as easy as it seems. We come to think of the way we do things as the normal way to do things, the right way to do things, the only way to do things, the logical way to do things. When I asked my mother to describe in detail how she made her *Krautrunzas*, a traditional German Russian dish from my earliest youth, she was baffled as to why I would ask: her conclusion was that, well, she made *Krautrunzas* the way one makes *Krautrunzas*. How else would you do it? Even the great folklorist Louise Pound, writing about plains pioneer Christmases in the late nineteenth and very early twentieth centuries, dismissed the subject by explaining that Christmases in that wilderness area on the American frontier were celebrated . . . the way one celebrated Christmas in that context. Well, thanks a lot, Ms. Pound!

I mentioned above my experience in visiting Artemia's pueblo in the bowels of the Yucatan, one of the most astonishing experiences of my life. Just months ago, twenty years after that experience, I contacted my hosts from that occasion and asked them to ask Artemia some questions about her pueblo and about that visit for me. They said Artemia was astonished that I even remembered going there. Why would that visit have been memorable, after all? It was just her pueblo. It was just her parental village and home. She grew up in the shadow of a Mayan temple that dropped me to my knees when I saw it. The foods we ate and the gardens we saw were, for her, everyday realities, even though they were startling revelations to me. So can we imagine that she had been astonished throughout her life when she saw the ordinary, everyday life Verne, Terri, and I led? No. Not really. Artemia has grown up in that world, too. It is she who is cosmopolitan, and we who are naïve.

38. *What History Teaches Us*

As I have mentioned throughout these pages, the notion that others hate us Americans "because of our freedom" is nothing but bumper sticker jingoism mouthed by fools who have nothing to say for themselves. Other nations and cultures hate us, and justifiably so, for our arrogance and ignorance. It would be sad if it weren't so comic, the way we consistently cut ourselves off at the knees because we can't remember which part of the axe is sharp. Knowledge is an asset, no matter where it originates. Despite those who insist otherwise, we do not know everything; other cultures know many things we do not or that we have forgotten; we can profit from paying attention to those things they know. It's as simple as that. So simple, in fact, that the hard part is understanding why anyone could miss the obvious fact, and yet we do.

In more than a few examples like this, we mainstream outsiders are the naïve and awed innocents. It is our hosts, the Natives, who are the sophisticates. When the lost, hungry, miserable, clueless Pilgrims met Squanto in Cape Cod Bay, they were confident that they were the ones with the superior culture, knowledge, and sanctity; the truth was, Squanto had been to Europe a couple times, knew English well, was urbane and educated . . . and the arrogant Pilgrims, smug in the certainty of their religion and culture, were the hapless boobs. You won't read that in your grade school primers.

It was allegedly Harry Truman who said, "History is just one damned thing after another," but I can't be sure of that attribution because history isn't clear about it. In fact, history is never clear about anything. Small wonder that Napoleon defined history as "a set of lies agreed upon" and Henry Ford said, "History is more or less bunk." It takes a dozen peers in a jury and a couple of alleged witnesses to doom a person to death or a lifetime in prison but only one historian to condemn a person to eternal infamy or fame. As a folklorist I am always baffled by people who put such faith in the written word, certainly in historical studies, but have little or no confidence in oral history. I imagine the error is double: we think, "Seeing is believing, so if it's in print, it must be true." And we imagine that oral tradition is like the old party game of Gossip, in which a sequence of people whisper a story or sentence secretly to the next person in line and the story as it winds up at the end of the line is compared to the story as it began; everyone is amazed at the distortions accidentally (or, let's face it, intentionally) introduced in the narrative. That is the way *written* history, not *oral* history, works.

A general writes an account of how a battle went and, not remarkably, he almost always comes out looking pretty good, even if the universal judgment of all witnesses is that he suffered a complete rout. Later, historians—probably having few other accounts to rely on but even with a larger mix of data presuming that the person who was actually there and instrumental in the event should know the facts—base their work on his account. And so history based on lies continues—or may even be further embellished. A historian writing a book faces reviewers, editors, fact-checkers (maybe), peer evaluation within the discipline, and possible correction or protest from the people he or she writes about or people who have information from other sources (including first-person experience), but once history is written, right or wrong, there it is, rarely corrected. The printed word has an impressive memory, but it tends to embrace error as easily as it does truth.

Oral history is not at all like that, contrary to popular belief. First, human memory is more impressive than we might think. We have lost a good deal of our ability to recall long narratives as we have come to rely increasingly on print, but the fact remains that the human mind is still capable of retaining remarkable amounts of information. I forget names but I remember stories, and especially jokes. I'm famous for it. Some people memorize the Koran. Others memorize poetry, legal opinions, or classroom lectures. Moreover, the truth of oral history is rigidly enforced. Oral history is recited again and again. Most of the people in the audience have heard the story before, perhaps thousands of times. Rarely does someone hear an oral historical narrative for the first time. Many in the audience may know the story as well as the narrator and be eager to serve as stern, critical guideposts to keep the truth in place. In fact, in many cases in the human narrative process oral materials are considered sacred and *must* be recited accurately or their efficacy suffers or is lost altogether. Folklore is almost never conveyed like the story in the game Gossip, passed confidentially or even secretly from one person to another and so on down the line. Folklore is public property, while formal, scholarly history is a personal holding.

What do we know, for example, about the "facts" of the battle of the Greasy Grass, so-called Custer's Last Stand? For generations, in fact, the very nature of the encounter was completely misinterpreted by calling it a "massacre." The Lakotas, Cheyennes, and Arapahos were gathered in a domestic village—a large village, to be sure, but populated by families who were not expecting or prepared for an attack. Two military units—the Indian warriors and the Seventh Cavalry under Custer—met in pitched battle. The correct term for the event is "battle." On the other hand, the slaughter by that same U.S. Army unit, only a generation later, of unarmed, freezing women, children, old men, and a few tired warriors near the present village of Wounded Knee was at the time and for many years afterward widely characterized as a "battle," with many U.S. Medals of "Honor" distributed to the craven butchers, when the clear evidence is that it was a savage crime—mass murder.

The histories of the Battle of the Little Big Horn were written almost entirely by white historians, none of whom were at the battle, while the oral histories based on accounts by hundreds of people who *were* there—whose accounts were rigorously supervised for truth because individuals' reputations rested on what happened at that battle and what exactly they had done on the scene—were discounted because they were not *written*. To this day the accounts preferred by many scholars are made up of the guesses and self-serving distortions of non-Indian narrators rather than the fastidiously maintained oral accounts of the Indians.

Historical distortions get chiseled in stone as they are passed on in the context of popularly held history, becoming scarcely recognizable when compared to what actually happened. All one needs to do to see the nuttiness is to watch the human-interest reports on any local television news report. Only two weeks ago I cringed as a news report showed a local church "educating" some of its children about the life of Jesus by having the tykes actually "live the life of Jesus." There they were, dressed up in their mothers' cut-down chenille bathrobes, neatly scrubbed, eating—we and they were told—the very food that Jesus would have eaten. Unleavened flat bread? Yeasty wine? Figs for sweets? No—and I swear I am telling you the truth—they were feeding the kids . . . beef jerky! Never mind that Jesus probably never tasted beef in his life. Goat maybe, lamb—but beef? Not to mention, *jerked* beef? I doubt it. And yet now there is a clutch of children running around thinking that they have actually learned something. And I guess they have. They've learned that history is, indeed, "lies agreed upon."

Every Thanksgiving I watch with dismay the usual reports about school programs telling children the story of the Pilgrims and Thanksgiving. Days spent misinforming students about virtually every phase of seventeenth-century Indian and Pilgrim life—what they wore, what they ate, what they did, what they said, their intentions and understandings. It's as if there is a concentrated effort to turn history 180 degrees so that not the slightest fragment of truth is left. People insist on observing the "original meaning of Christmas and Easter" without the slightest sense of the irony; both holidays and many of the practices associated with them are pagan in origin. (The word "Easter" does not appear in the Bible; the word refers to Ishtar, a fertility goddess, which explains all those bunnies and eggs.)

Local and recent history fares no better. Even reputable museums sometimes offer distorted interpretations of history. Plains pioneer history is shot through and through with error, cheerfully passed along day after day as presumed fact by teachers, books, museums, and ordinary citizens. The courageous pioneers came to this vast, empty, brutal landscape and with hard work created something from nothing. And now we have a long, deep history that celebrates their success. Clutches of fourth graders are herded through museum re-creations of sod houses and come out astonished at the horrible conditions of pioneer life, peek into mock-ups of Pawnee earth lodges and are struck by the primitive nature of life there. And then I presume they all have some beef jerky and know that they have indeed tasted genuine pioneer life. They haven't.

They go away utterly ignorant of what the sod house really was and, most egregiously, of what life in it meant. Yes, the sod house was humble, it leaked dirt, snow, rain, and fleas. But it belonged to the builder, who before he came to the plains had lived in a landowner's shack that wasn't much better, farming six acres of rocky, rooty land that wasn't his, starving, knowing his children would never know any better. Look at the photos in my book *Sod Walls*—all those people standing proudly out in front of their shabby, sagging, humble, small sod houses . . . all their possessions dragged out into the yard for the photographer, things that belong to THEM. And all that land behind them? That's theirs too. The dogs? The horses, the wagon, the rocker, the pump organ, the well . . . all theirs. These people are not lamenting their poverty but celebrating their wealth. (Ignoring for the moment and for the purposes of my point here that history lies to us, as do photographs, if we don't start with enough information about what the photos are about.)

Beyond the pride and wealth illustrated by the sod house, there is another, crucial consideration: the remarkable efficacy of sod construction in the plains environment. One might imagine some contradiction here: on one hand I say that the Pawnees, Omahas, Poncas, Otos, Lakotas, and other Plains Nations considered the plains a garden land of abundance, a generous mother of plenty. On the other hand, these folks were not stupid: they also knew that the plains are a demanding, harsh environment that does not tolerate fools easily. So they learned how to live with the plains, on the terms of that environment.

For one thing, they build earthen houses. As I noted in *Sod Walls*, the sod house's roof construction is almost precisely identical to the construction of the dome of Omaha and Pawnee earth lodges. The first sod houses recorded built in Nebraska were constructed by the Mormons at Winter Camp on the Missouri River, just north of where the city of Omaha is now, just south of the great Omaha Indian earth lodge villages. They were constructed after the Mormons had visited the Omaha camps. It could be a coincidence, of course, that the Mormons then built sod houses and sod fronts to dugout houses, probably the first in America built by whites—if you put overwhelming faith in coincidence, which Richard Fool Bull did call the White Man's True Religion, after all.

The plains are murderously hot in the summer, and grass fires moving faster than a man can ride on horseback were a constant danger—as they can be today, too, even after the land has been mostly tilled, divided by roads, and mowed and grazed to a fuzz. Winters here are arctic. As I write this, at noon on a February day, it is five degrees below zero with a forecast tonight of twenty-eight degrees below zero, wind chills well into the forty-below-zero range. The wind has piled drifts up to twelve feet high. The Highway Department has given up on clearing the roads. We are warned that exposed skin will become frostbitten in a matter of minutes.

What better response to such conditions could one devise than . . . an earthen house? But the homesteaders had come from another world (and were headed toward yet another). The Swedes, Czechs, Germans, Poles, Danes, even the settlers from the eastern climes of North America had never experienced (except possibly at sea) such vast, open vistas and isolation as they did once they set sail on the great Sea of Grass called the Great Plains. Day after day they struggled on landholdings greater than they could have possibly imagined in the homeland. In most of their native countries farms measured less than ten acres in size, sometimes as few as five or six. They often were so clogged with roots and rocks, mountains and forests that even only parts of that were arable. And suddenly here they were, in possession of 80—maybe 160—acres of open, rich, reckless, treeless, fertile ground just begging for tillage. They worked endless days and into the nights in the fields, richer than they could ever imagine, exhausted to the edge of endurance. (For the best extended depiction of this in the best form I know, read Ole Rølvaag's *Giants in the Earth*, which incidentally is based on extensive interviews Rølvaag did with pioneer Scandinavian settlers in southeastern South Dakota.)

Now, with all that in mind, imagine just for a moment the image of a man coming home from eighteen hours walking alone behind a plow across the prairie in the blazing sun, wind, and blowing dirt, and thinking, "Hey . . . know what sounds good? Let's fire up the grill and cook and eat outside tonight! And then maybe go camping with the kids or take a walk in the park!"

God, how they must have lusted for their family's warmth, the cool and dark sod house, the quiet and respite from the wind. And in winter all the more. I have some personal experience with this: for almost forty years I have had and cherished a fine old log house built in 1872 by Civil War veteran Tom Bishop about twenty miles west of Lincoln, truly on the frontier at the time. I moved Bishop's house out to my land on the Loup River, where I have spent long, long hours. I have worked long days planting trees in the cold and in the heat, cutting wood in the wind and snow, being beaten into the ground by a crushing sky, experiencing firsthand what the homesteaders called "Wind Sickness." And when the time came to retreat to the small (nineteen by twenty feet), dark silence of that log house with its enduring and comforting warmth or coolness, I never felt oppressed. I have spent wonderful times there with two, three, even twenty friends, during blizzards and heat spells. Long winter evenings with no electricity, light by kerosene lantern, heat from our Buck's Hot Blast potbelly stove, rejoicing in games played with my children: "If you could have dinner with any . . . oh . . . three people living or dead . . . who would they be?" Never for a moment feeling the deprivation visitors to museums or readers of history books automatically presume the plains homesteader must surely have felt because, well, they didn't have the pleasures of the life that . . . gulp . . . we have in our modern homes with all their "conveniences."

One might logically ask at this point, if sod construction was such an appropriate response to the harsh plains environment, why was it abandoned in favor of what is revealingly known as "balloon construction," the flimsy web of two-by-fours one sees going into modern construction and being blown to splinters by passing tornados? Let's look at the progression of plains construction history: Log houses were superlative. My log house was built of oak and walnut and it is to this day, 140 years later, a remarkably solid building. But it didn't take long for Nebraska to run out of oak and walnut logs suitable for dressing for house construction, you can be sure. Stone? Only in the easternmost edge of the state. Brick? There is excellent clay for brick firing, but in the frontier years and well into the modern era coal and petroleum fuel for firing brick were simply not available. Even sod had its limitations, since it could be employed only where there was suitable sod—tough, root-bound soil that had never been tilled—and only where the soil was itself firm and not the excessively loose, sand-based ground west of the ninety-eighth meridian (roughly west of Grand Island but out of the Platte Valley). Where there was sod suitable for construction it was a one-time resource; once the surface of the prairie had been shaved of its centuries-old sod, it was no long suitable as a source for more sod for house construction. It would take another thousand years to recover. That is, new grass would and does grow on plowed ground, but sod suitable for house construction was limited in quantity and once used up it would be many, many centuries before that same ground was again at that point of root saturation. Later there was a short period of baled-hay construction, especially during the period of Kinkaid homesteading, roughly from 1904 to 1910.

So to a certain extent balloon construction of framed dimension lumber was something of a final solution, especially once the railroads made transport of milled lumber available in much greater quantities than the few water-driven sawmills in Nebraska could make from what few trees remained in the state after harvesting for log houses, railroad ties, and fuel. How, then, do we explain the predominance of wood-frame construction across the plains? It doesn't take an expert historian or field worker to see from extant old and new houses or the remains of older houses in decay and ruin along the highways and roads that this construction has been the standard for well over a century now. And anyone who lives in an older frame house (or sadly, even many new ones) knows they are poorly adapted for the plains climate—hot in the summer, cold in the winter, like a sieve in wind, incredibly flammable, and vulnerable to termites, mice, squirrels, birds, snakes, mosquitoes, flies, raccoons, and groundhogs.

Just as the courageous but rather dim-witted homesteaders did not want to eat Indian food, neither did they want to live in Indian mud huts or burrows in the ground. They came to the plains to become kings and masters, and to reflect that wealth and power they needed a fitting palace to live in. Efficiency? Of no particular importance. Comfort? Doesn't compare in the least to image and prestige. In fact, then as now the whiteman wanted to demonstrate success with conspicuous consumption, a reckless squandering of resources and wealth. If you doubt that assertion I invite you to take a short tour of any new housing development, urban or rural. Drive a short distance on the highways out of my little home village of Dannebrog. Every hill is blistered with monstrous palaces and castles, each housing far fewer people than there are rooms in the entire house, with towering, huge windows bleeding heat and cooled air, inviting in the wind and dust, the surrounding ground scraped clean of trees that would mitigate the harshness of both winter and summer—but they are splendid billboards for obscene wealth and distorted priorities. Again, you won't read that in many booster-based Nebraska history books. The real function of most historical education is to convince children that the historical mythology their culture holds to be true is true, reality be damned. Homesteading and the frontier were based not on heroic conquering of an empty, free, wasteland but the theft of that land from the rightful owners and the gifting of it to people who, by and large, have not done well with their ill-gotten property.

39. *The Empty Frontier*

Not long ago a long letter appeared in some of our state's newspapers from a man in the irrigation industry who supported the looting of our water resources because, he said, irrigation is what has permitted us enlightened people to make something out of the "uninhabited wasteland" (his words) we call the Great Plains. You know—the very land the Pawnees and other tribes celebrated as their mother because of its generosity and beauty, the land that fed them and housed them well (while pioneers starved around them because they weren't about to eat "Indian food"). The land was not uninhabited. It was a home to thousands and a landscape in which they lived comfortably and which they loved. In their eyes it didn't need conquering, taming, or subduing. Many Native cultures were agricultural societies with large cities and villages. A further argument often used as a rationalization for seizing Native lands is that, while the land was being used in a casual sort of way by the Indian inhabitants, it was not "developed," not being used to the full extent possible. When that idea pops up I like to suggest that it would justify Chinese, Indian, or Japanese invasion and occupation of the United States. They could then apply their more intensive agricultural practices and make the land truly productive, since we are not using it to its full capacity. The notion of legitimate seizure of underused territory really loses its appeal for the frontierophiles when the discussion turns in that direction.

The Homestead Act was in fact a massive theft to begin with and then a monstrous welfare boondoggle when the land was virtually given away, in many cases to settlers who did not succeed because they did not understand the land or the agricultural methods suitable for it; the people who already lived here did. Far from being courageous, many frontier settlers came here because they were greedy and not very bright. Or they fled the rule of law in the states, preferring the lawlessness of the territories. If the homesteaders and new settlers came, as many claimed, to find religious and political freedom, they also, like the Pilgrims, did what they could to impose a new religious and political tyranny on the land they invaded and occupied. That may be a lesson we are still learning as the land and water resources are squandered and the misinformation continues. Nebraska's farmers no longer "feed the world," as is claimed (just recently by the governor, who one would think should know better, in a news story on our local television station), but fuel America's prodigal and arrogant insistence on the automobile, resulting often in the spectacle of a 120-pound woman driving a huge, gas-gobbling suv to her daily exercise workouts.

When I was told I would be given a Hunkapi, or kin-making ceremony, I did some preliminary research on the process, reading especially carefully Marla Powers's monograph on the Hunkapi. She notes that the whiteman isn't often blessed with a Hunkapi because among many Lakota elders "the white man is still considered a passing phenomenon." And so he might be, sooner than we think.

Homesteaders not only had no understanding of the land they came to, they also had no knowledge of the people who lived here, to whom the land rightfully belonged, who could have saved the new-comers a world of trouble if they had bothered to sit down and listen. A standard cliché on the plains tells of the pioneer woman alone in her sod or log house, making doughnuts. She suddenly sees a hideous face at the one small window in the hut—a savage Indian. (I am using the words conventionally used in such folktales.) She screams, but the Indian casually opens the door and walks in. (Sometimes it is a troupe of warriors who come in, or an entire Indian family.) The terrified white woman offers each of them a doughnut, hoping to distract them from murdering her or subjecting her to the expected "fate worse than death." But then she is dismayed as they proceed to help themselves to all the doughnuts on the table. So, still hoping to save her life and honor, she goes back to making doughnuts, and her visitors go back to eating each and every one as it comes out of the lard, until her entire supply of flour is gone. At that point, the story usually continues, the husband comes rushing in and chases away the Indians, but not before the head of the Indian family (or band) offers him six ponies in exchange for this woman who makes such wonderful food. Hahahahaha. As if a white woman would ever agree to go off with the lowly Indians.

And that's the kind of courage we've come to expect from our pioneer forefathers.

Well, not exactly. There are no doors to knock on in a tipi wall. So it was customary and only courteous to open the flap and peek into a tipi to make sure a visitor wasn't walking in on a private moment. If visitors came hungry into a Native household of course it was presumed they would be fed, especially if there was clearly an abundance of food there in plain sight. Like all those doughnuts on the homesteader's cabin table. And to this day at many tribal gatherings (especially among the Pawnees) it is understood that one eats what there is to eat; it would be insulting to do otherwise. If the settlers had ventured into an Indian village, they would be fed to the point of bursting and would be expected to eat at whatever lodge hosted them, as abundant reports describe. I myself have come from a wonderful meal where I was a guest of a Pawnee friend and stumbled into a social gathering like a handgame meal, only to be fed again—and to have it made very clear that to reject what was being served would constitute a major error in social protocol.

The doughnut incident might have actually happened once, or several times I suppose, but certainly not as often as told by amused descendants who use it as an example of great-grandmother's courage in the face of certain death. It is actually an example of her cultural ignorance. Which social system is better? The one with universal hospitality and sharing? Or the one where visitors—especially Indians—were objects of fear, contempt, and historical amusement? Cultural ignorance (or even the reverse: rampant egalitarianism) hinders our ability to make such judgments. But reason and survival can provide some evidence. The Pawnees lasted a lot longer on the plains than most homesteaders and perhaps will wind up outlasting white society—it remains to be seen.

Upon initial contact on the frontier and even today Native culture was and is understood as "primitive," when in fact it was highly developed, complicated, and even advanced. The Pawnees didn't use the wheel but hauled their belongs on pony or dog drags, two tipi poles raised on one end to the animal's shoulders, the other ends sliding along behind. Primitive? There were no roads on the plains and the soil was soft. Wheels on wagons dried out and fell apart, bogged down at river crossings or in drift dust, or were pounded apart on the uneven trails and open ground. Wagon after wagon failed on the Oregon Trail, but for centuries pony drags and before them dog drags carried nomadic Indian groups from one camp to another without any such trouble. One could argue that the Indians were the ones with the advanced system of moving their goods. Native religions were intricate and highly developed—although not, of course, "right." Their foodways were clearly superior to the whiteman's. Their arts, from music to dance, costume to carvings were at least equivalent to the skills of the typical eighteenth- or nineteenth-century white citizen and to my taste far superior. I would invite anyone who thinks otherwise to visit a museum or look at a book illustrating beadwork, painting, or carving (like catlinite pipes) commonly used in tribal life at the time.

Even our calendars function as a serving tray for historical insult. Doubters can ask any Native about his or her enthusiasm for Columbus Day, when we celebrate the bringing of "civilization" and "true religion" to these shores by missionaries like Columbus, Pizarro, Cortez, and their ilk. Yet when there are efforts to establish a special day, week, or month to recognize Native Americans, as one might expect, a firestorm of protest arises. Why should Indians have a special day? Because every other day of the year is *not* a special Indian day. In fact, almost every other day of the year is a whiteman's day of the year. At least Cinco de Mayo is increasingly celebrated, even in Nebraska, and sure enough, there is always some rockhead writing a letter to the editor of the local newspaper, unhappy that even one day is a special day for someone other than him. Probably the same genius who howls at the treasonous display of the Mexican flag on Cinco de Mayo and then drives off in his pickup truck sporting the Confederate Stars and Bars, a blatant symbol of the worst treason against this nation of ours in its history.

40. *Indians Today*

I think I have made enough of the diversity of America's Native population. One cannot speak of "the Indian" or say things like, "The Indian position on this issue is . . ." or "Indians hate . . ." or "You can count on Indians to . . ." As with non-Indians, there are national, regional, religious, gender, tribal, clan, and family differences from one person to the next, as well as the inevitable individuality of human personalities and experiences. And yet there are some common experiences and a common history stemming from patterns imposed on that experience by the larger forces of the invading white culture and then a fairly monolithic U.S. government.

For example, the U.S. government hunted the Mohawks to the ground like animals and murdered them, as it also did the Lakotas two hundred years later. They were the enemy, and killing the enemy is what we do. On the other hand, the Pawnees were not simply noncombatants in relation to the U.S. government, they were military allies. They wore the uniforms of U.S. military forces and fought side by side with U.S. troops; yet the Pawnees, too, were hunted down, murdered, betrayed, disenfranchised, and sent into exile.

Most American Indians have been removed from their traditional lands and their sacred landmarks. Most have had their religions attacked, mocked, or outlawed. Most tribes have a long history of abuse at the hands of non-Indians—from the introduction of plagues to rape and exploitation of their women, from the expropriation of intellectual property to theft of resources—from the arrival of Columbus to the present day. These kinds of experiences are common to most American Indians, and we can therefore look at them as consistent histories with consistent impacts (although still with varying results because of all the other variables mentioned previously).

One could argue that, what the heck, lots of groups of Americans have gone through trials like this. Sort of. But not quite. While African Americans had a longer, more pervasive, crueler history of slavery, Indians, too, were kidnapped and used as slaves. My own German Russian ancestors worked at miserable stoop labor in agricultural fields, were robbed of rightful wages, suffered discrimination, and were mocked for their clothing, language, and perceived ignorance. Their citizenship and patriotism were seriously questioned during the two wars with Germany (and later Russia) and through most of the twentieth century. Somali, Hispanic, Bosnian, and Afghani immigrants to America this very day still suffer the unjust abuses that seem ever with us as long as stupid, cruel, and frightened people constitute a substantial segment of our society, if not a majority.

Such trials are not a matter of ancient history for Native Americans. Not only the results but even the conditions leading to those results remain in force to some degree. Consider the few milestones below—not so much as markers of progress but as painful reminders of how slowly justice is being realized.

African Americans were given the vote in the Fifteenth Amendment to the Constitution in 1870, although many were effectively unable to exercise that right until almost a century later. Women won the right to vote in 1920—admittedly, disgracefully delayed. American Indians got right to vote in 1924, but even well into the 1960s in some southwestern areas of the country, Indians were denied the vote in direct defiance of federal law. Indians were not allowed to buy alcohol or firearms starting in 1897, and that policy was not reversed until 1953. It should be noted, however, that Indians were allowed to carry firearms in World War II, which they did valiantly.

Perhaps the most egregious violation of Indians' human rights was at least addressed and corrected legally (if not in actual practice) with the judgment in 1879 in U.S. District Court in Omaha that Indians are—it is hard to write this without genuine pain and embarrassment—persons in the meaning of the law. Denial of the Indians' status as part of humanity enabled the federal government to ignore the right of habeas corpus for Indians. The case, *Standing Bear v. Crook*, is well documented and widely known now. Briefly, in 1877 the Poncas were removed from their traditional territory in northeastern Nebraska and exiled to Oklahoma Territory. They asked permission to return but were denied that basic right of travel. One band defied the prohibition and returned to their traditional tribal lands in Nebraska, where they were arrested and removed again by troops under General George Crook. The trial of Chief Standing Bear of the Poncas is famous not only for Judge Elmer S. Dundy's decision that Indians are indeed persons in the meaning of the law but also in the magnificently eloquent plea in which Standing Bear declared his humanity and begged for his basic rights. I consider the case a major moment in Wannabe history, too, because General Crook was so offended by the arguments of the court (that Indians were not actually human beings because they didn't dress right—which is to say, like whites—and because they worked on Sundays) that he threw his substantial weight behind Standing Bear and the Poncas during the hearings.

All of this means that American Indians, despite differences among tribes, clans, and families, do have historical and contemporary experiences in common, and as should be clear, those experiences lead to different problems than other segments of American society face. At this very writing the Nebraska legislature is threatening to disregard these important facts and lump Indian concerns and problems together with those of "other minorities." Many legislators arrogantly disregard the very real fact that all "minority problems" are not the same. Mexicans have issues with naturalization, language, and immigration; Indians have problems with repatriation and reburial of desecrated remains, tribal sovereignty, tribal law, and reservation status. In one legislative hearing an oblivious representative sputtered, "Why can't you Indians and Mexicans just work together on your problems?" My old friend Mick whispered to me from behind his hand, "For the same reason the basketball team and the football team don't practice together!" Another solon noted that the state's cattlemen's associations seem to take care of their own issues just fine on their own; why do Indians always come running to the government with *their* problems? Maybe, uh, because the cattlemen are rich and the Indians are destitute? And yet it is out of ignorance like this that our laws arise.

41. *Indians as Americans*

One of the first things to strike any prospective Wannabe when first encountering modern Native culture is the deep and sincere patriotism of many Indians. That would seem strange considering the long history of hostilities between Indians and the U.S. government, indeed between Indians and the white American public in general. Why would an Indian honor at all the government and population that have treated him or her with contempt for centuries? Almost fifty years ago, as I sat under the shade arbor at a Sun Dance on the Pine Ridge Reservation, I asked Edgar Red Cloud about this historical contradiction. How could it be that I saw the American flag fluttering everywhere around the circle, witnessed a profound respect for veterans of the U.S. military, and heard declarations of patriotism for a nation that had treated these very people with such contempt? How could there be such respect for the flag that had flown over the troops that had slaughtered women, children, and old, sick men, not far from where we were sitting at that very moment and not all that long ago (at the time, only eighty years earlier). Mr. Red Cloud considered my question for a long moment and then explained that to him the flag represented not the government that had perpetrated atrocities against his people in the past and even today but stood in his mind for the land, and the Lakotas love that land no matter how cruel its occupiers have been. In fact, Mother Earth was theoretically and maybe even legally still his.

An additional part of the intense Native patriotism and reverence for the American flag is the element of the military so often associated with that flag. Strong elements of warrior societies still live within many Native communities, and indeed, there are specific warrior societies within some tribes—the Tiapiah Society among the Omahas, Pawnees, and Kiowas, for example, various veterans organizations like the American Legion, and even associated groups like the War Mothers among the Omahas and Pawnees. There are ritual responsibilities and privileges specific to veterans, such as raising and lowering the flag in public displays like powwows and even in the quiet solitude of the morning, when they also sing the tribal flag song. Within some tribes, like the Omaha, when a piece of regalia is dropped in a dance arena only a veteran can retrieve it. An outsider should never make the mistake of presuming that whatever animosity existed in the past or persists between the U.S. government and its most abused citizens, the Indians, has led to a disrespect for the U.S. military or the flag or has limited their patriotism in the most general sense.

Nor should Indian dedication to the United States as a nation be seen to conflict with Native "nationhood"—so-called tribal sovereignty and individuals' insistent affiliation with the tribal nation. On the other hand, an outsider's confusion about all this "Omaha Nation" or "Pawnee Nation" is certainly understandable: it is confusing and even contradictory. But it is not the flippant nonsense of athletic allegiances like the posited "Husker Nation," meaning the University of Nebraska Athletic Department and its rabid followers, a metaphor insulting to the concepts of both nation and Nebraska.

Tribal nations were established as sovereign political entities in the course of U.S. encounter and occupation of Native lands. Their establishment allowed for war to be waged against Natives by another sovereign nation, the United States of America. The United States cannot wage war against its own people or ignore the guarantees in the Bill of Rights and Constitution in dealing with U.S. citizens (although in the wake of George W. Bush that presumption is no longer absolute). As long as American Indians could be seen as foreigners, even on this, their own land, they were fair game for war and abuse. That legal condition has continued, even though it is now perceived as an anachronism. In fact, it is now seen as offering an occasional economic or political advantage for Indians (in regard to casinos and gaming, enrollment advantages in health care, tribal commercial endeavors, intergovernmental exchanges, and self-governance, for example). What was a truncheon used against Indians is occasionally now a tool for tribal advantage and is therefore tenaciously held by Native individuals and tribes.

Non-Indians sometimes see this leverage as some kind of easy advantage, as charity, or as "special treatment." Well, yes, in a way it is, but like labor union gains, it was hard and expensively won through trade-offs involving the loss of land and other privileges—pennies on the dollar. Long-overdue payments (or more likely, partial payments) and settlements for land lost in questionable treaties, "sales," and "voluntary removals" are often seen as welfare, but no non-Indian would consider it welfare if she were to sell her home for $1,000—theft under another label—and then receive only $10 of that, a century after the sale. And yet that is not an exaggeration of what some government payments to Native tribes sometimes are, scarcely gifts or charity. It is a profound and total mistake to think of such belated payments and arrangements as charity or unfair advantages instead of delayed and inadequate justice.

I come to these questions from the perspective of one who has long had an association with Native Americans, has put some time and energy into examining Natives' situation, and is personally involved with Native issues, so I believe that the situation of American Indians in the greater American culture is substantially different from that of other minorities and substantially more strained, difficult, and troublesome for all of us. While some of the hurdles faced by Natives are the same as those of any other American of color, some conditions as bad as those of any others among the disgracefully poor in this wealthy nation, some political disenfranchisement as hopeless as that of others who are already powerless, the difficulties faced by all Native peoples in America are in many ways unique. And they are in many ways worse because they often relate to culturally inherited and sometimes proudly held cultural goods and as such are not easily nor willingly changed. My German ancestors gladly left Germany in the eighteenth century to follow Catherine the Great (a German) to Russia and new settlements along the Volga River and around the Black Sea; a century later they were glad to leave Russia to come to the American steppes, the Great Plains. The same cannot be said of American Indians: in no case did they enthusiastically, hopefully, or even willingly leave their traditional homelands to resettle in much different, inevitably harsher landscapes at the point of bayonets. The loss of sovereignty, status as a separate political unit, would constitute a loss not only to the Native people holding it but potentially to all Americans, indeed to all citizens of the world community. It is through sovereignty that many of the problems of these conquered, displaced, disadvantaged, abused populations can be addressed. Many of the problems are based in ignorance, sometimes innocent, sometimes deliberate, but sovereignty gives American Indians at least a shred of shelter against the harsh and fickle winds of the non-Indian world.

Imagine, for example, being a Pawnee, exiled from lands stolen from you in Nebraska and Kansas and moved to Oklahoma. You have reason to visit your ancient traditional lands and for the first time see the rivers and hills that were sacred to your great-grandparents. You visit museums and see "artifacts" of your own heritage but removed from their cultural matrix and now behind glass. You read the labels on the items—printed in English. Then, as you read the local Nebraska newspaper in that same language you have to swallow hard as you read letter after letter from area Know-Nothings. Some crow about how immigrants to this land—now *their* land!—should at least show the energy, courtesy, and patriotism to learn the language of this, their newly adopted land. You know—just like the Anglo-American homesteaders, soldiers, and missionaries learned the Pawnee language when *they* came here as immigrants to a foreign land. Wow. What gall, you think.

You don't have to be Pawnee or Indian to be a victim of the arrogance in such attitudes. Forty-some years ago I had a moment of realization when in one day I attended an elegant (elegant for Nebraska, at any rate) coffee at a university president's home along with other new faculty and then gathered with some Omaha Indian friends for a traditional handgame. At both events people had dressed in their best Sunday clothing. The food was plentiful and delicious. There were differences: the president's reception was a good deal quieter, but then at that site we were acquaintances but not close friends, while at the handgame there was laughter, singing, dance, and more comfort, even though there were guests from another city enjoying our hospitality.

You can already sense the contrasts between the two occasions, and they would seem perfectly logical, considering the nature of the gatherings and the relationships among the people attending them. But that wasn't the heart of my epiphany. At one point during the fun and excitement of the handgame, two uniformed city policemen walked into the room. The singers went silent. As a middle-class, mainstream white man I had never experienced a situation quite like this. The police stopped at the open end of the large room and slowly looked around at all of us sitting around the edges of the room, as one does in a handgame. We "Indians" sat silent as the police then slowly walked around the room (in the wrong direction, one might note, which is to say counterclockwise around the drum, an invitation to ill fortune for all of us, not that the police knew or cared), looking at each of us in turn. We didn't say anything, nor did the police. The only sound was the slight crunch of their shoes on the naked pavement in the open room. Having completed a circuit of the room, the police left, still not having said a word.

I imagine they had been notified of some trouble outside of the building where we were having our game and were simply looking for the people who had caused the problem. But even at that moment I wondered. Would the police have done that silent walk around the room at the president's reception? Even if there had been an assault in the mansion's driveway? How about a murder? Would they have entered the room without seeking permission or explaining why they were there? Without apology? Without a word of greeting? The next moment I was more Indian than I had been only an hour before. I had a new feeling in my heart—the bitterness of prejudicial treatment in a state where our official motto is Equality Before the Law.

Yes, anyone of color may have had that same experience, probably many times, perhaps as a matter of course. Sometimes the events are uniquely Indian, however. As I noted previously, the history of institutionalized victimization is recent for American Indians, within the living memory of many of my elder friends, and is distinctive to Native Americans. Poverty is rife everywhere without regard to race, it seems, but without question the most economically distressed areas and populations in America today are its reservation lands and the tribes on them.

Now and then someone with no awareness or sensitivity performs a pseudo-minstrel show in black face, but they rarely do it a second time because the reaction to such boorish behavior excites instant negative reaction. I cannot imagine anyone doing a public parody of Jewish religion or culture unless it came as an esoteric statement from someone like Kinky Friedman; there is, after all, a large, structured organization specifically dedicated to responding to actions based in anti-Semitism. Cultural mockery is going out of style. Too slowly perhaps, but at least those who practice it learn quickly that their behavior will not pass without reaction. While some offenders shrug off objections to their racism as "pc," political correctness, respect for other cultures is little more than common civility.

Not so with Indian culture. In fact, I would guess it is the rare weekend sports fan watching television who doesn't see at least one bonehead wearing a warbonnet, with painted face, waving a foam rubber tomahawk, prancing around like an idiot, and . . . mocking Indian culture. That kind of racist buffoonery is not simply accepted, it is expected. Sometimes entire stadiums and arenas are filled with non-Indians imitating what they believe to be Native behavior in a derogatory way. Their excuse? As often as not, in apparent surprise and confusion, they explain they are actually "honoring" the "First Americans." During a recent flap at the University of Nebraska about precisely this sort of cultural mockery a young Native protested the ridiculing of his people and his history. The good news is that the yahoos did apologize; the bad news is that then a major newspaper editorial objected to the presumed "insult" the writer believed was being thrown at the young men mocking Indians! Insulting other people, cultures, and histories has become for some a basic civil right, while decent civility is an offense against the rights of racism, cruelty, coarseness, and bigotry.

42. *The Land*

My German kin came from a basically feudal society in the German colonies along the Volga River in Russia, and the transition to American culture must have been enormous for them. I have what must remain a distant admiration for my mother's father, Johann Flach. He came to this country as a young man; I know nothing of his life in Russia. He quickly learned English well enough to serve as his community's translator; he wrote poetry in his new language; he entered a contest selling newspaper subscriptions in hopes of winning the prize, a new automobile—in 1917! Leaving virtual serfdom, he made efforts in this new land with its new freedoms to organize a union for migrant laborers in the sugar beet fields of western Nebraska and Kansas and eastern Wyoming and Colorado—his friends and neighbors—against the prevailing and powerful forces of the railroads, contractors, landowners and managers, and sugar companies.

But Johann Flach was a white man. He knew the general values and customs of Western civilization even in Russia. German is not English, to be sure, but then German is not Lakota, either. My grandfather Johann left behind relatives, the church he had attended all his life, perhaps a home that had been in his family for generations. But he did not have to see those institutions then co-opted by another people.

Of course they were, but he was not there on the Russian steppes to see the violations of his dreams and past. He was thousands of miles away with even bigger dreams in the New World. He did not have to see the graves of his revered ancestors desecrated. Indians have seen exactly that. Imagine the feelings that must course through Pawnee or Omaha or Lakota blood when they see ceremonies on television where "centennial farmers" are honored for living on land that has been in their family for a hundred years—land that was taken from Native families after they had lived on it for many centuries, taken from them through processes that were at best questionable, at worst naked theft. Imagine seeing those relative newcomers, actually uninvited invaders, running their plows and planters over your family's graves and the rubble of your villages and fields and then being celebrated as the people who "brought civilization and agriculture" to the blank slate of an empty wilderness!

Non-Indians express a deep affection for the land, although more often and most specifically for their own land. And yet the language of land acquisition and ownership on this continent expresses not so much a tender mother-child relationship, as is the case in most Indian nations, but an act of conquest: "the winning of the West," "conquering the land," "taming the land," fighting, struggling, waging literal warfare to bring the land to its knees and to bend it to the master's will. The recent mining of the land's greatest resources—water and soil—to the point of profligacy and the self-destructive exploitation of those resources to, of all things, manufacture fuel for automobiles seems to be closer to the relationship between a prostitute and her pimp than one of tender affection.

How many geographical sites in North America are held by non-Indians to be sacred? Where does God visit non-Indian Americans in our current geography? Some see God's *hand* in places of extraordinary beauty, but in the whiteman's theological geography God visits North America most often at battle sites where brothers have met to kill brothers. Our lands are sanctified by human gore, blood, and merciless slaughter. How dare even a man of Abraham Lincoln's humanity use words like "consecrate" and "hallow" for the obscenities of a blood-soaked site of carnage like Gettysburg!

All across the Great Plains there were (and are) sites considered sacred by various tribes, and they understood all too well that these God-given, divine-visited springs, hills, rivers, and rocks were theirs. Such sites were generally also respected as sacred by other tribes, including enemies. Not only have many such sites been physically desecrated but some have been further violated by unconscionable actions like dubbing a sacred mountain in the Black Hills with the name of a murderer of the very people to whom it belonged—Harney Peak in the Paha Sapa, or Black Hills. The blasphemy could not be more blatant.

There is a popular notion that Indians didn't understand the concept of "owning" land, so vast regions were not really, well, *stolen* because they weren't actually *owned* by the Indians in the first place. They may not have held deeds in safe-deposit boxes, but tribes most assuredly understood what territory was within their hegemony. They knew where their sacred sites were and where there were resources like flint and pipestone, sites where hostilities were to be avoided because they were held as common "property." Indians may have had a different concept of how one holds possession of land and how the boundaries and areas were measured, but they learned very quickly and to their pain what the whiteman's concept of ownership was and is.

I remember vividly the moment I stood at the bow of a large ocean-going ferry from Gedser, Denmark, to Grossenbrode, Germany, and through the thick fog caught my first glimpse of Germany, my people's homeland of two centuries before. With no connection other than a historical one, with a separation of centuries and at least two emigrations removed, the first sight of my motherland through the fog brought tears to my eyes. I have seen Pawnees come here to what was our home and tree farm and first see and feel the soil of their ancestors, to splash over their heads and drink the water of *their* native and sacred river. I have seen their tears and the passion on their faces. I have heard their prayers and songs. I love this land and I, too, have thought of it as sacred. As mine. My feelings and those of the Pawnees were close to each other.

But not the same, I can assure you. A Pawnee family once stood here by the graves where over a thousand of their ancestors now again rest in Pawnee soil and to the clapping of the father's hands quietly sang a song about this very land. They were not alone in their tears. Just as I know a bit of the feeling of being rejoined with one's native soil, I also know just a bit of the pain of separation from it.

A quartet of young Pawnee powwow circuit singers and dancers once stopped by this land that is now theirs. They visited the graves where their ancestors have been put to rest and then, as seems to be a requisite part of pilgrimages to this returned land, they asked to be taken to the river. When we arrived at the bank and looked across the broad, clean, fast-flowing water, they prayed but then were clearly driven to do more. They thought about the situation and talked over what they would do. The river's sandy bottom is uneven at best, and despite my assurances that even in the channel the river is rarely more than two or three feet deep they were understandably reluctant to wade into the unfamiliar moving water with their drum. They did something extraordinary, and I only regret that I alone of the non-Indians on the farms and in the villages around us was there to witness it. They waded out to the center of the river where the water was just deep enough to come to midthigh, and they sat down on the sand beneath the water. In unison, sitting there chest deep in their river, they slapped the water gently with their open hands as if it were their drum, and they sang. They sang songs to their ancestors and to the land and river as they sat there in the river and on their land, in sight of the hill where a thousand of their people lay at rest. Ownership was not the issue; the Pawnees at that point owned it again. Their presence on it, however, was a moment of great power and emotion. For all of us.

My ancestors had a fresh start in this new country; Natives have been left with the wreckage and rubble of what was theirs. But why, some ask, can't Indians quit living in the past and move on into the future so they can enjoy a good, prosperous, truly American life? (Which is to say, like me!) Because those opportunities are not always open to people with dark skins. Because they still have the evidence of the injustice before them every day. Because the victims of any crime always remember the offense longer than the perpetrators do. Because the offenses not only are recent but continue. Because the ways of the American mainstream may not be as attractive to others as they seem to us, nor the old traditional ways as undesirable. Because such decisions should be up to them and not to others.

43. *The Real Wonder of It*

I f there is a wonder in all this, at least in my mind, it is that there is not *more* anger. In my long life and long association with Native people I have rarely experienced anything but warm welcomes, generosity, kindness, unexpected trust, laughter, and brotherhood. I'm not at all sure I could be as generous if I were in the Indians' shoes. In fact, I have been in small ways. I was once with a distinguished group of tribal elders and political and religious leaders when we went for a quick meal at a franchise restaurant. You would recognize the name immediately—a plain, lower-middle-class place to get an ordinary meal. We had just attended an important business meeting so we were all relatively well dressed—sort of western causal dress clothes, slacks, western-cut shirts, bolo ties. We sat and waited, talking quietly, studying our menus. Time passed. We sat at our table until it became evident that we were not going to be asked for our food order. Everyone else in the room had a waiter and had received their meals while we sat, slowly realizing what was happening. I imagine my Indian friends recognized the situation much sooner than I did because they were used to this kind of treatment, while I had never experienced it. I was furious and wanted to make trouble, but my wiser, more experienced Indian friends calmed me and said it was much easier simply to move on and try another place to spend our money. I was the angry one. I have tried to learn from them, not always successfully.

Of course, there are angry Indians too. Sometimes unreasonably so. Sometimes the most indignant "Indians" are Wannabes like me, perhaps all the angrier because the people who behave badly look like us, are our "blood" kith and kin, and along with being offended, we are embarrassed for our own kind. In my case, unpleasant situations based in racism have given me reason to be ever more grateful for my Indian associations, for lessons from people who know much more about being Indian than I do.

It may seem curious, but it is something worth thinking about: sometimes being Indian gets in the way of grasping exactly what it means to be Indian. That is to say, yet again, viewing a culture from within is sometimes more challenging than having the wider perspective of watching it from outside.

44. *Eloquence*

It's complicated, but sometimes Indians not only don't understand the whiteman but moreover don't understand how the whiteman sees them. For example, one of the first things that struck me as I moved more frequently and deeper into Omaha culture was Omaha eloquence. Many surveys have been taken, more for public amusement I suspect than scientific curiosity, that show that of all the things Americans fear—death by fire, cancer, terrorism—what they fear most is public speaking. I made my living as a public speaker for banquets, conventions, and other gatherings for many years, and it always amazed me that a group of thousands of educated people, of whom surely at least a dozen would have had interesting things to say, would rather pay me handsome fees than get up and speak themselves. Small wonder—few of them were any good at it when they were required only to do something as small as introduce me from the head table. A microphone apparently induces mental paralysis in most Americans.

Not so with the Omahas, or for that matter as I have since found, most Natives. Eloquence is not just prized, it is expected. From everyone. Prayers and introductions soar floridly at even small gatherings. At powwows the humor and language skills of announcers, or as they are sometimes called, "criers," are as polished as those of our finest orators.

For a moment consider the run-of-the-mill politician in our system, scarcely able to get through a sentence without sounding as if he or she were speaking in an unknown tongue; a brilliant orator like the U.S. president at this writing, Barack Obama, is a rarity and all too often is suspect precisely because he does use the language well. Many Americans, amazingly, prefer an inarticulate clown like Obama's predecessor or any of a number of his current detractors, finding their violence to the language (you know, that language they want to make "official") somehow legitimizing.

There are times set aside at every Omaha gathering for speaking. A hand signal is given by a person who wants to say something to those gathered, an open hand raised slightly above waist level and swept forward toward the person in charge of the meeting. Upon being given a brief spoken acknowledgement the speaker rises and says what he or she has on his or her mind. An apology is usually given for asking permission, perhaps an expression of gratitude to the elders present or to the scorer's table at a handgame, and the statement is made, seldom hurried, never terse. Upon finishing the speaker acknowledges the group and thanks them for their attention and again takes his or her seat. The crowd may in turn express approval with a muttered "Uda! Uda!" (Good! Good!).

I was once at the drum at a handgame between two local Indian clubs, an informal, friendly evening for laughing and feasting. I usually sat beside a particular friend of mine because he is a good singer and also because he was so quiet, so shy that I felt he might appreciate my presence, too. So I was amazed that evening when my friend made the gesture requesting permission to speak. He rarely had anything to say to anyone at the drum, yet he wanted to stand and give a public oration! He was given permission and stood.

His speech was remarkable. He said, roughly (this was more than forty years ago so my recollection is not exact), "I want to thank the elders here for allowing me to stand and speak before them. I also give thanks to those at the head table for this chance to speak. My father has told me that it is time that I should stand and speak, for that is what an Omaha does. You know I have little to say but it is important that I learn how to say what I need to say. So I stand before you now. I ask you to forgive me for my clumsiness in finding my words. I know it is difficult for you to listen to my words here tonight but I thought that while the food is still being prepared, this might be a good time for me to stand and speak …"

He went on like that for perhaps four or five minutes, a relatively short speech for an Omaha. He said virtually nothing, and yet he was speaking and that was what was important for him. And for everyone else. Everyone there knew what this meant to this young man and to them. He had faced his unease and was, as he said, doing what an Omaha does. When he spoke his closing words and took his seat at the drum again, the chorus of "Uda! Uda! Uda!" rang especially loud and firm. Everyone beamed. He had risen and given a speech. It didn't matter what he spoke about. He had spoken.

Pick up any book on Native American speeches (I am especially fond of *I Have Spoken*, by Virginia I. Armstrong, and *Touch the Earth*, by T. C. McLuhan, but there are dozens of anthologies of Indian speeches) and you will quickly see that eloquence has long been a strength in Indian culture, even when speeches are given in English, a second language. You will probably be as impressed as I have been.

But perhaps I should not have been. Again and again I have heard amusement, disapproval, and even contempt from my Native friends for this common reaction from the whiteman. Many Indians even feel this admiration for the skills of oratory is a slap in the face. Why is the whiteman surprised that an Indian can be well spoken? Why is there an expectation, of all things, for Indians to be inarticulate?

I understand that point of view. You'll have to admit, they are right. Why *is* there a presumption of poor speaking ability when it comes to Indians? I understand the indignation among Indians, but I also see clearly the reasons for those expectations. Just as eloquence is the tradition within Indian cultures, so too is the lack of eloquence within the non-Indian mainstream; even more important is the mainstream understanding that Indians are even *less* articulate than the rest of us.

That being the presumption, when the opposite proves to be true we are understandably surprised.

Those understandings may now have changed, thank goodness, but throughout my youth they were constantly reinforced. Hollywood Indians were always mute or inarticulate. That was one of their primary characteristics. You know, Tonto (Spanish for "stupid," incidentally), with his grunts, "Me go now," and "Heap plenty white man come." Indians were always—*always*—portrayed as inarticulate. When I was young, our local television station had a kiddies' cartoon show every afternoon, and one of the stage props was a white man with a blanket wrapped around him who simply stood behind the pseudo-cowgirl hostess of the show, never speaking a word. You know, the ever-reticent Indian. He was referred to as Caliga the Wooden Indian. Victor Mature, Marlin Brando, or Sal Mineo—not one white man playing an Indian role spoke well. The notion of an actual Indian playing an Indian, perhaps even as an Indian of his own ancestry, is a relatively new screen concept. In comic books, on television, on the big screen, the Indian never spoke even his own language well. He grunted. His sentences were never more than three or four words long. (I must note that one wonderful relief from this indignity was the hilarious send-up of the Hollywood nonsense by Mel Brooks in *Blazing Saddles*, where he played the role of an Indian chief—a Jew in [as it were] "red face," speaking . . . Yiddish! It is said that the beadwork on *his* warbonnet read KOSHER. That gives him a lot of latitude in my book.)

The conclusion has to be that while the common perception of Indians and their lack of skill with language is not just wrong but *very* wrong, there are plenty of reasons why even an educated and open-minded non-Indian would approach Indian society with that erroneous understanding. It could, after all, be worse: the outsider could dismiss Indian culture without ever noting that error and continue with the wrong and insulting notion he or she started with—seeing Indians as inarticulate, sullen, and dense, when precisely the opposite is true.

45. *From Presumed Inferiority to Rampant Egalitarianism*

Despite blustering insistence from some social scientists that they are indeed *scientists* because they approach the examination and explication of culture objectively, those declarations ring largely hollow because culture is not something that allows absolute objectivity. However hard we might try, it is simply not possible to shed a lifetime of immersion in one or even several cultures and study another without the distortion of the ever-present lens of previous experience. Whatever context one comes from and whatever context is the target, they are both slippery, constantly shifting footholds. There is no constant that can serve as a base from which to view a variable; each platform can be seen only relative to the other. What's worse, each platform not only is moving relative to the other but is in constant transition itself. And the pressures and forces behind those cultural changes are so complex that the task of sorting them out becomes more theological than scientific.

Similarly, the methodology and mythology of "science" is constantly shifting as the culture within which it rests changes. I have watched the trends of scholarly and academic ethnographic research during my half century of interest in Native culture and have found that the "scientific models" are as elusive as the cultures themselves. While I have commented on "political correctness" previously as only an alternate term for common civility, a growing, overwhelming, generally well-intentioned but ill-designed tendency toward rampant egalitarianism does not help us understand other cultures.

Everything is *not* equal. A dear friend and fellow scholar once chided me for my advocacy of certain qualities of Native American culture, namely the pan-Indian precepts about time and property that I discuss elsewhere in these pages. He insisted that all cultures are equal, just as all languages are equal. The curse of rampant and misunderstood egalitarianism has become a hobble on progress in understanding other cultures. All languages are to a great degree *adequate*, but that does not mean they are *equal*. Who could argue sensibly that Bantu music is no different from Inuit music in complexity and magnificence? The African musical traditions feature hundreds of instruments for making many different sounds, complex rhythms, and tonal combinations, sometimes layered one on the other. The Inuit have one instrument, a frame drum, and one rhythm, 1/1. The two cultures may be equivalent in their adequacy—that is, they speak to and fulfill the needs of the people embedded in them—but they most assuredly are not the same. Mainstream American culture has virtually no traditional "folk" music—that is, music that is transmitted from one person to others by oral tradition. Our mainstream culture has almost no tradition of riddle, proverb, or folktale other than the modern legend (unfortunately mislabeled "urban legend"). The tall tale once prospered in America, but it has faded almost entirely away except as a vestigial remnant despite the constant and utterly impossible assignments of grade school teachers to "write a tall tale." In a lifetime of studying the tall tale on the plains I have yet to meet a single person who is skilled at *inventing* tall tales, and increasingly there isn't even a tradition of developing and conveying a body of such humor forms. Teachers requiring children to invent tall tales are essentially asking their charges to revive dinosaurs without having so much as the DNA. They should be jailed for child cruelty, or perhaps sentenced to composing ten or fifty tall tales themselves!

Mainstream America, on the other hand, does have a strong tradition of the modern legend, the riddling joke ("How many [fill in the blank] does it take to screw in a light bulb?"), and the punch line joke (as opposed to storytelling, in which the humor of a narrative lies in the style of the telling rather than in a punch line). Different cultures display different strengths, but the differences cannot be dealt with as flaws or advantages. They are simply differences.

Generally speaking, Native American culture has a continuing, strong musical tradition, a fading inventory of narrative and performance, and perhaps most difficult to detect and describe, a powerful momentum in belief and custom. That makes intercultural understanding even more difficult: a song is easily recognized as a song and a story as a story, but belief and custom are far more difficult to grasp as discrete cultural entities.

As I have also mentioned elsewhere in these pages, we tend to believe that our ways are natural and therefore that other ways are not. Stories can confuse someone unaccustomed to that narrative form. Songs that are in fact very complex and expressive may seem like just so much noise (think of the wahwahwahwah and ki-yi-yiki-yiki imagined to be the sound, and gibberish, of American Indian song), yet we still recognize the story as a story and the song as a song. But the way we respond is quite another story. Our way is not just the right way but the only way; any other way is, well, perverse. I have described the minor behavioral differences between mainstream, generally white culture in America and Native custom in terms of the usual gestures of a first meeting—the relative firmness of a handshake, the gesture of eye contract, and the casual use of first names.

If those three, minor differences in micro-behavior constitute problems when moving between mainstream white and Native culture, one can only imagine what enormous difficulties more substantial cultural differences—differences big enough and central enough to be seen as Weltanschauung, a way of seeing the world—can and do cause in cultural encounters. As I have used only three minor cultural differences to illustrate that point above, I will now turn to a very limited number of larger cultural problems, leaving to your imagination how much more complex and troublesome the greater inventory must be.

46. *Time*

M y first example of a cultural attitude, a way of seeing the world, is obvious enough and distinctive enough to have its own name— Indian Time. Natives are sufficiently aware of the phenomenon and its impression on people from other cultures that they take it into consideration within their own lives, although that does not mean they see any particular reason that it should in any way be changed. When announcing an event to a Native audience, the reality is dealt with as a legitimate factor: "This Tiapiah Society Gourd Dance Sunday will start at 1 p.m. White man's time! Be sure to be there. Don't be late or you'll miss it."

"Whiteman's Time" means that the schedule will be pursued with dogged determination. Not ten minutes early or ten minutes late. Keep your eyes on the clock. Proceed as if this announcement is the very will of God. You can arrive early, but even if everyone is in place and ready to go at, oh, 12:30, nothing will start until the magic hour of 1:00 p.m. arrives. Ten minutes after 1:00 p.m. people will start to get nervous and twitch if the ceremonial hasn't started. More than fifteen minutes after the time set for the start of the occasion and people will start to grumble and perhaps even begin to gather up their belongings and leave.

"Indian Time," on the other hand, means, "Leave your watches and clocks at home. We'll kick things off when everyone is there and comfortable," when it seems like time to start. And if that happens to be at 2:00 p.m., well, that's okay too. We'll just plan on having a good time all afternoon without being obsessed about what the clock is telling us.

Whiteman's Time. Indian Time. Which is "correct"? The usual non-Indian argument is that there would be nothing but chaos without a clock's measure. Really? That might be true in some situations, but it certainly can't be considered the Eleventh Commandment, brought down from the mountain by Moses. There was, after all, a time when both Indians and early white explorers of this continent would say with reasoned logic, "Okay, I'll meet you at the forks of the Platte River next spring," and that was precise enough. Anything more precise would have been nonsensical. The buffalo didn't move on a schedule more precise than that, nor did the rains and snows. The real question perhaps is, "Who's to be master?" I often quote one of my favorite musical groups, The Incredible String Band, who in their song "Time" have Time say sardonically to Mankind, "Once I was your slave . . . and now you are mine."

Is the truth in those lyrics a barb aimed at Indian Time or Whiteman's Time? Is our mainstream servitude to what was once a tool really something to be proud of? Or embarrassed by? It does not take much observation or analysis to see how painfully cowed we have become by the seconds, much less the seasons. A clock tells us when to eat; wouldn't hunger be a far more rational indicator? We fidget and twist in our seats because our clocks tell us we should be agitated, even if we have no place we need to be, nothing urgent we need to do. Wouldn't our time be better spent relaxing and enjoying the company of good friends and family?

We non-Indians are manipulated by mechanisms strapped to our arms or hanging on walls. Or not strapped to our arms or hanging on walls. At locations where the priority is to move people along and get them out of the way, for example those tiny tables at airport fast-food windows where one stands and gulps down terrible and expensive food, there are no clocks. They want you to eat and get out of the way for the next desperate traveler frantically checking his watch every few minutes. Is that good for us? Forty years ago I came to know and understand Indian Time and decided it just might make my own life easier. I put away my wristwatch and never strapped the manacle back on. In forty years I have felt no loss.

In airports and in my own life I have instead worked to develop a clear mental image of a stick shift at my right hand. When I feel myself tensing and straining with anxiety about what my master Time wants of me, I consciously think about my situation at that moment. Do I really need to know the time, much less the exact time? Is there reason for me to fuss and fidget? If I can't come up with a good reason, I mentally shift down into Indian gear and relax. If an unexpected storm strands you in an airport, as they have so often me, what good does it do to flail about, pace, and stew in frustration? None. None. So I consider the moment an opportunity to rest easy, to think, to watch my fellow mainstreamers flit and fret, and to practice one of the most useful elements of being a Wannabe—Indian Time.

Which system of time is more logical? It certainly isn't always Whiteman's Time! I was once camped for a long week on the Omaha tribal powwow grounds, enjoying the food, music, dance, and friendship of my Omaha family and friends. Mostly. There was still a certain amount of whiteman in me, I was to find. I woke one night in my tent to hear cheering, yelling, and revelry, apparently all around me. I listened, and it sounded for all the world like I was camped in the middle of a ballpark, somewhere around second base. I raised the flap on one of the small windows in my canvas tent and looked around. To my amazement I found that, well, I was indeed camped on second base in a ballpark. Literally. And the game was going on all around me.

The next day I remarked at my Indian family's campfire over our morning coffee, "Uh, I guess there was quite a baseball game last night." My friends chuckled and commented that there was indeed a ball game, and there was some conversation and surprise about how I didn't come out of my tent and join them watching the game, especially since I was pretty much in the middle of it. A friend gently explained that it seemed so whiteman of me to sleep during the cool of the night and then sit around in the sun during the heat of the August days. Wouldn't it make more sense, they asked without asking, to do my outdoor physical activities under the full moon, when it was cool, and then sleep under a shady tree in the breeze when it was hot? Well, yes, I suppose it would have made more sense. But my clock told me it was time to be in bed. The next day I shifted into Indian gear; I lounged and napped during the heat of the day, and that night I joined the activities around the campground, showing who was master in this situation—not my watch, but me. Take *that*, Mr. Time!

47. *Property and Gifts*

Even if you have never met an Indian or participated at all in Indian culture, you can at least imagine the problem the conflict between Indian Time and Whiteman's Time can cause . . . for Indians, because they are far and away a minority within our culture. Many, perhaps most, modern Indians have managed to adjust to the dominant time system, but especially among elders and more traditional Indian populations, particularly in the insular context of the reservation, the disjunction between the two persists. And the whiteman inevitably, perhaps even understandably, has come to see that his concept of how time works, and what time is, usually prevails.

Less obvious to both the Indian and the whiteman are our mutual understandings of what constitutes wealth, how resources are distributed, and what exactly a "gift" is, again as obvious as that would seem to both societies. Imagine the relief when tribes like the Omahas first heard the precepts of Christianity. Of course—feed the hungry. That only makes sense. Provide for strangers and the poor. Certainly. No problem there. It is easier for a camel to pass through the eye of a needle than for a rich man to go to heaven. That pretty much sums up the traditional understanding within Omaha society. One's reputation depends not on what one accumulates but in one's generosity. Open hospitality—that is, a welcome to all comers—is the Omaha way. So many precepts of theoretical Christianity were easy enough for the Omahas to accept. After all, that had always been their way of life.

What the Omahas didn't understand, and what few Christians today seem to grasp, or admit, is that while all the Christian stuff about charity, the importance of the poor, the anathema that is wealth is an *ideal* within mainstream Christian populations, it certainly is not our custom. Actually, it's probably not even an ideal but some kind of vague throwaway line. In practice, no one accepts these ideas as a way of life. Does anyone seriously think that people who give away all their wealth are more virtuous than rich people whose wealth is on display, the more ostentatiously the better? Sure, the guy sleeping under the highway overpass is a better candidate for salvation and heaven than the one living in the starter castle fronting on the country club golf course. No American seriously believes that. Give away everything you own? When hell freezes over! We even have a phrase for our historical misunderstanding of the nature of Indians and gift giving—Indian giving, suggesting a lack of appreciation for a fair exchange, the value of a gift, the importance of reciprocity in giving, the importance of hanging on to what we have, and especially what we are given.

In this situation I'll have to admit that I have weighed cultural goods and have come down at last on the logic of Native values, even though I still find myself hopelessly bound by mainstream conventions. That is, I understand, appreciate, and even work to embrace Native customs when it comes to property, possessions, and gifts, but there is always the pull of my upbringing, perhaps of my Germanic genetics. Again and again I find my Native friends chuckling or even gently reminding me when I don't think to transfer my actions into Indian modes while moving within Indian circles. An old Oto friend, Benny Butler, once gave me a beautiful ribbon shirt, and I blurted out, "Thank you so much, Benny. This is a beautiful shirt and wonderful gift. I am going to wear this only for special occasions and keep it as a treasure forever." Benny was stopped in his tracks, as *he* had to do the cultural downshifting and try to think like a whiteman. "Roger," he said, "this is an *Indian* gift. You don't need to keep it forever to show

how important it is to you. Or to me. You would in fact show me honor by passing it along to another friend sometime."

The value of a gift for an Indian (at least the Indians of my narrow experience) lies not in its potential for possession but in its potential as a gift. Even after I had moved within Omaha tribal society for a few years I was surprised on an occasion when, out of affection and knowing that food constitutes a gift of particular value, I put together a very nice peck basket of fruit and other foods for a friend of mine. As is customary, at a time in a handgame's schedule for gift giving, I signaled to the official at the game that I would like to step forward and speak to the crier. I said quietly to him in the center of the gathering that I would like to present this gift to my friend. He conveyed that message to the people at the game and my friend came forward and accepted the gift. I was quite proud of myself as I returned to my seat—and, I suppose, waited for words of praise and gratitude for my gift. Rather nicely done, if I say so myself.

But my friend did not retreat to his seat. Instead, he spoke to the crier and the crier then announced that my friend was passing along the gift I had just given him—to another person at the handgame! What? Well, I can see how much the gift means to *you*, I thought. My surprise must have shown on my face because another friend leaned over to me and explained, "Frank and his family are so pleased with your gift that he feels it is something he would be proud to pass along to someone else." Oh, yeah, that's right. *The value of a gift is in the giving.* The virtue goes to the giver. A gift's value is only demonstrated and emphasized when it is then given to someone else. You know—Indian giving!

48. *The Gift of Giving*

I am getting ahead of myself. Let me briefly outline some of the precepts of gift giving within the Native circles with which I am most familiar—Omaha, Lakota, Ponca, Winnebago, Pawnee. First and perhaps hardest for the non-Indian to understand much less practice is that prestige is gained not by acquisition and possession but by giving. The mainstream sees that as wasteful and profligate. Indians have so little to begin with, and yet instead of saving and taking care of themselves they apparently give it away without concern for thrift. They receive money, perhaps from a tribal legal settlement with the federal government, and instead of salting it away for a rainy day, they give it to relatives or they blow it all on a huge meal for the entire tribe and wind up with even less than they started with. At every Native occasion with which I am familiar a time is set aside for speech making and for gift giving. Non-Indians fidget at powwows when the speeches begin and long recitations are made of gifts being given, from money to the drum to a beef for the next powwow. What happened to the music and dancing? they ask, not realizing that what they are seeing is at least as distinctively Native as the dancing and music. Money is passed from hand to hand at honoring dances and the ever-present "crier," or announcer, receives information quietly conveyed to his ear from a donor, then strides to the microphone or front or center of the arena and loudly announces the gift. While modesty in some gift giving is seen as a virtue in white culture, remember that prestige is gained in Native circles with such gifts and they are therefore announced so the contribution to one's prestige can be recognized.

An honored and successful tribal member dies, and at the memorial service the widow's family drags everything out of the house, including the deceased's clothing, household goods, kitchenware, and even furniture, and distributes it all to the assembled family and tribe, leaving the widow impoverished. What sense does *that* make? Well, it makes a lot of sense if you consider the cultural logic of possessions. The prestige of the family and the man himself is weighed in balance not with what he has but with what he gives. Money flows from the Indian community to the hands of the widow and her family and is redistributed as gifts. Beyond that, there is also a remarkable logic of death and mourning within the process that certainly would not occur to a non-Indian but that makes far more sense than is immediately apparent. Imagine the widow returning to the home she shared with this man—perhaps her mate, partner, friend, and love all of her life. She looks around her and sees his chair, his pipe, his favorite coffee cup. Everywhere her mind is wrenched back to what was—his clothing in the closet, his shoes, his tools, his rifle. Every possession that is hers was his, and each is drenched with now-painful memories.

A culturally brilliant alternative is to be rid of those things in an automatic process inherent to the culture: dispersing all those possessions is not something she chooses to do but something that is done, understood to be a part of what happens when someone dies. Her house is emptied of all that pain, which now lies on the shoulders of her family, community, and tribe.

But how is this woman to live now with no money and no property—not so much as a coffeepot in her kitchen cupboards? Well, that is not the end of the process. Soon gifts begin to flow in the opposite direction—linens and towels, dishes and kitchenware, chairs and tables, brought as gifts from others in the community—and soon the bereaved woman is restored. In a way at least. But with new property, free of painful memories. The process is not, in fact, a foolish squandering of property but a perfectly logical way to deal with death, pain, mourning, and restoration. Is the mainstream, non-Indian way of dealing with such things really superior? In my opinion it is not, and this is one situation where I believe we can make cultural comparisons for better and worse. The Native way is superior.

Jesus said, "It is more blessed to give than receive." Does any whiteman actually believe that? Very few. But it is commonly held as truth within the Indian nations I know. Seriously. They actually believe that. And what's more, they practice it. The whiteman unfamiliar with Indian culture gets huffy when he gives gifts to an Indian and receives not so much as a word of gratitude. But wait a minute—if it is more blessed to give than receive, then shouldn't it be the giver who is grateful? He, after all, is the one receiving the blessings! Try for a moment to understand the logic of that. It isn't an easy worldview to understand, much less adopt, and yet it is essential for the Wannabe. If you can't deal with that basic reality, then there is very little chance you will grasp larger and more complex cultural complications.

The mainstream non-Indian begins to grouse after two or three years of sending a simple Christmas card to someone and receiving nothing in return. A gift of no value, and yet we expect a reciprocal gift. Within the Native cultures with which I am familiar the understanding is precisely the opposite: one is expected to maintain an informal accounting of what has been received from others in order *not* to appear to be reciprocating. The common non-Indian phrase for it is "*exchanging* gifts." That's what we do. Sometimes families or work or social groups make the understanding explicit: "This year we will limit our gifts to office colleagues/cousins/club members to $20." As an Indian once explained incredulously to me, "*We* call that 'buying things.'" It most certainly cannot be seen as giving a *gift*.

49. *The Fabric of Sharing*

I believe this cultural tradition of sharing, generosity, and gifting is based not in idealism but in realism, a conscious philosophy of generosity. It was and to some extent still is a pragmatic system in support of a community's survival. The path to survival, it should be obvious, is not isolation. That, in fact, was the ultimate punishment among many Native tribes—exile from the community meant one was on his or her own, easy prey, with no supporting context, a candidate for death. It's an old idea: *e pluribus unum*. We hang together or we hang separately.

In America we have lost, or are at least losing, the idea that we are a community. The new thinking seems to be the utterly obscene Ayn Rand social perversion that we are each on our own, and devil take the hindmost. No Native tribe or village or lodge could survive with that attitude. (Nor, eventually, can we.) I see modern Americans insisting that entire segments of our mainstream culture, usually the poorest and most oppressed, are not deserving of health care or education, as if plagues and epidemics somehow recognize economic castes, when in reality the welfare of the whole body of society depends on the health of each individual.

The strength of any Omaha or Pawnee village or lodge or Lakota family or band depends on the strength of each member of that group. It very quickly became evident to me as an outsider a half century ago that the same was precisely true, even in the twentieth century, for the small, insular Native enclaves in America, whether on a reservation or within a city's population. Whatever the *moral* imperatives of feeding the poor, elderly, and young, survival of the individual or the group comes down to the welfare of all. Those who have must share with those who do not or none will survive. Call it socialism if you will, as the selfish and greedy scream now, but it is foolish of them to think for even a moment that they can exist in comfort for long while others starve.

Thus, at most Indian gatherings, from huge powwows to small prayer meetings, those who have the resources, be that a small bag of fry bread or half a beef, provide food. And those who are hungry eat. Not as charity, a truly ugly notion, but as a birthright. You know, "life, liberty, and the pursuit of happiness." The common welfare—that includes food in a rich nation. Coming from the mainstream, I was struck at handgames when the food, no matter how meager or generous, was put in the center of the gathering as a common holding and then divided equally to each and every person, young and old. As babies slept in their cradleboards, their dishes were set out and they received equal portions. All of us. Each of us. Sometimes there are honored guests who are perhaps served first, and sometimes those honored guests are given something special like sliced white grocery store bread rather than the browned, redolent fry bread from a bushel basket, but everyone is fed. And it is always a "feast" no matter how much or how little there might be. To this day I make a point of reaching into the basket as it passes by me and violating etiquette by taking two pieces rather than the permitted one. I then apologize that I accidentally, uh, seem to have gotten, er, *two* pieces in my blind groping. Everyone knows I do it and that it isn't accidental at all. It is not just another whiteman's greed but a genuine affection for Indian food and Indian ways. If there is fry bread on my plate when the food distribution ends, I consider it a feast.

One can scarcely argue with the practicality of this arrangement in which those who have, provide and those who need, receive. It is not simply biblical, political, or social but practical. It is almost certain that at some point, sooner or later, the person who has plenty and brings it to the communal table will fall on hard times and be the one coming to the feast with an empty bowl. There is enormous comfort and confidence within a society where one never fears hunger or ever being hungrier than someone else.

50. *The Spirit of Giving*

There is also a spiritual dimension to this cultural custom, but I am reluctant to make an issue of it. I came to my Native experiences with a strong skepticism. I am not inclined to believe things I cannot see, feel, witness, or prove. That can be a more confining perspective than one might imagine, because once there is a proof or witness, one is pretty much obliged to follow through and make some admissions. My feelings are personal and I am not interested in convincing anyone else of anything; since my convictions and suspicions are based on personal experience, I can only imagine that others will have to have their own personal experiences to arrive where I have.

Despite my strongest resistance to the notion, I have been dragged kicking and screaming into an unavoidable conclusion that there are greater powers swirling around us, that those powers are conscious and operate their wills with us, that we are too intellectually puny to know much more than that there are such powers, and if we do see anything of those powers we are capable of seeing only tiny snippets of an enormous entity too huge for us to understand. That is, we can see only a small part of these forces, and we can't understand even those small portions. Nor can we even come close to understanding the greater truths precisely because only some people, in some cases, are able to see those splinters. In fact, people who insist they know the most—or everything—about the nature of these forces are precisely the ones who know the least, because the first and most basic rule is, It is too big for you to understand. Now or ever. Start there.

Our only meaningful reactions to the realizations that may arise within or from Native experiences are awe, fear, and gratitude. The only meaningful statements about spiritual realizations are questions because our best answers are at best guesses. There is a mystic element to gift giving. Aside from the practical economics of it, the social function and recognition, and a stated personal satisfaction, deep within Native thought there is also a subtle understanding that there is a larger mechanism at work.

I will use a personal experience as an example of this aspect of Native views of gift giving and property. The experiences of the day were too much to be dismissed as coincidence, and so I have wrestled with the events as a *woableza* (the Lakota term for "realization," or epiphany) or powerful experience clearly beyond the ordinary, even unexplainable without referring to the workings of greater powers that are normally in operation. I was once spending long winter weeks at my ancient log cabin in the woods along the Middle Loup River of Nebraska. I enjoyed the long, cold days, warmed by a wood stove, with little contact with the outside world, a kerosene lantern for light, and books, a pen, and paper to keep my mind occupied. Every day or so I walked the mile and a quarter through the deep snow, sometimes on snowshoes, up to the little town over the hill for the mail, maybe for some pancakes and coffee or a couple of beers with friends. On the day in question I found in my mail at the post office a letter from a dear friend, a Wannabe like me who had spent a good part of his life immersed in Navajo culture. We have a lot in common.

He had written me about a serious problem, one that required me to put on my Wannabe face and think not as a whiteman but as a Native. I wasn't sure even that would help me answer his dilemma. Long before, he wrote me, he had been given an eagle feather, a profound gift in Native circles and a symbol of immense respect and honor. The feather was a gift of particular importance because it had been passed along to him by a valued friend to whom it had been given by a very powerful Indian figure, one whose name you would almost certainly recognize but which I will keep private to protect my friend and the elder before him. My friend treasured that feather, as anyone (especially a whiteman) would. You know, it was one of those prized possessions he would "keep forever."

But he had found himself in an unusual and moving situation and was compelled by his own heart to give that beloved feather to another person. That happens. Despite one's strongest inclinations and presumed solid intentions there are times when something else speaks, as was the case with the unique developments leading to the return of our own home and land to the Pawnees. My friend was tortured. He didn't regret that he had given the feather away; it was something he absolutely had to do. But having done it he wondered about what he had done and why and how, now that this treasure was gone, he would replace it in his life and heart. "How," he asked me in his letter, "does one ever get back an eagle's feather of this beauty and power once one has given his away?"

Wow. I don't know. Perhaps one simply accommodates his spirit to the fact that the gift has been given. Maybe the feelings of uncertainty about this transaction would be more Native if the focus were on the blessings that had come to him or would come to him as a generous giver. Perhaps . . . well, I don't know. As I said, I have no idea how the greater mechanisms of the powers around us work, or why, and so I'm scarcely in a position to make even a wild guess. I can say for certain that I have never been successful in my own life at seeing what was coming at me, even though sometimes the outcome seemed almost inevitable after the fact.

I wrote all this to my friend, knowing I was offering scarce comfort, no explanation, little hope, no solutions. I simply don't know how one regains a gift like that once it is given away. I finished my letter in the quiet of my snowbound log house and decided to take a walk down by the river to stew on what my friend had asked me and maybe find some peace myself in my futile effort to help him. His problem had now become mine.

I walked through the woods and snow, reached the bank of the river, and watched the wide span of ice stretch and pop. I walked slowly, rolling my friend's problem over and over in my mind. I passed under a huge old cottonwood leaning over the riverbank and blocking my way. I dropped down the short bank and continued along the old channel under the tree. And there on the ground I saw it—a perfect, large, clean, gorgeous . . . eagle feather! It is the only eagle feather I have found in my seventy-five years of life. In disbelief I picked it up, the only human being to touch this beautiful thing that had soared as part of a great, giant presence over our river. It was exquisite. It was an unimaginable thing I held in my hand. I would have been awestruck at any time to find an eagle feather like this, but to find one at this very moment, and such a beautiful one, seemed far beyond physical possibility. I stood there a long time looking at it, praying, crying, imagining, gushing gratitude to Coyote the Trickster, my Little Brother, who had given it to me as an answer to my friend's inscrutable question.

Again I thought of Richard Fool Bull's words about the whiteman's actual religion being a total and unreasonable trust in coincidence. My friend had asked me a difficult question I could not answer: How does one regain a treasure once one has given it away? I had rolled that puzzle around in my mind and gone out to where the answer might be: at the river, with the great old trees, on an ancient Pawnee campground. I asked the question of the great powers there. And with the force of a four-by-four slammed across my forehead—no way possible a coincidence—the Powers gave me the answer: to receive a gift like that, you give away a gift like that.

Few people reading this will believe my story. I know that. Whenever I tell it or write it, I get the same response: "That story about the eagle feather, did that really happen?" Yes. And again and again. Imagine for a moment what your emotions would be the moment you decided—or realized the decision had been made for you—that all you had worked for, all you loved aside from your family and friends, was gone. And not lost, but given by your own hand. The house you love, the land, the trees (tens of thousands that you planted yourself), the river, the pond, the coyotes, turkeys, and eagles ... gone. You gave them away.

How is an asset, a treasure like that ever recovered? It took me a lifetime and a lot of pain and struggle to obtain and develop this paradise, and now it is gone. How can you ever recover it? You can't. But it is still yours. But even better. And more profoundly yours. My wife, Linda, and I returned all we owned—our house and land—to the Pawnee Nation some years ago. Without knowing exactly why, we gave away the most valuable possession we had. Now thousands of Pawnee elders rest here again; now what was once sacred only to us is sacred to an entire people. Now the land rings with prayers and songs of visitors, of the elders themselves, of the Little People and of the spirits. Where we once moved in love, pride, and amazement, we now find awe, inspiration, and blessings. What we may therefore think of as idealistic hope—to give is better than to receive—may actually be little more than practical advice, as basic as, "Buy low; sell high."

How does one acquire greater blessings? Easy. Give greater blessings. I had been given an answer to my friend's and now my question, how does one replace a gift of great value after it has been passed along? Brace yourself. You will be amazed. That very day I walked back up to town and the post office to send my friend his new feather. Now we all understood. I can write about it here, but I have to wonder—does this really make sense to anyone else?

51. *Squaring the Circle*

There are thousands of disjunctures between Native and mainstream culture, some as apparently trivial as how one's coffee is sugared (at Native gatherings like powwows and handgames coffee usually comes presweetened, often a surprise for the non-Native), others as culturally pervasive and individually jarring as the relationship of humans with the matrix of nature around them. I have selected only a few examples, hoping that readers seeing these will extrapolate them to a larger universe, realizing not only how hard it must be for a Native to deal with the mainstream culture but also that it is even harder for a prospective Wannabe to deal with and seek acceptance within the much smaller, much less powerful, much more removed, and, I would argue, so often much more logical, reasonable, and attractive minority culture of Native society.

"Transculturation" (or simply "culturation") used to be the term for the ideal of helping poor, benighted Natives come to understand and adopt the mainstream's glorious and presumably far superior ways. It seemed so reasonable, so logical, so easy: Let's just help the Indians become more like us and so enjoy all the cultural benefits we do. For a Wannabe the problem is the reverse: How do I shed the burdens of what I was born, raised, and educated with and come to understand and operate within the equivalent or, to my mind, even more elegant and civilized forms of Native culture? And how do I gain the understanding, acceptance, even approval of those who have every reason to have nothing whatsoever to do with me or anyone like me? I've said it before: Being a Wannabe is complicated. It certainly isn't easy.

Just as there are degrees of being Indian, being German, or being flexible enough to overcome cultural differences, just as there are differences from person to person, tribe to tribe, region to region, year to year, generation to generation in the degree to which one is mainstream, German, Catholic—or traditional, Oglala, Yuwipi—there are vast differences in the visibility of cultural differences themselves, apart from who the carriers and practitioners of custom are. The conflict between Indian Time and Whiteman Time may be difficult to rationalize or anticipate, but it is obvious in practice: Indians are less obsessed with time than mainstream non-Indians. Differences in concepts of property and gift giving are not as obvious, but they are noticeable when seen from the outside and called irrational, discourteous, or utterly incomprehensible—whether an Indian seeing white indignity at not receiving a Christmas card or a whiteman watching his special gift to an Indian friend being "regifted" to someone he has never met before. It is overt. It may be subtle, but it is not opaque.

Another example of cross-cultural disjuncture is a perception so deeply ingrained that neither the whiteman nor the Indian may recognize its profound impact in understanding themselves and others. I'm not even sure to what extent this historical perception persists today. It is so subliminal that I don't believe anyone could have stated its influence a century and a half ago when it was clearly dominant within Native culture, if not so strongly within the non-Indian mainstream, nor even today when it probably—we can't really know—is in decline within Native culture yet its obverse is overwhelming within white culture.

The factor I have in mind is the shape of things: Native understanding of the world in the round contrasts dramatically with the whiteman's dogged insistence on relentless rectilinearity. With few and notable exceptions the roads in my county are laid out rigidly on a grid, north and south, east and west. As I drive and in out of town, I can measure the annual equinoxes by watching for the sun to rise directly behind me, right over the middle line of the highway through town, and then to set that evening down the middle line of the highway headed west out of town. At noon the sun glares directly down the main street like the shadow on a sundial. At night Polaris stands directly north above that same main street. There are, of course, certain problems in laying out a perfectly right-angled, straight-line grid on something round—say Earth, for example—and so south of our place on the gravel road between our town and Grand Island there is a quarter-mile jog to make the adjustment necessary to keep that flat grid operational on a sphere. To better understand this point, try gluing a sheet of ruled graph paper onto the surface of a basketball.

Just as we worship time, we bow deep to the straight line and the right angle. "He walks the straight and narrow." "I got a square deal." "He is a straight arrow." There is an equal lack of respect for the circular. A quick, short signal for "crazy" is to spin one's forefinger in a spiral around the ear. "Crooked" is dishonest, in contrast with "straight." A good deal is fair and square. A bad deal is crooked. "Going in circles" suggests confusion. A square dealer is honest. Beating around the bush is not. Draw a picture of a house. What are the chances that you depict a round structure? Less than 0.0001 percent, I would guess offhand. Church? Same thing. Barn?

In the 1960s I did a major study of round and multisided barns as a traditional, if minor, architectural concept. The advantages of such designs were so many I could hardly list and discuss them all:

More volume for the same amount of materials (as counterintuitive as it might seem, a circle with a circumference of forty feet has considerably more area than a square with four, ten-foot sides—that is, with the same amount of walling: 127 square feet compared to 100 square feet)

Much stronger construction (a cylinder being more stable than a box; a mailing tube is stronger than a mailing box)

Easier to lay out (no calculating of side lengths or right angles; a
  piece of string tied to a center stake will do the job)
Less wind resistance
More compatible to animal (and human, for that matter) movement
Easier interior function for activities like feeding from a central
  bin or silo
Less waste in building materials ("square" requires "squaring")
Fewer internal obstructions (a cylinder can stand independently
  without internal bracing)

I located as many round and multisided barns as I could in Nebraska—about forty, as I recall. I also examined such barns throughout the United States, many more in the West than the East, even
though fewer barns in general were built east of the Missouri River,
as the general use of and need for barns lessened as modern agriculture moved westward across the continent. I also located and studied
round, octagonal, and multisided houses and put them to the same
considerations. The advantages and efficiencies of this architectural
design are hard to deny, although there are problems with it as with
any design, primarily stemming from builders' unfamiliarity with the
basic ideas of circular building and geometry.

The ultimate question about such construction turned out to be
not so much why anyone would build a round or multisided building
as why would one *not* build a round or multisided building? Far and
away the answers were not architectural or structural but cultural: We
build square barns because that's the way one builds a barn. A barn is
square. A barn that isn't square would look—well—silly. People would
laugh. I can't imagine how I would work things in a round building. I
don't understand how it stands up. I've never seen one like that before.
A round barn? Not for me!

In America things are square. And straight. Wherever they are
not, they are notable. Convincing farmers to convert to soil-saving
contour farming, curving and curling to match the rounded profiles
of the land, and to abandon relentlessly straight courses of plowing

was a major philosophical struggle in American agriculture. Farmers prided themselves on their skill in plowing absolutely straight lines. Plowmen were judged by the rigidity of their furrow. Formal contests with substantial prizes judged that farmer best who plowed the straightest line. And suddenly there were these "perfessor" fellers, these "gummint" people telling farmers to plow in a curve. Round. It seemed to be an insane, upside-down world.

There is a farmstead near here that does not sit compass-straight to the north-south highway. The home and buildings are arrayed at an angle to the straight north-south road that passes by it. People note and comment on it because, well, it just doesn't seem right. A main street through my hometown of Dannebrog, Nebraska, takes two slight angles as it drifts through the tiny village—and since it is Roger Welsch Avenue you can imagine that it does indeed get its share of comments about being "crooked," "off-center," and "on the bias." The nearest town of any size is Grand Island; it was founded as a railroad town and therefore its streets were originally set parallel or at a right angle to the rails. That pattern persisted until the railroad was no longer the central element of interest and economics, whereupon the streets took on the God-given rectitude of absolute east-west, north-south orientation. The curiously angled central business district complicates the divinely inspired, compass-dictated grid around it and never fails to confuse people, inciting confusion and drawing comment.

That is the white world—east and west, north and south, right angles. Straight as an arrow . . . uh, I mean bullet. If you are in a building—especially a house or office but even a library or bookstore—as you read this, stop for a moment and look around you. In most mainstream American contexts you will see squares—square rugs, square floor tiles, square ceiling blocks, square picture frames, square walls, square doors and windows (and through the square panes in the square windows I see a wall of square bricks and blocks), square tables, square machines (I am staring at my computer screen and sheets of paper my printer is spitting out—all square, squared lines, "justified" margins), square files, square file cabinets, gridded air conditioning and heating vents, square books, square television to my right, square bookcases to my left. How does that affect my thinking and outlook on life? I have no idea. It is too arcane for me to fathom. But can we really live in a world of such relentless rectilinearity and remain unaffected by it? That is even harder to fathom. Indians too now live in this squared and straight matrix. But it hasn't always been so. In fact, not all that long ago the Indian world was precisely the opposite—round, curved, oval, rolling, circular.

How much of an effect did that have on the Indians' way of thinking? At least enough to be formalized within religions even now. The Sun Dance arena is round, as is the powwow ground, the opening to the east just as it would have been in a tipi, earth lodge, wickiup, or igloo. It is the circle of life, within the hoop of the universe. The "road" of the Native American Church is not "straight and narrow," but an arc. The sacred drum is round, the "sacred herb," the consecrated host of the Native American Church, is round, it is round stones that are held sacred and that speak to Man, where possible graves are round, and dances are round. On the plains the sod houses were square; among the Inuit both the ice igloo and the sod summer igloo are round.

Indian = round; whiteman = square, with some notable and note-worthy exceptions like the Tiapiah Society Gourd Dance, which is historically modeled on white, rectangular, rank-and-file military ma-neuvers with the intent of capturing through imitation the whiteman's military magic. But still, the rank-and-file Tiapiah dancers move in a circle around the drum.

Black Elk, through the words of John Neihardt, made the issue explicit in *Black Elk Speaks*:

[Square] is a bad way to live, for there can be no power in a square. You have noticed that everything an Indian does is in a circle, and that is because the Power of the World always works in circles, and everything tries to be round. In the old days when we were a strong and happy people, all our power came to us from the sacred hoop of the nation, and so long as the hoop was unbroken, the people flourished.... Everything the Power of the World does is done in a circle. The sky is round and I have heard that the earth is round like a ball, and so are all the stars. The wind, in its greatest power, whirls. Birds make their nests in circles, for theirs is the same religion as ours. The sun comes forth and goes down again in a circle. The moon does the same, and both are round. Even the seasons form a great circle in their changing, and always come back again to where they were. The life of a man is a circle from childhood to childhood, and so it is in everything where power moves. Our teepees were round like the nests of birds, and these were always set in a circle, the nation's hoop, a nest of many nests, where the Great Spirit meant for us to hatch our children. But the Wasichus [whites] have put us in these square boxes. Our power is not in us any more.

Round just can't be right in the whiteman's world. Nor can square ever be right in the Native world. This is not a trivial issue for either culture. It imposes mind-sets on each culture, each and every member of that culture, and absolutely influences currents and countercurrents between cultures. It is hard for us to think outside our circles. Or squares. I once heard a well-educated, bright young woman state that Pawnee pottery had a round rather than flat base because "Indians didn't know how to make flat bottoms on their pottery." Uh, please—how difficult is the concept of a flat bottom on pottery, after all? So then why would the Pawnees have persisted in something as impractical as pottery with round bottoms? If you set it down, it falls over. No, only if you set it down on a flat, level surface like a tabletop does it fall over. But the Pawnees would have set their pottery down not on something flat but on something uneven—the ground. And what would then make more sense than a rounded bottom, which could be set stably in a small depression easily scooped in the ground with a hand or a bone or shell tool? Thus the pot wouldn't fall over, even on a slight incline or uneven ground or . . . anywhere. Far from being impractical, a rounded pot bottom was a logical and practical adaptation to everyday function and environment.

Even more dramatically, what was the impact of moving in only three or four generations from a universe completely understood in the round to one completely diagrammed in the straight and square? Again, I don't know and can't imagine, but it almost certainly had some effect. If we in the mainstream do not even notice how rigid our geometry is, can it be any different within Indian society? Do Indians have any impression at all of the enormous transition that has taken place in their cosmology over the past couple of generations? Are there vestiges of the old ways still submerged within individual personalities or tribal ethnologies? What does an Indian feel in his or her soul when he or she is in the tipi at a prayer meeting or a round community hall or school meeting room built on the model of the earth lodge, in the powwow circle, or under the Sun Dance arbor? Echoes from the past? If not, why then do these round structures persist in a context where straight lines and right angles so totally dominate every other structure and pattern in life and environment?

52. *So, How Different Are We?*

Mentioning, much less discussing, racial differences is taboo in today's America, another manifestation of rampant egalitarianism. We are all supposed to be the same. Well, we are not. Men are not the same as women. I find that obvious, but then I'm old-fashioned, I guess. Indians are not the same as other races—I cringe and look over my shoulder even as I write those words that are not supposed to be said or written. And, all differences are not cultural. That is to say, there *are* physical differences between races, just as there are between genders. This does not lead to the conclusion that one race is therefore inferior to another, or superior. Just different. What's so wrong with that?

I have an adopted daughter who is Native. She came to us when she was an infant, and almost immediately we were concerned that she might have been abused when she was in institutional care (which was the only care she had had until she became my daughter). I hope I do not embarrass her here with what could be seen as a rather personal physical detail, but I think it is worth mentioning as an example of a clear difference between races and one that persists in an atmosphere of mainstream ignorance. When she came to us as an infant, we found at the base of her spine a large, vivid bruise. We rushed her to a doctor, worried about her health but also concerned that a later examination might suggest that *we* had been the abusers. That was almost fifty years ago, so my memory is not clear on the exact details, but I have a vague recollection that our doctor was unsure of what had caused the bruise or when, but he did some investigation and learned that it was natural. It even has a name—the Mongoloid spot—and it is a common phenomenon with Native babies that quickly fades away with age. Other physical features are common and unmistakable. Why do we pretend they are not? Especially when the features, if not the differences, might be important in dealing with who we are? Or who *they* are? Whoever "they" happen to be.

Enough beating around the bush. Let's talk alcohol. Indians do. It's not as if *they* have missed the obvious. Perhaps that is another distinctive feature of Indians—they are honest about the obvious. More likely, it is like Richard Fool Bull's description of how Natives perceive patterns and powers where the whiteman sees only coincidence: "It is within all of us but the white man has had it educated out of him." One of the reasons I have enjoyed being accepted within Native circles is that I have heard discussions about the peculiarities of the whiteman. It is always a bit unsettling, to be sure, because I naturally wonder if my friends are talking about *me* when, for example, they discuss why white men smell so bad. The agreement in at least one such discussion at an Omaha drum where I was sitting was that it's because of our body hair. On that occasion I was glad to be wearing a long-sleeved shirt! Various clues within the conversation suggested that I was not the topic of the conversation but was simply being included as one of the curious speculators—actually a fairly flattering position to be in, as I considered it even then. We could talk together about why white people smell bad because . . . I am not a whiteman. I'll take that as a compliment any day.

I also sat in on many conversations about the devastation caused by alcohol in Indian society and why it seems to be so much more a curse with Indians than within non-Indian societies. Perhaps this is the Es-Ex Factor at work once again: what might be a forbidden topic outside of Native circles is permitted when it is Indians considering the problem. That is, Indians do not want outsiders showcasing the problem of alcoholism within Native culture, but it is too obvious and pernicious for them to ignore.

And it must be noted, they do not ignore it. No one works harder at avoiding, correcting, mitigating, and dealing with the problem than Natives themselves. Most reservation governments have imposed prohibition on their own people on their own lands; while there are Native bootleggers and still operators, the worst of the problem is non-Indians profiting from alcohol sales on the margins of reservations (as in the notorious White Clay, Nebraska, where liquor sellers prey on the residents of the Pine Ridge Reservation, which is within walking distance, just across the Nebraska–South Dakota state line).

Why? Why does alcohol seem to be so much more destructive to Native societies than white? I have heard various Indians suggest that a cause could be the poor diet so prevalent on the desperately poor reservations and in urban Indian communities. Where "commodity foods" are distributed to Indians, the governmental consideration is not what foods would be best for a healthy diet but what foods happen to be in surplus. Or is Indians' difficulty with alcohol a cultural consideration? Again, I have heard Indians talk about what they see on television: nicely dressed non-Indians plucking canapés from waiters' trays, swirling a dry martini, munching the olive, and conversing with elegant and aristocratic people on balconies overlooking magnificent urban skylines. That sure isn't the way life and drinking are on reservations! Perhaps it is the type of alcohol available in Indian communities—high in alcohol, low in quality, drunk not for social elegance but for rapid escape from the depressing context of the poorest areas of our nation. Or is the plague of alcoholism within the Indian population a painful consequence of poverty, despair, prejudice, frustration, alienation, or cultural change imposed too fast (if imposed cultural change ever occurs at an acceptable pace)? Or all of those things? I can't imagine how such factors could be quantified.

Could this weakness to the effects of alcohol be a matter of genetic disposition? If it is taboo in today's culture to speak of racial differences, it is even more dangerous to bring up the notion of genetics and genetic dispositions. Small wonder: heredity has been used in Western culture for centuries to suggest the inferiority of target groups. And yet within Indian circles one can't help but notice the difference. My German ancestors, for example, have been drinking alcohol for generations. Centuries. Probably even millennia. As often as not they drank before battle, intensifying the process of genetic selection. If your Viking or Vandal great-great-great-grandfather couldn't handle alcohol, heading into battle with his war axe might have been a terminal impairment. And thus endeth that branch of the family tree. As a result, somewhere out there on the twenty-first-century hereditary twig is me, perfectly capable of metabolizing substantial quantities of bourbon and still maintaining at least verticality and, usually, a sense of civility in social situations. On the other hand, most of my Native friends' family experiences with alcohol are remarkably recent and occasionally but not customarily before lethal combat. Isn't it at least conceivable, worth considering, that there is a physical element to the differences between the Germanic and Native genetic dispositions for dealing with alcohol?

I was once chilled when sitting at a handgame drum next to a dear friend of mine, as sweet and gentle a man as I ever knew. I had read in the newspaper earlier that week that a man with his same name had allegedly killed a law enforcement officer on the reservation. By way of joking, I said, "Russell, I read about that policeman who was killed on the reservation by that guy with the same name as you. He is going to give you a bad reputation. Is he maybe one of your relatives?"

Sweet, gentle Russell said, "Roger, that is me. Never drink alcohol with me. In fact, never drink alcohol with any Indians. It can be dangerous." I had nothing more to say, and Russell didn't need to say anything more. I have had white friends who self-destructed with the agency of alcohol. I've had white friends die and, sadly, I have had white friends who killed—and I mean murder, not just automotive manslaughter—when their judgment was blurred by alcohol. I have had Indian friends who are connoisseurs of fine single malt scotches and with whom I have spent quiet, civilized evenings sipping at excellent whiskies. Generalizations are always put to the test by such contrasts. But anyone who has spent time within the Indian community knows there is a problem there with alcohol. Something is wrong. I don't know what it is. I don't know if anyone does. Is there a genetic disposition within mainstream white culture that is absent within Native culture? Or is it the other way around? Is there a Native "allergy" or a non-Indian immunity to this long cherished but incredibly toxic product? The point in these pages is that a Wannabe needs to be aware of this problem, not make it worse, avoid it, never break a tribe's rules about alcohol, and mind your own business otherwise.

53. *What We See*

Differences exist between any two different cultures. There are differences between genders. And people. My wife, Linda, is an artist; she sees the world in terms of visual frames. She sees things I do not see. My world is about stories and words; I have a feel for hearing and remembering good stories when I forget everything else. (I should also note that I still rely on Linda for her sense of precisely the right wording of a truly good story. While I can remember the narrative in its widest outline, for the specific wording that makes it more than just a story I depend on her.) I enjoy hearing stories and I enjoy telling stories. Above all, I see the world in terms of its stories. We see the world not at all for what is (presuming there is such a thing as "what is") but only for what has meaning for each of us as individuals and as products of a specific culture.

When my son Chris was a toddler, we lived in a house surrounded on three sides by horse pasture. Horses fascinated Chris and they therefore defined his world. We were once visiting my parents' home when Chris began to point insistently at the cupboards in my mother's kitchen and literally scream over and over again, "Horsie! Horsie! Horsie!" But there was no horse. Not even a picture of a horse. I looked carefully. No horse. But Chris insisted. What could he possibly be seeing? Finally I lifted him up and, holding him horizontally like a metal detector, moved him toward the area of the cupboards where he indicated an interest.

Finally he pushed his forefinger against a plastic toaster cover on the cupboard. I looked closely at the cover. Buried almost microscopically in a geometric pattern, there it was—a cubistic image of tiny horses. My natural conclusion, of course, was that my son was a genius, perceptive beyond normal human capabilities. The truth was that his world didn't include things like red lights at busy intersections or flashing low-oil warning lights on automobile instrument panels, clouds signaling approaching hailstorms, ten-dollar bills lying under a park bench, attractive members of the opposite sex in skimpy beachwear, snakes sunning on a hiking path, an old friend at a corner table in a crowded tavern . . . the things that might attract the attention of an adult in our culture. Chris saw a world in which "horsies" were paramount.

All of which is to say that many of the mystic skills attributed to the Noble Savage were not some sort of magical talents that were the birthright of Natives but simply a matter of what was important and noteworthy in their environment. Think, for example, of the oft-cited skills of Native trackers and scouts. The Lone Ranger was a pretty savvy gent, to be sure, but when it came to tracking down the bad guys or knowing from the tracks exactly when the stagecoach last passed this way, it was up to Tonto to put his ear and eye to the ground. That has become a Hollywood Indian joke now and is even resented by many modern Natives, but like so many stereotypes, it had some foundation in fact and history. It was not by mistake or misunderstanding that the U.S. Army recruited and widely used Indian scouts, most notably my kin among the Pawnee Nation. Indians saw the world in terms useful to themselves and the military but not immediately obvious to non-Indians, and so they looked . . . mysterious. Indians were great trackers and scouts. But those were skills culturally taught, learned, and practiced, not somehow mystically and genetically inherited.

54. *Indians and Deeper Truths*

More resented, more pernicious than stereotypes of Native tracking skills is the less specific whiteman's notion that Indians are somehow supernaturally imbued with deep mystical insights. I am scarcely in a position to get huffy about this since my own religious life, and for that matter my understanding of life and the human role in this earth's processes, has been profoundly affected by Native religion. There are at least two factors in operation behind the widespread interest, participation, and involvement of the whiteman in Native spiritual issues: the profoundly powerful nature of Native religions and the generally unsatisfactory nature and political structure of mainstream non-Indian religions. Especially among the young, an experience in Native religion or even the slightest exposure to the surface elements of Native philosophy can have a life-changing impact. Indians frequently dismiss this as so much romantic nonsense, but that is, in part at least, because the Native spiritual world is a matter of course from their perspective.

Moreover, many Natives resent the constant assault on their culture, spiritual and material, by the whiteman. A further complication is that the whiteman's preemption of Native rituals and philosophies is often for profit—truly a blasphemy—and in the process of adapting them commercially they become sadly distorted. Witness recent New Wave theft and abuse of the cleansing nature of the sweat lodge. Unfortunately, the result may be tragedies such as the one at Sedona, Arizona, where on October 2, 2009, a botched sweat lodge ceremony by non-Native, inept, high-dollar, commercial "ritualists" who provided ethnotourists a "sweat lodge experience" resulted in two dead, nineteen hospitalized. In this way, "spirit centers" too often become seen not as desecrations of Native culture and religion but as examples of the inherent error of Native beliefs and customs. That is, people who see reports of such misuse of the sweat lodge and presume that the problem is all this claptrap about the sweat lodge, *not* the preemption and abuse of the ritual and instrument by pathetic clowns. Would it make sense to discuss the Catholic Mass as an example of poor nutrition and alcohol abuse? Then why is Native use of sanctified objects like the peyote cactus so often thought of as abuse of "controlled substances"? I can attest from personal experience that that is absolutely not true and that the misuse and abuse of substances like tobacco and peyote, whether by Indians or non-Indians, is absolutely contrary to their proper and reverent use and function within the Native American Church.

Native spirituality and spiritual knowledge are therefore subject to double misinterpretation: whites misunderstand and abuse them as commercially exploitable or are overly romantic about their inherent nature and efficacy, while Indians accept them as the normal way of such things and dismiss the idea that they are anything at all out of the ordinary. To Natives, they are special and sacred and yet still pretty much the norm. Traditional elders are surprised that an outsider, even a Wannabe like me, would not take for granted the presumed facts that rocks are alive and speak to us, that there are "Little People" still living around us in deep woods and remote barrens, just as they always have, and that animals play an active role in our destinies and have a very special relationship to humans, acting as emissaries, protectors, seers, or threats beyond the physical. Many young and modern Indians, to be sure, dismiss notions like "special medicine" as foolish superstition; others, frequently elders but even some younger Natives, accept them as such obvious truth they are not worth mentioning or, knowing they are held by the outside world to be ridiculous myths, keep such beliefs to themselves.

Such beliefs are so different from the thinking of mainstream Americans (who have their own, equally ridiculous superstitions, I should note) that one might think it is hard for Wannabes to cross the chasm from "science, good sense, and true religion" to outright "superstition" or "magic." All it takes, however, is one conversation with a rock, undeniable evidence of activities by Little People, or a couple of opportunities to experience the remarkable and unavoidably genuine relationships between animals and Indians to have one's long and confidently held attitudes shaken, if not changed. I have seen absolutely incredible encounters between bison, who often have a special importance to Plains Native peoples, and Indians that I would have sworn beforehand were completely impossible. But the impossible did happen. My Indian friends and kin speak of these occasions and events, but rarely in non-Indian contexts, knowing the skepticism and even ridicule that would almost surely result.

How can we explain those kinds of phenomena? More often than not, we don't. We don't even talk about them. We can't explain what we can't explain. They can only be accepted as matter of course, dismissed as serendipity, or quietly held as secrets within a circle of sympathetic minds. I am old enough and confident enough to share at least a couple of the dozens, perhaps hundreds, of such experiences I have had or have seen that have convinced me of what should be obvious to everyone: I don't know everything, and neither do you. And neither does anyone else.

As I write this, I am having cardiac problems and will be headed to the hospital shortly for the installation of a pacemaker. That is remarkable technology. For all the joking I am doing about it ("I am holding out for a pacemaker–TV remote combination—or at least a garage door opener") the truth is that I am very impressed by the ingenuity of humankind in the development of such machinery and the skills of the people who can install bionic parts in the human body.

The first time I had a "cardiac event" (as it is gently referred to), like most men I delayed telling Linda about it for a week or so, until I had no choice but to pack a hospital bag and head for our family doctor's office, knowing full well I wouldn't be going home for a while. I was rushed from the GP's office to the nearby hospital emergency room and treatment began at once. There was concern not only about the irregularity of my heartbeat but also about the possibility of clotting that could have taken place during the unnecessarily long delay in getting proper care. The medical priorities were to stabilize my blood pressure, regularize my pulse, restore the sequence of my heart's contractions, and slowly erode the blood clot in my heart without dislodging it.

Things didn't go well. Days passed and nothing seemed to be progressing in my treatments. Heart monitors showed no progress. Finally the cardiologist came to my bedside and listed a series of unpleasant options, each worse than the other, it seemed. He said that if there was no progress by the next morning, more drastic procedures would be necessary. I decided to call in my own treatment protocol and asked my wife to call my Omaha son, who is a Native American Church "roadman" (or church ceremony leader), and ask him to do what he could. My personal religious history is one of general skepticism. While Native religions had already had a profound influence on me, I approached each and every change in my firmly and fondly held cynicism with determination not to give up my lifelong doubts. At that point I considered prayer a personal comfort of questionable theological effectiveness—a kind of "what harm can it do?" attitude.

My son Jeff told Linda that he had that very day received a gift of blessed tobacco and he would instantly burn some while praying for me, and that night my Omaha family would pray and sing for me. Well, that's nice. And I appreciated his love and care. After all, what harm could it do?

Within the hour a nurse rushed into my room to check the monitors, which seemed to be malfunctioning; they were showing that my heart had suddenly kicked into "sinus," or normal, rhythm. Hmmm. In the morning the cardiologist came in to tell me that overnight everything had somehow jumped back into suitable synchronization, and while they would hold me awhile to make sure the new status remained stable, my heart had somehow gone back to normal. He asked if I had any idea what had happened to cause the reversion, and I admitted to the doctor that I had asked Linda to call my son Jeff and ask for Native American Church prayers and rituals and they had apparently started to work the moment he began them. Wisely, the cardiologist said only, "I want that man's phone number."

Coincidence. Could be coincidence. But even less likely is another experience I had with my son Jeff that is simply too preposterous for mere chance. I was fortunate enough for thirteen years to be associated with Charles Kuralt as an essayist on his wonderful creation CBS *News Sunday Morning*. Millions of people got used to seeing my face on their television screen on Sunday mornings. I received letters and notes from a lot of them, almost all friendly. One day I found a large package at our post office, and when I opened it I found a beautiful pipestone pipe. An enclosed note explained that the sender had had this pipe for many years and when he saw my image on his television screen, he had this overwhelming feeling that I should have that pipe. So almost against his will, he was sending it to me. He had no idea why.

Well, that was nice but, you'll have to admit, a bit strange. I leaned the pipe against the side of our living room fireplace and there it stood for a decade or more, gathering dust and just being beautiful. I almost forgot it was there. But then one day I got a curious feeling myself that I should dust the pipe off, package it, and send it to my son Jeff. Almost against my will and certainly without any particular explainable motivation. I didn't hear from Jeff for some time. It is not unusual not to get a response to a gift in Indian contexts because it is the giver, after all, who is the recipient of any presumed blessings.

Many months later I was at the Omaha powwow and camped in the side yard of my sister-in-law Naomi, mother of my son Jeff. I wondered aloud if he had received the pipe because he still hadn't said anything. As I recall, he never did, either; it was his beautiful wife and my daughter-in-law, Colleen, who said, why yes, Jeff had received the pipe. In fact, he had been working with a Winnebago road man on the songs and complications of the particular "fireplace" or church mechanism, its songs, rituals, and "instruments," and had gone to an uncle of his to ask what kind of gift would be appropriate for his teacher by way of thanks for the guidance. His uncle told him a pipe would be in order.

Jeff didn't know where to obtain a pipe, but someone had told him that a cache of pipestone had been buried many years before for just such an occasion; then it could not be located. In fact, there were indications that it might have been paved over under a concrete driveway and might not become available for many years. Frustrated, Jeff and his uncle returned to his home in Omaha for the evening and found waiting for them . . . my package. Jeff said, "I wonder what Dad Roger sent us," and his uncle matter-of-factly said, "I bet it's the pipe you need." No one there had any way of knowing what was in that package.

Jeff opened it to find the pipe. He made some adjustments to it—it was too ornate for his taste or for church use—and used it as the gift to his mentor. I asked Jeff if he wasn't, well, surprised that precisely at the moment he needed a pipe, he received a pipe. Didn't that strike him as a remarkable coincidence? Because it certainly struck *me* that way. He said no, he didn't. I told him that a person I had never met sent me that pipe many years before and that suddenly, out of nowhere, I had had this feeling I was to send it to him, and then there it was, on precisely the day many years later that he needed that pipe. How can we account for so remarkable a series of events? Surely there are limits to coincidence.

Jeff had no explanation for it but did mention his suspicion that it was his natural father and my brother Alfred "Buddy" Gilpin Jr. who, from "over the fourth hill," that mysterious place where we go after death, had directed me to send that pipe, and before that it was Wakonda, the Great Mysterious, who had known what that pipe was destined for and had instructed some stranger in Colorado to send it to me.

Would it be any more logical to consider all that coincidence than to see it as something designed and directed? Not for me. Or for Jeff.

I have no other way to understand it. For Jeff it was simply the natural course of things, directed by the remarkable irony inherent in the powers within the Native cosmogony; for me the event was another of the undeniable facts I encountered as a Wannabe that became a part of my own understanding of how the universe works.

55. *Conclusions*

So, what are we to make of all this? Are Wannabes a good thing or a pain in the rear? And if so (either option!) for whom, the Indians or the Wannabes? Is there anything to be learned from Indians? From cross-cultural exploration? Or are we too late to take lessons from the frayed relationships between Native Americans and, as my comedian Hochunk brother Louie likes to describe us, "boat people"? Where is all this headed, or are we doomed to live with this tragic historical failure, this wretched failure to learn, forever? Should we non-Indians, and for that matter Indians, simply try to forget the details and hope that sooner than later the Indians will just fade away, lost in the genetic stew, and all Wannabe questions will disappear along with them? Or will the whiteman destroy himself or enough natural resources that, as the Lakotas predict, he will simply go away and Native Americans will again reclaim what is rightfully theirs—this land? Why do some of us become Wannabes? What is it we want? Or need? What can we do to make our role useful to ourselves and to our Native friends and relatives, or can we do anything at all? What are Natives to make of all these non-Indians hanging around eating fry bread, sitting in the circle at prayer meetings, learning and singing their songs, perhaps learning their language so well that they wind up teaching it back to the tribe's own young? Writing books? What more is there to learn? What haven't we seen? What have we foolishly dismissed as coincidence or superstition? Is it too late for us to learn? Or too early?

To begin with, or perhaps better to end with, my own hope is that we can stop making the same mistakes over and over, mistakes that Columbus, Cortez, George Washington, Abraham Lincoln, state historical societies, anthropology professors, historians, grave robbers, artifact collectors, reenactors, legislators and legislatures, do-gooders, do-badders, and churches have made. Indians are human beings who can and should expect the civilities and general respect due any other human being. Not as "charity" or "tolerance" but as a human right. Perhaps they are not possessed of some mystic truth hidden in crystals and feathers that we can coax into our own bag of tricks through imitation, but just like any other single person or entire nation or society, they almost certainly know something I do not. Something that would be useful or even just interesting to me, perhaps something as trivial as the knowledge that chewing on a willow stick on a river bank while fishing can ease a headache or that milkweed soup or cattail asparagus is damn fine campfire fare when everything else has been lost in the rapids after the canoe capsized. Or something as cosmic as "there is a god" and "that god has a remarkable sense of humor."

Perhaps from the isolated enclaves of reservations, Indian towns, single log huts down unmarked roads on South Dakota reservations, in quiet gatherings at urban Indian centers, in hushed conversations with a new brother while sitting on a dark curb in a reservation town staring at a flat tire and knowing there is no tire jack or spare tire, you too will learn something so jarring, be changed so fundamentally that life will never be the same for you. Maybe even never the same for others who learn through you. It can happen. I know that for a fact, because it has happened to me.

From ancient ways of thinking that persist in the isolation of oppression and poverty and in the obscurity of a dying language, by the grace of one man's or one people's generosity we can learn why America is better off as an all-you-can-eat buffet than a culture-leveling melting pot. As Wannabes perhaps we can better see the absurdity of official languages, official religions, and oppressive majority rule, when a far better course to enlightenment and survival—even delight!—is a diversity of wealth and of ideas and ways. From ancient societies maybe we can again learn the meaning of family and the value of elders. In becoming aware of how painfully arrogant and ignorant we are, we can perhaps regain the gift of humility. In beautiful religions and cultures we are reminded that even great America is nonetheless a human construction and a vulnerable one at that, more likely to fail from greed, hate, ignorance, and pride than from any outside attack. Rome, Greece, the dynasties of China, Egypt, and the Incas, and the Third Reich all thought themselves inevitable, invulnerable, exceptional, and eternal, a product of the will of the gods, a manifest destiny, and yet they are gone. Our empire is no more "God's will" than theirs were. Or no less. That is visible in the squandering of our precious and irreplaceable resources, our constant warring, and our selection of our leadership more, it seems, for its comforting stupidity than for its commanding virtue or wisdom. The words of Lakota elders that the whiteman can be dismissed as a passing phenomenon may be more a matter of prescience than humor. Very early in my folklore and museological studies I began to see old and different ways not as errors to be overcome but as alternate technology that may be out of fashion for the moment or even obsolete but is worth knowing and remembering for a time when it might again be useful.

Just imagine, insofar as you can, what we don't know. One day spent among the Inuit is an introduction to a world of knowledge otherwise unimaginable. The technology of harnessing dogs, much less the making of a sled for a team, is beyond our invention no matter how "well educated" we are. Mr. Richard Fool Bull's vast knowledge of medical and food plants was encyclopedic. Virtually any Omaha's song repertoire is greater than the finest and most accomplished operatic singer's. And yet when we run up against such remarkable knowledge, as often as not we dismiss it as unworthy of knowing. Like the homesteader on the plains or the Viking in a Greenland settlement, we starve in the midst of a bountiful garden.

Some of my first work in folklore was in the area of folk architecture—round barns, sod houses, log houses, baled-hay construction—the humblest of buildings erected by the most unsophisticated of designers and builders. When I came out the other end of each and every new study, however, my opinion had turned 180 degrees. What I had approached at first as expedient, crude, and primitive turned out to be a remarkable technology when examined with any care at all. The round barn was not just rare and peculiar but structural and utilitarian genius, too early abandoned as the barn frontier was reached (a bit west of the Missouri River and out onto the Great Plains) and barns were no longer practical or were rapidly became impractical for that region's farming system and resources. There is an enormous difference, I insist, between the log *cabin*, with its unpeeled logs and rude corners, meant for only short habitation before falling in rot and mold back into the earth, and the log *house*, with debarked and squared logs and carefully cut corner notches ingeniously designed to exclude moisture and long outlive the builder. My own log house, just below where I sit as I write this, down along the Loup River bottoms was built by a Civil War veteran named Tom Bishop in 1872. It is as solid now as it was when Bishop and his family lived in it. That is not a hut, not a cabin. It is a *house*, and it will outlive me as it did him. It will also outlive every modern house built in this entire county since the Second World War. Which, then, is the "primitive" technology?

The plains sod house is almost universally depicted as uncomfortable, filthy, temporary, and fragile. Many were. The construction method was, after all, geographically limited—to build a sod house one needs suitable sod. Weather is hard on unshielded sod walls, and yet I have found in my lifetime dozens that stood up well into their hundredth year. Can that be hoped for the modern modular, manufactured, trailer, or double-wide house? The sod house spoke to its geography, times, and resources better than one might expect, just as the Omaha, Ponca, and Pawnee earth lodge did before that (and with much the same construction system, one might note). And certainly better than the modular, manufactured, trailer, or double-wide house mentioned before. Homesteaders new to the plains needed something to protect a family from the wind, heat, cold, and attack, from the crushing sky and withering distances. The sod house did that, and well.

When the logs were all cut and gone, when the earth no longer yielded suitable sod, where there was no clay or fuel for firing bricks, beyond the lines of supply—that is, in Nebraska's Sandhills—the baled-hay house was invented. Cheap, easily and quickly built, sturdy, safe, quiet, warm in the winter, cool in the summer, baled-hay houses were never numerous in the sparsely populated, largest sand dune area in the Western Hemisphere, but again, the technology served its purpose. Some still stand and are lived in today. In fact, my early research into this construction method has led to a boom in new baled-hay construction. (Look up "baled-straw [or baled-hay] construction" on the web; the form is far from dead.) If I ever found myself in a situation where I needed to build quickly a solid, comfortable, inexpensive shelter (and if I were not given another fine old oak and walnut log house like Mr. Bishop's) there's not a doubt in my mind but that I would turn to baled-hay construction.

At every turn in my curiosity and research, as I examined one thing after another in traditional culture, gone or persistent, I found that I was looking not at failed experiments but genius and complex technology, set aside for the moment on the shelves of history but with every promise of one day being useful again. Food, weapons, tools, architecture, religion, song, medicine . . . doesn't matter.

I once worked as a consultant for the Living History Farms complex east of Des Moines, Iowa, in its earliest planning stages. On one occasion we were wrestling with the problem of where agriculture was likely to go in the future. Reconstruction of the historical farm of 1820 and initial settlement was pretty well planned and in development; the farm of 1890 or shortly thereafter, anticipating the transition from animal power to steam and internal combustion power, was even easier to reconstruct since that history was relatively recent; but what of the farm of the "future"? (I place the word in quotation marks because at the time the future was 2000.) Would the farm of the future be a huge, industrial, petrochemical intensive, technologically complex factory? All of it was guesswork at the time, and our task was to guess.

As a folklorist, not an agriculturist, futurist, or scientist, my vision was different from the vision of those who were ag experts—different enough, in fact, to be ignored. I suggested that as museum visitors took the path from the farm of 1900 to the farm of the future, there should be a fork in the road, one to Farm of the Future A and the second to Farm of the Future B. Path A would go to the technologically based factory farm of the futurists' ag-industrial dreams; Path B would lead the visitor back to the farm of 1820, a small subsistence farm that could survive the aftermath of the ruinous soil and resource (especially water) mining technologies of Future Farm A. I believe that in Nebraska we are moving resolutely toward path B.

56. *Repositories of Wisdom*

How many worlds of information from the Native past and present were lost to the whiteman because of his arrogance and ignorance? How many troves of information are we still losing day after day by not listening to the wisdom of intellectual giants like Fool Bull, Iron Shell, Charles Trimble, Louie LaRose, Joseph Marshall, Francis Morris, and hundreds of others like them? Where would we be today if the white invaders in this hemisphere had listened and learned? What worlds of knowledge were in the libraries of Incan, Mayan, and Aztec codices gathered, piled, and burned by the Spanish, who settled only for gold and slaves instead of far more valuable knowledge? What did the Pawnees, Lakotas, Winnebagos, and Omahas have in their oral histories that might have solved the mysteries about possible proto-explorers of the Western Hemisphere? Chinese? Welsh? Vikings? Having ignored those questions before, we now have no answers and have to rely instead on the speculation of crackpots and, in turn, their critics.

Like the Mayans, the Pawnees were constant and vigilant astronomers in a day when the night skies were brilliant, and perhaps when cosmic events took place about which we now have no knowledge at all. What did they know that we don't? Surely something. We, after all, know so little. As it is, a good deal of our modern pharmacopoeia originated in aboriginal and ancient plant uses—digitalis, aspirin, penicillin. What has been lost through the insolence, nonsense, and ridicule of bleeders, alchemists, patent-medicine peddlers, and quacks? What foods would we have known if our ancestors had listened and learned? What ideas and theories of aesthetics and form in art? How many songs have we lost? What literature? What wisdom? What truth?

How can our insistence on ignorance possibly continue? And yet it does. I call it the Limbaugh Syndrome: if Rush Limbaugh doesn't know it, then it can't be true. That is, his presumption has become the presumption of his enormous following, too. Even when his random or drug-induced fantasies are immediately and apparently false or later proven to be completely erroneous, since it is Rush's idea, crazy or not, it is embraced. There are worlds of things I don't know; there are galaxies that a drug-addled blowhard like Limbaugh doesn't know. I don't listen to this clown any more than I would to the gibbering of sparrow, but I was once trapped in a car with a friend who hung on Limbaugh's every word. Limbaugh was ridiculing the idea of global warming, buffoonishly wondering if these ignorant scientists think the earth is warming up because they have the temperature records that cavemen and Indians kept, as shown on the thermometers on their cave and tipi walls. Hahahahaha.

See? Limbaugh doesn't know how temperatures and climates of the past can be determined, so it follows, in this manner of thinking, that no one does. Because Rush knows everything . . . He doesn't know about tree ring studies, lake bottom silt samplings, ice cap drill core collections, geologic stratigraphy. Limbaugh doesn't know about such things . . . so they don't exist.

I once heard an anthropological expert comment on a huge glacial boulder that sits on a pedestal outside the main (north) door of Morrill Hall, the Nebraska Museum, on the university campus in Lincoln. He stroked his beard thoughtfully and concluded it was a modern fake, because Indians could not have carved the petroglyphs on it with the primitive tools available to them. The stone is extremely hard pre-Cambrian gneiss, an erratic carried to Nebraska (Cedar County) by the great glaciers. The petroglyph carvings (or more precisely, rubbings and peckings) are geometric patterns, lines, grooves (possibly for tool fabrication), some probable animal and bird effigies, and the almost universal human expression of self-realization—a handprint!

The expert insisted that because the Indians of the proposed time of the boulder—post-Pleistocene?—had only stone and wood tools, they could scarcely have incised the images into this extremely hard stone. I noted that the Egyptians built the pyramids with only copper tools. And that nothing is harder on the Mohs scale than diamonds, but we cut diamonds. With other diamonds. Why couldn't a Plains proto-Indian have carved the figures on the boulder essentially using grinding powder and fine grit from that same boulder? That is, a hardwood peg like oak or Osage orange dipped and pointed with minute fragments—dust and grains of the equally hard rock—from the boulder itself could have been used with patient pecking to cut into the boulder itself, at the same time and in the same process producing more of the small grit that could be used for even more incising. That, after all, is pretty much how it is done. Everywhere. By many peoples from then to now. He had no answer to my question, or for that matter, no respect for my reasoning behind it. But since he didn't know about such techniques, and his culture and science are presumed to be so superior, he presumed no one could know them, least of all a bunch of ignorant, "primitive" natives.

And that from a professor of anthropology.

Ancient technology was ancient, to be sure, and slower, perhaps one could even say primitive, but to dismiss it as impossible is a real mistake in grasping the nature of technology. But milkweed soup, pecking at rocks, log houses, and round barns are limited, perhaps trivial examples and examples only of alternate technology, of thinking differently about small physical problems. That kind of trivia is not at the heart of Wannabeism. No serious Wannabe I know considers issues like those to be a central motivation. Which is not to diminish the interest, fun, wisdom, and surprise of each and every one of the smallest details of learning about any other culture. But for many of us the most remarkable and important results of being a Wannabe are the enormous questions about the nature of life and the powers that swirl around us on this earth, the things that seem beyond our understanding, where Native culture can sometimes be the granite dust on the end of the pecking stick that allows us to penetrate just a fraction of a centimeter deeper into the mysteries hidden within the greater rock.

In the end, that is, to my mind, the rationale for the Wannabe—to learn greater truths. The small, surprising bits of information that come to the cultural traveler along the way—the remarkable advantages for parent and child of the cradle board, for example, or the intelligent handling of a campfire (a nice, big, open fire for poking, staring into, and warming, but a small shovelful of coals carried away from the traffic of the camp for cooking—I learned that from my aunt Lillian Sheridan in 1967)—are delights that serve the Wannabe for a lifetime, but ultimately it is the greater experiences and changes in the worldview of the Wannabe that are life changing and perhaps, hopefully, eventually even society changing.

In the field of agriculture there are institutional seed banks where diverse varieties of beans, corn, squash, wheat, whatever are preserved not simply as a matter of idle curiosity but as fallback sources of genetic varieties that may be needed later. I see cultural enclaves like Native tribes as the same kind of repository. I will never understand the fools who resent new ideas, perhaps from cultures new to them; the more ideas and directions that are available and explored, the better the chances of refining, fine-tuning, and improving one's life and culture. And therefore the life and culture of all of us. Petrification is the final stage of death for a culture as surely as it was for the dinosaurs. To invite that kind of oblivion willingly has no excuse. Exposure to and appreciation of other ways changes us in ways that cannot be predicted, because we don't recognize or understand them until we are suddenly smack in the middle of the change. Suddenly we need something we couldn't possibly have anticipated, and we can only hope that someone, somewhere has, even by accident, saved that crucial element.

Who could argue that in coming to understand Native appreciation of the role of elders, or for that matter children, in the family structure our own families might be strengthened? In my own experience, I was confronted with the problem of a child who was going through the usual gauntlet of misery offered up by childhood and adolescence, exacerbated in our case by the factors of the child being adopted and being Native. After trying all the mainstream solutions, I began to think in terms of my Indian friends and how they faced similar problems in their families. Children who are problems or have special needs are frequently "farmed out" to another family. Sometimes it is simply a child with a special need, one perhaps who has a talent for singing traditional Native songs but has no source of instruction within the family. The child is simply sent off to live with another family for a while, the idea being that perhaps just the change of scene might give a new direction to the child's life, offer a time to reassess options, or even provide those new opportunities. The white mainstream often interprets that Indian process as a lack of love for children, something like casting children aside, but precisely the opposite is true: it is an act of love.

In my case, I was fortunate to have Comanche friends in Oklahoma. They raised horses. My daughter loved horses. So uneasily I asked my friends if they would take my daughter for a summer, put her to work, let her work with horses, let her be away from us—her mother, her father, her siblings—for just a while, to let her live within a Native family, let her learn how to get along with the horses, another tribe, and another family. And that's what we did. I'm not sure the experience turned my daughter around, but it certainly did her no harm. And it widened her world, always an asset.

As I have noted, we often think of our own culture not as a culture among other cultures but as the "natural" or "normal" way of doing things. Moving across cultural lines into another society makes it clear that this is a false perception, that there are many, equally legitimate, sometimes more useful ways to see things. Would myopic fundamentalists be quite so certain that they want creationism taught in the schools if they had any idea at all that theirs is only *one* story of creation and that there are dozens, maybe hundreds of other ideas about how the world came into being and humans came to populate it? Each as sacred, venerable, and "true" as their own? I suppose not, since an equal element in zealotry is absolute and unique knowledge. But at least the knowledge that talking about "creationism" might lead to Navajo, Omaha, or Lakota ideas of where we all came from might cause the biblically based creationist to slow down the rush to destroy the wonderfully wise idea of separation of church and state.

And that is only a beginning. Isn't there some sense, even likelihood, to the idea that genuinely held, honestly practiced, ancient ceremonies and formulations might be based in actual experience and hold a truth that we in our society have not yet encountered or understood? Isn't it possible, as I have suggested, that we don't know everything and that there are unseen paths to unknown treasures that we can find only by opening doors hidden within other cultures? Or not hidden at all but lying right before our eyes and ignored?

Why not learn what we can from sources other than ones familiar to us? Why not learn what we can from successful cultures, just as the Great Plains pioneer could have learned so much from Indian people living with them in the same geography and at the same period in history? Nor is that only a historical potential. Native culture persists today within the matrix of the greater culture, but still with dimensions the mainstream avoids or scorns. I don't get the impression that our mainstream, Anglo-American culture is all that successful or spiritually satisfying for many of its members. Perhaps a great number or even majority of its members. I am finding that enlightenment within Native ways. I have no reason to believe I am unique in my experience. Quite to the contrary, I have seen again and again cultural adventurers or lost travelers accidentally finding their way into Native circles and finding them to be not a wilderness but a respite, or even a garden like that the Pawnees considered the Great Plains to be. Not exile, but home. If nothing else, we can learn from other cultures, like those of the Native world, how enormous and wonderful life is in its variety and surprise.

As I write these words I am wrestling with issues of death within my own culture. I am learning that one of the greatest problems in growing old myself is not only my own physical decline but also the decline and death of friends and relatives. Mainstream American culture does not handle death well. Even as I wrote these words . . . the decline and . . . uuuh . . . passing? . . . No, Roger, the word is *death*—I found my mind moving through the maze of avoidance that we practice when we speak of . . . it. I lost my father a decade ago, and on that occasion I went to Native friends and family and asked them to help me negotiate my way through that loss, the first big, close loss in my life. Through them I found new metaphors to help me deal with death. My Winnebago brother Louie and my Omaha son Jeff and sister-in-law Naomi took time to talk with me about their understandings about death: that we pass over four hills in our life—birth and childhood, maturity, old age, and then the voyage over the horizon of the fourth hill into . . . what? Into something else. We can't know what lies beyond that hill, but we know it is a new adventure that may well open up into a new reality as challenging and wonderful as the one we stepped into when we crossed over the first hill.

Historically we know that the Plains Indians saw life as a circle just as surely as our people saw it—and still see it—as a straight line. Death was as much a part of and as unavoidable as everything else in life. It was there. You dealt with it or you didn't. And the aged might very well understand that when they were no longer an asset to their people they might become instead a liability. The concern of an old man was about the survival of his people, perhaps only fifty relatives or a thousand people he knew in their village, the people he knew all his life in this world. In that event he might well suggest to his family and the leader of the village or hunting party that they go on ahead, that he needed to stop a bit and would catch up with them later or return to the village in time for breakfast the next morning.

No one was fooled about what was happening and what was going to happen; there was no intent to deceive. He was going off to die quietly, in dignity, in the company of his Creator, to return to Mother Earth as quickly as possible (in vivid contrast to our own ghoulish intent to remain separated from the comfort of the earth for as long as possible, if not forever). There is a lesson we might well consider even today.

57. *What's in It for Indians?*

One might well ask at this point, well, sure, all this is fine for the Wannabe but what's in it for the Indians? That's a little harder for me to answer because I fear it's not much. The profit in being a white American mainstreamer in Native company, it seems pretty evident, is for the Wannabe, not the Indians.

I like to think that everyone has something to offer someone else. Even the most benighted whiteman comes to another culture, be it Inuit or Omaha, with something to offer. In my case, at least to begin with, it was a modest knowledge of how to work the academic system of student support, scholarships, and academic program design. Later my writing skills became useful and even important; political, social, scholarly, and business contacts came into play. While I never imposed those assets on my Native friends ("Sit down, shut up, listen, and learn"), when I have been asked for help I have done what I can to give it.

In a broader sense, Wannabes bring the same old stereotypes to issues and yet are also the ones who encounter realities with a sympathetic eye—that is, a romantic Wannabe may be precisely the person to reveal realities to both Indian and white friends because he or she is the only one who encounters and considers them. I may be romantic and naïve—okay, I *am* romantic and naïve—but I honestly believe there is value in brotherhood and trust. I believe we are somehow drawn to others by powerful agencies outside of us—the metaphor that serves me well for visualizing this external agent is Coyote the Trickster—that guide us to some of our fellow human beings. Or maybe it's "chemistry," which is to say some natural, explainable mechanism that produces "love at first sight." But there's no doubt in my mind that the phenomenon exists and it is not just the physical attraction a beautiful person has for someone of the opposite (or for that matter, the same) sex. The moment I saw Linda I could not take my eyes off her. At that point in my life I was surrounded by beautiful women. There was something more between Linda and me. I have also felt the same sudden linkage with many other men and women, without romantic intent: I meet them and quickly like them. In fact, I find that in my solitary life as an enisled farmer-writer I make friends in no other way. I have dear friends I have met only once, but the magnetism was instant, undeniable, and permanent. That is the nature of many of my closest Native relationships. To this day, forty-five years later, I have no hint whatsoever of why my Omaha brother Buddy Gilpin asked me to be his brother—and even more dramatically, gave me his name. My Lakota brother Chuck and Pawnee Idadi Francis are in the same category: they are men for whom I have profound respect and admiration but whom I would have never so much as presumed to hope to call my friend. Yet, out of nowhere obvious, they proposed that we be brothers. I have no explanation for that but hope that somewhere in the process they have found a reason that serves them to have me as an ally and brother.

Perhaps the Native community somehow enjoys in a small way—it would have to be in a small way—my company, in the same way I enormously enjoy its company. As for those Natives who object to sharing their culture, the first consideration for an outsider is to understand that reticence: in terms of the long and painful history between Indians and the whiteman, the reluctance to enter into yet another relationship or bargain, even if only cultural, is easy to understand. Appreciate those who are willing to share, listen to the objections of those who do not, keep their objections in mind, avoid actions that are clearly offensive, but in the end whether you are accepted or not depends on the Natives you have befriended and who have befriended you. After all, who do we most and best trust in such judgments: those whom we trust, respect, love, and are indebted to or those who oppose us? So I do what I can to be honest about calling myself a Wannabe to make it clear to everyone, Native and non-Native alike, that I am not claiming to have Indian blood but also to state explicitly my deep respect and admiration for Native peoples and culture. On the other hand, within Native circles I make it equally clear that I am Pawnee or Omaha, and that in keeping with the best of Indian culture I am willing to laugh at myself. There is a reason I was given the Lakota name His Medicine Is Contrary and am therefore allied with the Heyoka, the Contraries! I am obligated and pleased to acknowledge the gift I have been accorded by those who call me "friend" or "family," and I will resist firmly anyone, Indian or not, who suggests I deny those gifts and alliances. I am Pawnee. I am Omaha. I have no other option. It is what I am.

58. *So You Wannabe a Wannabe?*

It is my impression after many years of experience in Native and Wannabe circles that superficial, short-term, unambitious Wannabes quickly fall to the roadside. As I have already noted several times, it's not easy being a Wannabe! Frustration and confusion weigh heavy; sometimes the disregard or even contempt of Native peoples for those who butt into their lives and culture without regard for the damage they do becomes obvious or explicit and the Wouldbes are shown the way out of the tipi.

The Wannabes I respect and associate with are some of the strongest people in my life. Early on, forty-five years ago, Earl Dyer, a former editor of the *Lincoln Star* newspaper, was courageous in supporting Native rights when that certainly was not a popular position. He worked hard at making Native gatherings comfortable when he was in attendance, from prayer meetings to Sun Dances. The real secret is to approach Natives and Native culture with respect and innocence, with no agenda but to learn—sit down, shut up, listen, and learn—a formula I adopted early in my own relationship with Native friends. Kay Young, one of the strongest people I have known in my long life, became an expert in ethnobotany through her formal studies but much more importantly through her apprenticeship and friendship with Richard Fool Bull. Her love for Mr. Fool Bull was obvious. He knew that and trusted her with many things he would have shared with no one else. John Mangan came to the Omahas from Ireland as a worker in the domestic peace corps—that is, as a do-gooder. But he quickly learned the real lesson of Wannabeism: while he may have had knowledge or skills he could bring to the Omahas, they had far more to offer him. He is, to this day, always there to help as a teacher in the Omaha Nation school but also as a friend within the community and tribe; he has become Omaha not only in his foodways and other aspects of daily life but also in song and language, teaching those topics in the Omaha school. Barre Toelken was rescued by the Navajos when he fell desperately ill in their lands and wound up not only being saved but eventually transmuted into a Navajo in every facet of his life. Mark Awakuni-Swetland was little more than a kid hanging around Indians when I first met him, but he devoted his life to learning the language and ways of the Omahas, taking on a program of learning traditional ways much more rigorous than one would find in any classroom. And then he followed his immersion education in Omaha culture with a formal mainstream education, eventually gaining a PhD in anthropology and becoming a worker educating brother Indians and non-Indians in Omaha culture and language. (Often people who are at best mediocre students in conventional educational systems blossom and flourish when they encounter bodies of traditional knowledge.) Mick Maun, a brick mason and tile setter, was dragged into various Pawnee projects by me when I needed his construction skills and knowledge. I know for a fact that the last thing in the world he wanted or expected was to make this brief, practical connection into a life-changing personal concern, but that is what it has become. To his benefit and that of the Pawnees. And me.

These are not weak people looking for a psychological crutch or shallow imitators seeking ascribed status, not people without ideas hoping in their cultural adventuring to "find themselves." Just as traditional Native culture and knowledge have shown remarkable, sometimes unexpected, vitality even when embedded within modern cultures, so too has Wannabeism. I see a small but constant flow of emotionally strong, bright, energetic Wannabes trickling into Native culture, being accepted there, and becoming remarkable double agents for both systems and new sources of important information for all of us.

When I began my Pawnee association I presumed I was the only one on the prairies who cared about such things. Imagine my surprise, then, when I found a working scholar and committed Wannabe, Jean Lukesh, living just ten miles away, virtually in my neighborhood. Even with her doctorate, many honors and distinctions, and incredibly wide knowledge of the Pawnees, Jean Lukesh is not above serving corn soup and fry bread at Indian gatherings—not simply as a gesture of humility but, significantly, what a Pawnee woman does in such a situation. That is, Lukesh is a respected scholar in the mainstream but as a successful Wannabe, she is also a strong, respected woman.

Ronnie O'Brien, on the other hand, came into my life as a blank slate, violating (I thought) every one of the ideas I have included in this book as a suitable entry to Native culture. Working for a local tourism attraction, O'Brien contacted me about my work with the Pawnees because she had decided she wanted to host a powwow for the Pawnees. Even though she'd never been to a powwow. Groan . . . It was January and she was planning to hold the powwow in June. Double groan . . . She obviously knew little about the logistics and complications of the powwow or the intricacies of busting into Native culture or the politics of tribal organization. There was no way in hell her plan could succeed.

I underestimated the energy, goodwill, flexibility, and native adaptability of Ms. O'Brien. And of the Pawnees. She launched herself with utter innocence and humility onto the mercy, goodwill, and energy of the Pawnees—especially the Pawnee women. She not only brought off the powwow as one of the most spectacularly successful events in the summer calendar in 2009 but has been embraced wholeheartedly by the Pawnees. She is working now on a second powwow and other projects within among the Pawnees, like the regeneration of lost maize varieties. Almost as a side benefit of her blitzkrieg approach to Wannabeism, she has made an enormous dent in the education of everyone in her larger community, from children to the elderly, by bringing the Pawnee history of the region to the forefront. She is bright and energetic not an empty vessel waiting to be filled.

Gale Pemberton and Peggy Lang's route into Wannabeism was through proximity: they live in the same village I do and just a few doors down the street from what was to become (through their hard work) the Pawnee Arts Center. As I recall, we got to talking one day about a building that had been given to the Pawnees, then about some art objects that were stored there, and then how they could help me out by doing some volunteer work—for two evenings and one Saturday afternoon one spring. And before I, or they, knew it, they were working week after week, night after night, almost as a full-time job, managing, selling, cleaning, arranging, curating, and even lecturing at the center. They developed relationships with the Pawnees, and voila! There they are . . . inextricably linked with a tribe they had never so much as thought of before.

Successful Wannabes through history have been strong people who can deal with the wrenching of their perceptions of reality and understandings of life by shifting into another cultural gear without needing to assume control, exercise authority, or collapse in weakness under the constant and enormous pressure of being divorced from their customary and comfortable context. I think of the boldest of the frontiersmen, from John Colter and Jim Bridger to military men like General Crook, the many white and black captives who opted to stay with their Indian "captors" rather than return to "civilization" (a far more frequent decision than one might imagine), John Neihardt (a student of Black Elk), and the hundreds of French trappers and traders who came to the Plains Indians as allies, friends, and kinsmen and therefore prospered. No wonder so many French names echo within Plains Indian tribal enrollment lists today. All of which is to say, when we seek motivations for those who become Wannabes, personal weakness is most assuredly not one of those reasons.

Not everyone needs to be a Wannabe. I worked for the Smithsonian Institution researching German bands in Germany and the United States. I had wonderful times across Germany, in Freistadt, Wisconsin;

Friedricksburg, Texas; and Scottsbluff, Nebraska. I loved the music and the musicians. But at no point did I aspire to be a German musician. Or a Wannabe German, even though all four of my grandparents were German and my undergraduate and graduate majors were German. No offense—it just isn't my aspiration. There are people who visit a powwow and that's the end of it. They may have had a good time, liked fry bread, enjoyed the music, admired the dance . . . and then went home content with having seen something special. Nothing wrong with that. It is perfectly acceptable to enjoy Native culture, friendships, and understandings without becoming Indian. But for some of us, there is something within that drives us further and deeper. For us the question is not "Why would anyone want to be a Wannabe?" but "How on earth could I *not* be a Wannabe?"

However, it is important somewhere along the line, before it is too late, at some point when there is a feeling that lines are being crossed, that we ask ourselves, "Why?" I have explored some of the possible reasons throughout the preceding pages and suggested that we may not want to dig too deep within our own psyches, lest we learn too much about ourselves that we'd just as soon not know. There are people who simply like costume. They dress up in funny clothes to be party clowns, big game hunters, square dancers, Civil War reenactors, muzzleloaders. That's fine, but more caution is needed when one is a Wannabe. Clowns, rebs, and mountain men aren't around to be offended when imitation is not flattering or is even insulting, perhaps offensive and blasphemous. To enjoy dressing up on weekends is a not good motivation for being a Wannabe.

I have a feeling that one of the factors in my own long and serious association with Indians stems from my discontent with mainstream Anglo-American culture, empty religiosity, and weak family structure and a need to be with the oppressed and abused—that is, it is essentially a political motivation. Is that acceptable? I don't know. There's not much I can do about it. That's who I am.

Some of us are hopeless Romantics, with something of James Fennimore Cooper in our blood, a hope for a return to the Noble Savage.

I know that's a bit silly, but by acknowledging it I can avoid being influenced by it any more than necessary. Perhaps that is one of the benefits I gain from being a Wannabe and not just an idle observer: Indians, while not precisely like everyone else, are in fact still human beings, no more noble—or savage—than the rest of us.

People who have an attraction for Indians while nonetheless having obvious personal conflicts with the very idea of Indians utterly mystify me, on the other hand. I cannot imagine what goes on in their minds, unless it is pure Romanticism, completely devoid of a balancing sense of the real, a dream of the past resulting in contempt for the present. I have known specialists in the archaeology of Plains Indians who have never met an Indian. They are in heaven when they are in the field digging up dead Pawnees and their villages but have no interest in associating with the living descendants of those whose graves they rob, and perhaps even have an aversion to it. I have known historians who devote their lives to studying a tribe's culture and past while holding and exhibiting a contempt bordering on loathing for the very people they study. Even when they do have contact with living examples of the people they study and ostensibly admire or respect, they approach the encounter with overt paternal superiority. How does an attitude like that come to be? Shame on the part of the non-Indian? Fear? I have known the specific Indians in question, and they are genial, generous, certainly not to be feared, and yet the whiteman bristles from the beginning. I have no idea what that is about.

Only in the very beginning of my contact with the Omahas, in the first few weeks, did I come to Native culture as a scholar-researcher—if an undergraduate can ever aspire to those elevated levels. In an anthropological linguistics class I was assigned to transcribe and chart Omaha tribal kinship terms—something of a trick assignment no undergraduate would ever be able to complete, I should note, but I had a paid Omaha resource to work with on weekends. He became my dear friend and later a relative, and any suggestion of my presence within the Omaha community as a researcher, scholar, or anthropologist quickly faded away. I was among them as a friend. I enjoyed their company. My natural curiosity and my desire to be a courteous guest led me to observe and follow Omaha ways, but never in a systematic, "objective," documented process. I was just there, waiting after the handgame for some fry bread, corn soup, and conversation with friends.

Nor has this writing been an effort at a scholarly, scientific monograph. It's a memoir of my adventures among the Indians, along with advice and information for others who are certain to follow in my path. That's why the word "confessions" is in the subtitle. As seems to be the case with me, I learned the most from my mistakes, and my hope is to save others the same embarrassments.

A recent debate within the American Folklore Society, the scholarly organization that speaks to my particular training and experience, has showcased how something that may seem simple enough, even for the casual, non-anthropological Wannabe, can become mighty sticky at some point. Briefly, an old friend, Barre Toelken, wound up quite by accident involved with the Navajos and one family in particular. Along the way his friend and brother shared ancient and sacred stories with him. Many such traditional stories, however, carry with them restrictions about when they can be told—winter or summer, for example—and who can hear them—perhaps only certain clan members or only males within the tribe. Many years after Barre recorded the stories for his own use and perhaps for scholarly use, his dear friend asked him to destroy the recordings for fear someone might play and hear them out of proper season and therefore be injured, or that injury might come indirectly to Barre, to the tribe, or to his friend's family.

These stories were precious treasures, tales perhaps never otherwise recorded, not ever heard by anyone else, maybe dying with this one man and never to be heard by anyone again, either as recordings or live performances, lost to all humankind for all time. As you can imagine, Barre was deeply tormented. He had a sacred obligation to his friend, to whom the stories actually belonged after all, but he also had an obligation to the world of knowledge, to his beloved profession of folklore studies, maybe to generations of Navajos yet to come. He brought his torment to his colleagues in the American

Folklore Society and announced his inclination and intention to destroy the tapes.

Another dear folklorist friend of mine, Alan Dundes, was shocked and dismayed. How could this happen? Who would destroy so wonderful a treasure? Couldn't the materials simply be stored away, perhaps with full instructions about how they can and cannot be used, perhaps for centuries?

The debate became public, which is good because the issue of the ownership of culture is so important. At the October 19, 2009, meeting of the society in Boise, Idaho, I was asked to comment on the debate. It was easy enough to do that because I had been struggling with the same issues in my life, about when to speak and when to remain silent. The issue was complicated by my affection for both principals, Alan Dundes and Barre Toelken, two scholars for whom I have immense respect. The problem, like so many dilemmas, is that they are both right. We have an obligation to the people we love and who love us and so generously share with us their culture, and we have an obligation to our colleagues, our profession, and the world's body of knowledge.

Anyone who is a Wannabe is likely to encounter this same kind of conflict and wind up in a position of having to make his or her own decisions. In my case I came down on the side of my Native friends and relatives, bowing to the respect I have for the Elders and Powers (in the spiritual sense) and respecting the old ways of the traditions themselves (in the tribal sense). The decision was clinched for me when I remembered urging Mr. Richard Fool Bull to record his vast knowledge of plants and medicines or take on an apprentice to whom he could pass along his wisdom, so "it won't be lost to the future." Mr. Fool Bull chuckled at my naiveté and said patiently, "Roger, if we forget that willow bark cures headaches, does that mean willow bark no longer cures headaches? No, it simply means that for the moment we have lost that knowledge. Truth never dies." The destruction of Barre's tapes did not destroy the wisdom recorded on them. In fact, perhaps it is through the very agency of the Wannabe that the memories will endure.

What are the rules of engagement for a Wannabe in approaching a host culture? There are no rules. Each Wannabe comes with his or her own cultural inventory through which the other culture is bound to be viewed, and each culture approached is in itself different. Throw in a thousand other unlikely considerations like tribal politics, family feuds, economic conditions, bad weather, and the attitude of the visitor, and things can pretty much go anywhere.

When I am asked, as I frequently am, "Where is a good place to begin being involved in Native culture?" I suggest attending a powwow. Now, I know that a powwow is an artificial context. This is not the way Indians live on a day-to-day basis in America, and there is always a danger that seeing Indians in feathers, beads, and bells might only reenforce stereotypes. But powwows are an occasion when the Indian community openly invites non-Indians to visit their home ground and celebrate historical, family, and tribal traditions. A powwow is a nonthreatening context for cultural interface, and despite its drawbacks I encourage attendance as an easy first opening. If that works, it can lead on to other contacts; if it doesn't, there is no harm and both sides part on friendly terms.

If there is a danger within the excitement of a powwow it is for the Wannabe who lacks only a match to ignite his or her launch sequence. No doubt about it, even something as small and superficial as an afternoon at a powwow can become a life-changing experience. You may not come out the same person or even who you thought you would be. I have recommended that at the gate to all powwow grounds there should be a large sign reading BEWARE ALL YE WHO ENTER HERE; YOU MAY NOT COME OUT THE SAME PERSON WHO WENT IN.

On the other hand, while something as small as an afternoon at a nearby reservation's tribal powwow may have life-changing implications, there is a danger—I have seen it—that two hours at a powwow may produce not simply a Wannabe but an "expert." A visit to a powwow may be a start, but it is only a start. Moreover, observation is only observation, not participation. As is the case with so many museums, there is a conspiracy between the curator and the visitor, a dishonest agreement that the curator is actually teaching something and the visitor is actually learning something. The tour at a historical agricultural museum shows a flail hanging on a barn post and tsk-tsks about how primitive such a device is, how utterly impractical for actual threshing. A better museum takes that flail off the wall and has someone who knows what he or she is doing wale away at a pile of ear corn. The visitors will be astonished to see the ears virtually explode as the cobs fly and the grains separate. Wow. A flail not only works, it works well. The lesson is still not complete, however; now it's time for the visitor to give the flail a try and gain the further understanding that it does not work as well with a complete amateur swinging it but with a little practice it works much better, and with time and repetition it becomes remarkably effective. A glimpse of traditional technology is interesting, but its lessons are small and incomplete. Same with a powwow.

This is where a Wannabe's attitude becomes such an important factor. The tendency in mainstream culture is to take charge, ask questions, offer expertise, fix things, make improvements, tidy things up. That won't work for a Wannabe. Everything is just fine the way it is. A Wannabe's role is not to "fix" either the culture or practitioners of that culture. It is not a Wannabe's task to teach the value of keeping property for one's own use or the impracticality of Indian Time. A Wannabe's assignment is to adjust to the host culture, to learn and experience, not instruct and guide. A Wannabe is a guest or, if particularly fortunate, a friend. A Wannabe may have talents, skills, and ideas to offer, but must present them only when invited. Sit down, shut up, listen, and learn. Tattoo it on the back of your left hand. Learn to take "no" as an answer, or better yet, learn how to avoid putting your hosts and friends in a position where they need to say no. And if they do, take it as a way of helping you learn, not as a personal rebuff. Within the past year I pitched my tent on an Indian gathering ground and was gently but firmly told that I couldn't put it there because I would be behind a shelter, too close to where some nonpublic ceremonies would be conducted. Easy enough. I moved my gear, thanked my advisor, and felt I had learned something new, even fifty years into my lifelong relationship with Native celebrations and people.

Sophistication, education, smarts, cleverness, experience, and an eye for efficiency are of no use in Wannabe relationships. Our task is not to "fix" but to learn. The virtues of a successful Wannabe are innocence, luck, honesty, and humility. Sit down, shut up, listen, and learn. Don't push. Relax. Let your hosts be your guide. Listen and observe. That is, do what you can not to be a whiteman. Don't rush forward to introduce yourself. Don't immediately begin to call everyone by first names, an American custom that a good part of the rest of the world considers painfully forward, even rude. Don't jump into the dance arena and do your version of the Grass Dance.

Again there is the frequent experience of museum visitors who peek into a tipi or sod house exhibit and instantly draw the conclusion that since this dwelling is a tenth, a thirtieth, the size of their starter-castle home and doesn't gleam and glow with plastic and chrome that life in it was uncomfortable and even "wrong." Cultural and historical myopia so clouds the visitors' vision and understanding that their conclusions are simply flat-out wrong.

I have seen anthropologists, who should know better, do exactly what I am cautioning powwow visitors not to do, but perhaps under the cloak of being scholars and professional observers of culture. They jump into a culture for a few months, or even attend only five or six events like handgames, and are instantly experts. They aren't. They have only a very narrow scope on a vastly larger complex, and therefore their conclusions are at best incomplete, at worst utterly without merit. Once a person becomes a committed Wannabe, I believe the commitment is for life. That is why it may become, albeit gradually, an enormous, life-changing, personally shattering development. And once the transformation begins, you should be cautioned, it is not easily changed or stopped. Phony, short-term interest by a cultural visitor is easily detected and is quite understandably seen as exploitation, insult, or insincerity (because it is). This kind of drop-in behavior not only bears minimal results in any dimension—scholarly or personally—but jeopardizes more serious Wannabes in their efforts to truly understand a culture and participate in it.

"A little knowledge is a dangerous thing," the saying goes. I know for a fact that my own knowledge of Native ways is, by and large, incomplete and almost certainly in error in many ways. But there are degrees of error. I like to believe that I draw my conclusions from experience: things have happened in my presence and I have done my best to draw logical conclusions from what I have seen. That is not at all the case with many Wannabes. Far too many learn a little and then guess or presume a lot. That is dangerous because the guesses and presumptions are based in most cases on their own cultural matrix. The sum totals are inevitably wrong. We cannot guess what people might have thought or done in the past or what they think and do in the present on the basis of what *we* would do given the same circumstances. When I hear someone say, "I feel your pain," I want to scream, "No, you don't! It is not possible for *you* to feel *my* pain. You can sympathize, or empathize, but you cannot realize." I have written historical fiction and felt the actual agony of trying to put myself into another person's mind, in another time, in another culture, under circumstances I can imagine only in the most uncertain way. That is, I know the inadequacies of imagination. The well-meant but utterly impossible idea of "putting oneself in someone else's moccasins" is shaky business and must be undertaken with caution, not boldness. Especially in teaching or writing, where the results of error are not just personal but are transmitted to others who think they are learning rock-solid truths, when they are in fact only sharing another dreamer's fantasies.

A few months ago I received a letter from a writer wanting some advice about Native issues and traditions because he intended to write a book for young readers (uh-oh) about the life (groan) of a teenage (oh no!) Neolithic (gasp) girl. At this point I collapsed into a pile on my computer keyboard. I presumed, since the prospective author wrote me for basic information, that he was starting from nothing. He insisted that he intended to read a lot of material and pretty much become an expert in Neolithic Native life. And teenagers. And girls. Some people spend a lifetime at any one of those endeavors, we should remember.

I have seen this enough times to know how the thinking process goes: How different would life have been three thousand years ago? Humans are humans. We eat, we tell stories, we sleep, we love, we die. There you are. And we all react to those events pretty much the same. Don't we? Well, no. We don't. We can't even imagine what life is like for someone who is living under a bridge at this very moment. I have struggled for thirty years to understand my wife, fifty years trying to follow the thinking and lives of my children. We can only guess. And our guesses will still and always be 95 percent wrong. It is one thing when I am trying to understand why Linda says it is an offense against God to wear light-colored pants and a dark jacket, but it is quite another when a person is presenting naked speculation as informed knowledge in order *to instruct children.* That really should be considered a crime against humankind. I remember a few years ago when a young woman from the East came here for a week to learn about the plains so she could write a book about sod house life. The book was a disaster. There was never a chance for it to be anything else. (It was a critical success, however, because the reviewers, all from the East, too, were precisely as ignorant about such things as she was.)

Imagination falls short even when grounded in years of concentrated research; a week's visit is a sure path to a greater ignorance than that with which the speculator started. It has been my clear experience after five decades of moving within Native culture that one doesn't need much imagination to find plenty of excitement, plenty of interest, plenty to chew on intellectually and spiritually in what is actual, or at least what is perceived as actual. Indeed, I find myself falling further and further behind in coming to grips with all that I have seen, heard, and experienced. I have a lively imagination, I've been told, but I know that I could never invent anything nearly as remarkable as the realities I have found among Native peoples. Imagination falls far short of the realities. And I am grateful to my Native friends and family for showing me these new realities.

Dr. Jay Anderson is an academic and scholar who has led me in many directions in my life and opened many doors. On one occasion he invited me to join him in his work with the foods program at Plimoth Plantation, the museum that attempts to re-create the context and life of the Pilgrims in the year 1624. My task was to identify and catalog the wild foods inventory of the area and to develop a brewing program to match the extensive and vital processes of brewing in the Pilgrim village that should perhaps be given credit for allowing it to survive through the extreme trials of its earliest years.

We malted barley, gathered nettles (as a hops substitute), cultured yeast, cooked the wort, or beer soup, and worked with the cooper (at the original village that was John Alden) to develop beer vats, strainers, and barrels. To keep the brew working during the long, cold spring nights Jay and I lived on the museum grounds (appropriately, in the Brewster house), keeping the fire stoked, working the fermenting barley, and struggling to keep ourselves warm and occupied during the almost painfully cold, dark, and lonely nights in the empty village. We were in the village on the evening of April 15, the very day when the *Mayflower* lifted anchor and sailed for England, leaving its few, isolated charges alone on the shores of the new country.

Jay and I left our shelter, fire, and brewing beer and walked out into the village. We looked down toward the sea past the dreary, humble houses. We were cold, lonely, tired, dirty . . . but our thoughts were with the Pilgrims who had stood there in 1621 looking out to sea, watching their last solid contact with the Old World recede in the distance. And there they were, in the same silence we were knowing. I broke our quiet thoughts with words that have ever since served me as the rationale for my enthusiastic embrace of becoming a Wannabe: "Jay, I don't know how much we're learning about the Pilgrims, but I sure as hell get the feeling we're learning a lot about ourselves."

Other Works by Roger Welsch

Busted Tractors and Rusty Knuckles: Norwegian Torque Wrench Techniques and Other Fine Points of Tractor Restoration

Catfish at the Pump: Humor and the Frontier

Cather's Kitchens: Foodways in Literature and Life

Forty Acres and a Fool: How to Live in the Country and Still Keep Your Sanity

It's Not the End of the Earth, but You Can See It from Here

A Life with Dogs

Love, Sex, and Tractors

My Nebraska: The Good, the Bad, and the Husker

Old Tractors and the Men Who Love Them: How to Keep Your Tractors Happy and Your Family Running

Shingling the Fog and Other Plains Lies

Touching the Fire: Buffalo Dancers, the Sky Bundle, and Other Tales

A Treasury of Nebraska Pioneer Folklore

Ingram Content Group UK Ltd.
Milton Keynes UK
UKHW040429170723
425189UK00019B/259